Daire Whelan is a writer and journalist.
The author of two previous non-fiction books –
Who Stole Our Game? and *A Year with the Dubs* – his work
has appeared in *The Irish Times*, *Magill*, the *Daily Mail* and
the *Sunday Tribune*. A former award-winning producer with
Newstalk, RTÉ and Setanta Sports, he now runs his own digital
content company, LastCastMedia.com, and lives in south
Tipperary with his family and dogs.

THE MANAGERS

The Tactics and Thinkers that Transformed Gaelic Football

Daire Whelan

HACHETTE
BOOKS
IRELAND

First published in 2013 by Hachette Books Ireland
First published in paperback in 2014

A CIP catalogue record for this title is available from the British Library.

ISBN 978 1444 744 026

Typeset in Times New Roman by Bookends Publishing Services.
Printed and bound by Clays Ltd, St Ives plc

Hachette Books Ireland policy is to use papers that are natural, renewable
and recyclable products and made from wood grown in sustainable forests.
The logging and manufacturing processes are expected to conform to the
environmental regulations of the country of origin.

Hachette Books Ireland
8 Castlecourt Centre
Castleknock
Dublin 15, Ireland

A division of Hachette UK Ltd.
338 Euston Road
London NW1 3BH

www.hachette.ie

Contents

For Ryan,
the ultimate game-changer ...

In the end, just three things matter:
How well we have lived
How well we have loved
How well we have learned to let go.

Jack Kornfield, Buddhist teacher and writer

Introduction

Cold baths. Fresh fruit. Red meat. Never drank, never smoked – 'avoid the fags, anyone who uses them will never be any good'. In the morning, he drank water from the well, followed by a bowl of porridge, some bread and a small piece of beef or mutton cooked well. At midday, he had boiled mutton or roast beef with vegetables but few potatoes, always avoiding salty bacon and all fatty foods. His day was finished off with porridge, dry toast and milk. It sounds like the preparation and attention to detail of a champion athlete and it was – that of Maurice Davin, the GAA's first president, in the 1870s.

'His boxing experiences taught him the value of regular exercises in toning up and developing greater power in his muscles through using dumb-bells and clubs. He practised weight-lifting and fitted out what could be called a miniature gymn for use by himself and his brothers. He studied whatever fitness periodicals and manuals he could acquire and he worked out a strict diet for himself to be adhered to rigidly,' former GAA president, and Davin's biographer, Séamus Ó Riain, wrote.

Along with a strict diet regime, Davin focused on hydration, rest and keeping a detailed log of his training along with notes on his competitors. This was a man who held national records in the high jump, long jump, hammer and shot putt; a man who was a boxing champion in his hometown of Carrick-on-Suir in Tipperary before turning his attentions to rowing and then focusing on athletics where he came to prominence in his thirties.

If ever there was the progenitor of the modern Irish athlete, Maurice Davin is it. Trained in a variety of sports, focused on diet, rest and exercise, it is little wonder that Davin excelled in the sports he turned his attention to. The era of the twenty-first-century Gaelic footballer pushing himself to the limit, focusing his life around his sport in pursuit of success, is nothing new. Maurice Davin, in post-Famine Ireland, was doing exactly the same.

The foundation of the GAA and subsequent codification of rules for Gaelic football by Davin himself saw the game spread like wildfire around the country. Competition and games between neighbouring parishes was nothing new, stretching back hundreds of years, but rules varied from area to area with confusion and ugly violence often the by-product. The late nineteenth century saw the development of organised sport, giving a recreational outlet to the masses in the urban centres created in the wake of the Industrial Revolution, and, in Ireland, the GAA gave shape and purpose to Gaelic games.

From the first playing of the All-Ireland championship, team rivalries grew and the competitive instinct meant that those serious about winning were always looking for an edge over their opponents. Even in the early years, the question of style arose: some teams were more cynical in their pursuit of winning, while others were practising 'screw kicks' and other skills.

'The tension within the rules – how rules were applied, how rules are managed by referees, how the games are reshaped by people constantly seeking an edge, and redefined by players who bend the game to their strengths and weaknesses, it's a constant challenge and recurring theme,' says sports historian Paul Rouse. 'You can't go through a decade and not see match reports or see discussions in newspapers about style, about the rules, the organisation of the game, and it is a recurrent theme in Gaelic football, possibly not in the early period but certainly from later on, about the problems of Gaelic football, the bad stuff in the game. It's as if Gaelic football is about to keel over and die. These were the discussions going on over a hundred years ago!'

In many ways, the arguments haven't changed; the notion of purists versus pragmatists and a constant struggle between those who saw the game as primarily a catching-and-kicking one and those who placed an emphasis on the hand-pass.

When Kerry emerged as one of the first dominant Gaelic football counties at the beginning of the twentieth century, their catch-and-kick style began to be seen as 'traditional' and 'pure'. History, as they say, is written by the winners, and Kerry have had a long tradition of writing about their expertise and exploits on the field of play, starting with the publication of the sport's first manual in 1914 by legendary Kerry player Dick Fitzgerald. Entitled *How to Play Gaelic Football*, it was a book that laid out in thorough detail the different skills involved in playing the game properly. 'Gaelic football of the present day is a scientific game … when the number was reduced to fifteen a side science became the order of the day,' he wrote.

Fitzgerald's book spelled out clearly how players and teams could improve through scientific knowledge and focused training. While it wasn't the 24/7, year-long dedication that we see today, it did introduce concepts, such as having training camps in the run-up to All-Ireland finals, which became a growing feature of the increased requirements necessary to win at All-Ireland level.

In Fitzgerald's time, the most important person in the setup was the trainer who was brought in for the dedicated pre-final training camps. Usually, this was a renowned and successful sports star who had an expertise in training and whose job was to get the team up to peak fitness. As a result, previously unheralded counties were disrupting the perceived natural order of things.

Wexford, who had been hammered 4–4 to 1–3 by Wicklow in the first round of the Leinster championship in 1912, are the best example of this. They brought in Jem Roche, who had fought for the world heavyweight title in 1910, as their trainer before going on to win four All-Irelands in a row from 1915–1918.

Wexford's secret? Much the same formula that has proven so effective down through the years: good organisation from county board level down through to the playing team, coupled with very talented players and effective training methods.

Can it be as simple as that? In many ways, it can. Good organisation, ensuring everything is set up and in place for the players to perform to their maximum, comes from the top down, as does leading and innovative training techniques that will give players the edge in the fitness stakes. Combining these two elements with a particularly talented and dedicated group of players can ensure success no matter what the era. It's the hallmark of all winning teams: Wexford in the 1910s, Kildare and Kerry in the 1920s, Cavan in the 1940s, Mayo in the 1950s, Down and Galway in the 1960s … what stood out for each was their ability to develop new traits and habits, evolving from what went on before to give them the upper hand.

While the trainer and training camps became increasingly important, the role of team selection still lay with an unwieldy system of up to half a dozen selectors – the role of a single manager to pick and lead the team wasn't to evolve until the 1960s and 1970s. Players remained the stars of the day and the cult of the manager didn't emerge until the Kevin Heffernan–Mick O'Dwyer rivalry from 1974. From that point, the philosophy of a team was linked to the manager's personality; training, tactics and team selections all became the responsibility of one man and, in many ways, the team was a mirror image of his traits and approach to the game. Thus, Heffernan's belief in having a team of self-analytical players was reflective of his own playing days, while O'Dwyer developed a closer bond and warmth in his dressing room, treating his players as a father would his son.

Until then, the manager/trainer was very much in the background, Kerry's Dr Eamonn O'Sullivan being a case in point. Here was a man who trained Kerry for nine All-Irelands between 1924 and 1964, winning eight, and yet he was only called upon when Kerry were struggling. His legacy to the game is immense, combining his background in psychiatry with regimented training camps in the run-up to the finals, focusing on diet and rest as much as physical fitness itself. Outside of Kerry, however, to the ordinary fan, the name Dr Eamonn O'Sullivan would not have meant very much. Instead, it was the names of the hero-players such as Jim Brosnan, Jackie Lyne and Mick O'Connell that were the talk of fan conversation.

While managers may not have been the major talking point down through the years, tactics and style of play were, and just as it dominated in the early years of the GAA, so too the arguments continued to rage about teams employing the short hand-passing style rather than the catch-and-kick philosophy. The great Kildare and Dublin teams of the 1920s became known as 'machines' for their seemingly unbeatable hand-passing systems – Dublin won three-in-a-row and Kildare captured three All-Irelands in that decade. But these systems of play with their emphasis on teamwork were being derided in some quarters. Dick Fitzgerald is his book wrote:

Everybody knows that the tendency of the outdoor games
of the present day is to reduce the individual player to
the level of a mere automaton. In a manner the individual
in modern games is a disadvantage to his side if his
individuality asserts itself too strongly ... How dry is the
description one often gets of those great matches in which
perfect combination alone is the only thing commended!
In them there is no hero – no great individual standing out
from the whole field.

Fast-forward one hundred years, people have said the same thing about the rise of Donegal or Dublin.

This notion that those teams – most noticeably Kerry – practising a catch-and-kick style are the purists of the game has been in vogue for as long as the game itself, but as Paul Rouse and others have argued, sport is about the inherent tension in the rules, giving a team as much of an advantage as possible. Thus, the Armagh- and Tyrone-style of swarming in the early 2000s was about stopping the opposition's forward momentum and smothering them without fouling. Without a clear definition of the tackle in the rules, it was a tactic that proved to be very successful.

'Stairs and landings' is how the innovative coach John Morrison describes the game's evolutionary path. Some years it's incremental, then in other periods it takes bigger leaps to the next level. Developments in the game since the start of the 2000s have changed it utterly, to where, once again, GAA people are talking in worried tones about the future of the game, the lack of catch-and-kick and the dominance of the short hand-pass.

In the one hundred-plus years during which arguments over Gaelic football playing philosophies have been taking place, perhaps the biggest difference today is the fact that managerial mindsets are focused primarily on stopping the opposition first, with attacking and forward play a distant second. Going back through the decades when the hand-passing systems were successful, it was still with an emphasis on attack – it was the forward movements and inter-play that were unplayable, until another way was found to overcome those players and their tactics.

The modern game has switched its focus and stopping the other team from scoring is paramount, getting forwards fit and agile enough that they can track back and tackle is a necessary part of the forward's DNA. When Dublin won the All-Ireland in 2011, their wing-forwards were converted half-backs from a previous footballing life. Just as Dick Fitzgerald asked where the heroes in those playing systems that subsume the individual were, so too many ask if the genius of a Colm Cooper will ever be seen again. Are we coaching the sublime and unique out of players in favour of them becoming automatons who can only play the safe percentages? Derry's Joe Brolly, a harsh critic of the modern styles of play as espoused by Tyrone and Donegal, says players of the talent and skill of Donegal's Michael Murphy would give their right arm to play in teams that embrace an attacking philosophy, such as Crossmaglen.

Earlier this year, Kerry's Colm Cooper questioned the way the game is developing and wondered with his slight frame if he would have been given a chance. 'An unwritten requirement at the moment to be a GAA player is you've to be six foot four and built like a tank,' he said at a press conference previewing the championship season. 'If you look at most county teams, every guy is lifting big weights, has to be able to run and has to be able to tackle. He's taking over from the skilful guy that's five foot ten and slight build. If I was starting out again right now, I might not get the opportunity. You need to safeguard the skills of the game and the skilful players in the game.'

Yet, as the innovators ask, who is coaching the coaches? Where is the positive approach to the game? It is easy, say leading coaches such as John Morrison and Val Andrews, to show someone how to stop the opposition playing and to run five-yard, hand-passing drills, but where is the imagination and outside-the-box thinking that will coach players to attack creatively, score points and goals from out of nothing and embrace a philosophy of forward play first and foremost?

Managers are reflective of their time and place, and in a society that is focused on cutbacks, austerity and the bottom-line, it is little wonder that playing the safe option and taking no risks is dominant. Sport in general has been taken over by the numbers game: by statisticians, dieticians and tacticians. We're in a big-data society lived on the internet and run by machines that can measure our habits and movements and give us the information we think we want based on algorithms and predictive models. As a human society, we have been reduced to being measured in 0s and 1s, a way of living that is byte-sized, either black or white. Within this context, the data overload in sport has meant that nothing is left to chance: five-yard hand-passes are more likely than those kicked fifty yards because of the percentages game. There is no place for what-ifs in the modern manager's philosophy.

'Management is doing things right; leadership is doing the right things,' wrote the American management guru Peter Drucker in his 1954 book *The Practice of Management*, and, in modern sport, it seems leadership has taken a step back. Surrounded by teams of backroom staff, it is easier to delegate responsibility, but the true manager in the dressing room is the leader, the one who cajoles and inspires, who gives you a hard time and knows when to put an arm around your shoulder.

For the managers featured in this book, their success has been based on a mindset combined with a methodology that has enabled them to stand out among their generation. Yes, it is easier to succeed with a talented generation of footballers hungry to win, but to do it year in, year out, to drive the players on to keep winning even after they have succeeded, is a remarkable testament to the manager. Likewise, the manager who can see a purpose of dedication in a group of players, who, while not as talented as others, have the burning desire within to achieve more through the sum of their parts. It is in these dressing rooms that the talented manager can step up and provide the experience, attention to detail, knowledge and edge that sees them achieve their goals and more.

There are common traits among all the most successful managers – a talented generation of players, hunger from within, leaders on and off the pitch, a county organisation working in tandem from the top down doing whatever and however it takes to succeed, and the manager looking on, cajoling, coaxing, driven and determined. Management is the easy part; leadership is the key.

This book is not meant to be a definitive list of Gaelic football's winning managers – such a book would run into multiple volumes – but is an insight into those who have led the way since the rise of the manager and the beginning of the modern game with the emergence of Down in the 1960s. There were many successful teams and managers who could also have been covered and deserve chapters of their own (for future books, perhaps), men like Peter McDermott, Ray Morgan and Bobby Miller, who achieved remarkable success given the time, resources and talent to hand.

Once again, Gaelic football is in the midst of an evolutionary change and it could be a future championed by the technique, style and philosophy of Donegal's Jim McGuinness, one that shapes athletes into a unit of self-belief and drive that will run through walls for what their manager tells them. Under McGuinness, Donegal are the epitome of the modern in Gaelic football, cherishing the system, the athlete, the work effort and a game based on percentages. It is the kind of society we are living in today anyway.

And then there's Crossmaglen, and a handful of coaches coming through who want to see the game espoused differently, emphasising catching and kicking, where the individual is allowed to flourish – it's a philosophy that is inherently different to what has become the norm, and an approach that emphasises the enjoyment of playing, and watching, Gaelic football.

Liam Gilmartin is the oldest surviving All-Ireland winner. Aged ninety-two, he is sprightly and can remember clearly when Roscommon won their All-Irelands in 1943 and 1944. Their emergence came off the back of talented youth who were given their chance and took it with both hands. Asked about his career, about the wins and the All-Irelands, what stands out most for him were the moments of pure pleasure on the field of play.

> *There is a half a minute when the final whistle goes and which gives you something that is unbelievable, there is no description for it. You have won your second All-Ireland against Kerry, had a good game, and the world was all there and it was tremendous. As I walked through the crowd, through the sideline seats, they were slapping me on the back and an old man came up to me and caught me by the shoulders and said to me, 'Jesus ye were mighty', and that's the reward I got out of it. For those thirty seconds, everything was just perfect.*

A lifetime of habit and thirty seconds of perfection – moments we can all hope and strive for.

Part I

Purists and Pragmatists

'I gave it my body and mind, but I have kept my soul.'

Phil Jackson, eleven-time NBA championship-winning coach

Part I

Purists and Pragmatists

Chapter 1

'Like an explosion onto Croke Park'

Croke Park had never seen anything like it. Kerry football didn't know what hit them. GAA fans all around the country shook their heads in amazement. On the day, a record 87,768 spectators knew they had witnessed something special and unique. The traditional kingpins of Gaelic football had been humbled in an All-Ireland final by a county that had only captured its first provincial title the previous year.

On that sunny September day in 1960, Croke Park was bedecked with black-and-red flags, scarves and hats, the Kerry fans clearly outnumbered. For the Kingdom, All-Ireland final day was becoming a routine event of expectation – they were the reigning champions after all, into their fifth final in eight years and looking to add to their record nineteen Sam Maguires. The Kerry team sauntered onto the Croke Park pitch as if out for a Sunday stroll; Down burst out from the tunnel in the Cusack Stand, emerging like a bullet train arriving with purpose and intent. Kerry might have been used to final day, but they weren't ready for what Down would do to them.

Sixty minutes later, Kerry stood shell-shocked at the final whistle. On the scoreboard behind the goal, the result was there in black and white for all to read: Down 2–10, Kerry 0–8. The Kingdom had suffered its heaviest All-Ireland defeat. Down were All-Ireland champions.

When Kevin Mussen lifted the cup in front of the ecstatic players and fans, football observers knew this was no flash-in-the-pan victory. With their fluid movement and fast passing, allied with their modern training techniques and high levels of preparation, Down were heralding the future for inter-county teams.

Only a few years later, in 1964, their midfielder Joe Lennon wrote, *Coaching Gaelic Football for Champions* and launched the first national coaching courses at Gormanston College in County Meath. The 1960s were a breakthrough decade for Ireland in so many ways – television, *The Late Late Show*, The Beatles, George Best, civil rights, JFK … and Gaelic football wasn't to be left behind.

From the Hogan Stand, looking down on it all was the head of St Finan's Psychiatric Hospital in Killarney. Kerry hadn't called on Dr Eamonn O'Sullivan's training expertise that year but it wasn't long before they did come calling again, asking him to lead the Kingdom back to the Promised Land.

O'Sullivan had first trained Kerry to an All-Ireland in 1924 and, over the course of the next five decades, he was prevailed upon to take charge of team training camps for nine All-Ireland finals. In 1960, O'Sullivan's philosophy and approach to the game hadn't altered much from 1924. He applied his knowledge and understanding of medicine and psychiatry to enable Kerry teams reach their peak for All-Ireland Sunday. However, in terms of tactics, his adherence to zonal marking and traditional catch-and-kick was becoming out-dated in the rapidly changing modern game.

Despite witnessing Down's destruction of Kerry, O'Sullivan believed Kerry had nothing to fear. If they stuck to their strengths, they would win out. After all, he had encountered similar hype during 1955 and the final against Dublin, when all the talk had been about Dublin's roving full-forward, Kevin Heffernan, and how no one could stop the Dublin machine. With O'Sullivan in charge, Kerry had seen off the Dublin challenge comfortably and O'Sullivan saw no reason why he couldn't do the same with Down. But in the five years since the win over Dublin, the game had moved on and the unknown team from Ulster were the real harbingers of change.

It began with a man who had a simple but ambitious plan to reorganise the county's Gaelic football and make sure everything was in place for his county's senior team to win an All-Ireland – all within five years. Maurice Hayes couldn't understand why people's ambitions were so low.

There was a hugely defeatist attitude in Down GAA. The sum of their ambitions was to win the junior All-Ireland and people were being kept back so as to be eligible for the junior team.

Firstly, Hayes had to be in a position to instigate change and have men beside him who shared his vision. There was a younger generation coming through, men of the calibre of T.P. Murphy, Paddy O'Donoghue, Barney Carr and Arthur Doran, and they began working surreptitiously from within the organisation at first.

It was done almost subterranean. I think what happened was that, especially when we started talking about winning All-Irelands, most of the board thought we were lunatics, and they didn't want to be associated with defeat, but the one good thing was that those who thought we were mad left us alone.

Nothing less than a complete root-and-branch change was to be implemented if Down football was to go anywhere and if standards were to be raised across the board. As Hayes explains:

> We had people talking about a five-year plan, which is true in a way. But there was five years before that, of hard slog, of getting an inter-county league, an all-county league and breaking down divisional barriers, all based on the Kerry model of divisional teams. So the guys who were playing their hearts out on a junior team and getting the lining kicked out of them got a chance of playing with their peers, or at least better players, for a while. One of the problems was also that the minor teams tended to be dominated by college people because their selectors were priests and brothers. One of the things that we brought in was to give openness to guys like Doherty, Morgan and those guys. A few years ago an old man came up and said to me, 'You were the first to give the country boys a chance.'
>
> Calling it a plan, looking back at it, dignifies it with a strategy. But the rough notion was, you'd build it up for a couple of years, you'd get to an Ulster final. You'd lose it, but you'd learn enough to win the next Ulster final. And then you'd get to an All-Ireland semi-final where you'd get beaten, but you'd learn enough to go on like that. What that did actually was prepare guys for defeat as well as for victory – because if a defeat came, they knew that it was part of a progression and it wasn't the end of the world.

What they achieved in Down was more than just progression. By the end of the 1960s, a county that had never won an Ulster title, never mind an All-Ireland, had been provincial champions seven times and three-time winners of the Sam Maguire. But more than that, they had changed the face of Gaelic football forever, introducing new approaches to fitness and training, a new mindset to preparation and attention to detail, and a new thinking about the playing of the game. In short, it was nothing less than a complete modernisation of the sport.

Ulster football had been dominated by Cavan since the 1920s. There had been occasional wins by Monaghan and Antrim in the intervening years, but Cavan's dominance was coming to an end and other counties in the province were improving their lot and breaking the stranglehold. Armagh had won two All-Irelands in the 1950s, as had Tyrone and Derry, who made their breakthrough in 1958. Despite winning a junior title in 1946, the promise of Down football, it seemed, would go unfulfilled. Prior to their first Ulster title in 1959, Down had only had three appearances at an Ulster final, but as Hayes rose up the ranks of the Down County Board, finally becoming secretary in 1956, he was in a position to ensure that the ambitions and vision would be followed through.

'Initially progress was slow,' he admits, 'but winning the annual Wembley Tournament was a huge step forward. In 1959, we beat Dublin who were the All-Ireland champions and things began to take off from there.'

An Ulster final defeat at the hands of Derry in 1958 didn't spell the end of the road for Down GAA, it was merely the beginning.

'As far as I was concerned,' explains Hayes, 'they had cast themselves as second-class warriors, whereas there was this notion that Kerry men and Mayo men were all giants. I remember one day bumping into some Kerry footballers in Dublin, and there was a friend with me who, when we left the Kerry lads, said to me, "I know they are footballers, but who were they?", and I said, "You saw them last week playing in the All-Ireland." His response was that "they were giants of men" even though none of them were big guys. Because they were from Kerry, in people's eyes they were bigger than they actually were.

'And the second psychological barrier was Cavan, who dominated. If an Ulster team could beat Cavan that was it, that was their All-Ireland, after that they just wanted to put on a good show. It was about getting Down GAA over that line and getting them just mentally right. I think the difference was we made the players feel part of something, something that other people wanted to be involved in.'

Hayes, and those who shared his vision, decided that one of the best ways to make their players stand out and believe in themselves was by showing them that the county believed in them by treating them right in every aspect of the game and organisation.

In 1947, Hayes had played for Down in an Ulster hurling junior final in Clones. Picked up by a bus in Downpatrick at 8 a.m., he stood all the way to Clones because the bus was full of county board officials. Coming off the field, an official told the players 'to go and get your meal now because we are leaving immediately after the senior match'. The players replied, 'But we came here to see the bloody senior match.' Hayes says:

He told me to f– off and that scarred me for life. It was the one thing that we never did to our players. We said, if you got a group of guys together, and got commitment from them and committed to them, that you would treat them decently. If they were hurt, there would be adequate medical care. You were helping guys with summer jobs, you were taking them to decent hotels. That built up a tremendous team spirit. We started doing winter training. We had a doctor before other people had doctors.

Money was needed, but Hayes recalls that the cost for Down going all the way to the All-Ireland was only about €1,500 in today's money.

> *It was done on a shoestring. That was why the league was important, because you got money out of the league. You nearly needed to win the league to fund yourself for the championship and we had great voluntary help all the way through. We virtually had access to a hospital in Downpatrick where we had one guy, he was a surgeon, who just was interested in sports injuries. The physios could bring anybody in any time of the day or night. That was huge, there are people paying fortunes for that now. So that was one thing. The second was that employers were very decent; people would let them get it off or give you a car or something. There were no expenses for players, but what we did was we treated them decently.*

Hayes was also a friend of Dr Eamonn O'Sullivan, and could see some of his special qualities that Down also needed to incorporate into their approach.

> *What Dr Eamonn brought was psychological understanding of the needs of people and how people were different. He didn't train them all the same. I remember him waxing lyrical about a player's pectoral muscles one time. But he was just saying how with different people you had to train them differently.*

All the ambition and planning won't get you anywhere without the players, and the Down success in the 1961 final consisted of one of the greatest half-forward lines the game has ever seen – Paddy Doherty, Sean O'Neill and James McCartan, names that are revered around the country to this day. They played a fast, intelligent style of football that Radio Kerry's Weeshie Fogarty described as coming out onto Croke Park 'like an explosion'.

'There was no fear in the Down team,' says Joe Lennon, a midfielder on the three successful Down All-Ireland teams in the 1960s, whose books and courses on coaching completely revolutionised and modernised the scientific approach and methodologies to coaching Gaelic football. 'Paddy Doherty was one of the guys that exuded confidence in the Down team, as well as fellas like Patsy O'Hagan. Never was Down, not since I was playing, ever overawed by Kerry or anyone else. The most important thing was that Down was blessed with a lot of very talented players who knew their game and knew it inside out and were their own coaches, if you like. They did their own thing to quite an extent, they were self-motivated and they trained very hard and they knew their game and they were full of confidence. Now those are the things that got us through.'

Self-confidence, self-belief and self-motivation. Go back to Kerry and Kildare in the 1900s, Wexford in the 1910s, Kildare, Dublin, Kerry in the 1920s, Cavan, Galway, Mayo in the 1930s or Roscommon and Cavan in the 1940s, and these were the principles that stood the test of time. Combine them with an organisation that makes sure the players and team are treated correctly and you have a potent mix ready to go all the way.

In terms of training, Joe Lennon says Down weren't that different to other counties, but early preparation was key. 'The one thing that was different from other counties was the team started training earlier in the year, I think that is one of the most important things they did. They had a lot more training under their belts by the time the championship came around.'

Lennon's own dedication to the cause meant that because he was studying for a physical education degree at Loughborough

University in England, he had to fly back at weekends for county games until he moved back permanently in 1964.

Getting rid of the existing selection system and bringing in Barney Carr as manager was also integral to the county's future success. 'When I started off, the whole county board selected the team,' says Hayes. 'There is a man who – actually, I still have to bite my lip every time I think about it – he was the most bigoted, the most unreasonable person and when his man was voted out at right-back, he just turned his back to the meeting and read his breviary. You had all these guys pushing for their own teams, you couldn't do anything. We eventually got the selectors down to three.'

It's no surprise that Maurice Hayes was to have such a successful career after he stepped down as county secretary in 1964, going on to be, among other things, Northern Ireland's Ombudsman and Boundary Commissioner, Permanent Secretary of the Department of Health and Social Services, and a member of Seanad Éireann.

'There was no planning or organisation, but Maurice Hayes came along and changed all that,' remembered the team captain, Kevin Mussen, in a newspaper article written by Michael McGeary in the *Belfast Telegraph* at the time. '[Hayes] was the organiser, a man who knew exactly what he wanted and how to go about it. If anything was out of place, he was first to correct it. In a sense, his decisions were ruthless simply because he was convinced of the righteousness of the vision he had of us winning an All-Ireland, though he did consult with Barney Carr and others in the management team. We were blessed though to have had a man of such vision.'

Barney Carr's role as manager was also vital. Now in his ninetieth year, he set out his story in *Summerhill, Warrenpoint: A Memoir* in which he revealed the bitterness and antagonism that developed between himself and Maurice Hayes. In 1958, he joined

Hayes and Brian Denvir on the three-man selection committee and
agreed to take over as tactical coach with trainer Danny Flynn and
Dr Martin Walsh as medical adviser, also on board.

'I was conscious of my own lack of experience,' he wrote.
'However, I was confident that I knew football and how it should
be played. We trained two nights a week and we had a series of
challenge matches. The biggest tactical thing that we did was that
we got the ball to the forwards. You don't tell fellows like Paddy
Doherty or James McCartan how to play football. All you want is
them to get the ball.'

But Carr did bring outside influences to bear on the technique and
style of Down's play, utilising player mobility to beat more static,
zonal systems as espoused by Kerry and Dr Eamonn O'Sullivan.
It was Carr's soccer background and awareness of the incredible
Real Madrid team of the 1950s, which won five European Cups in
a row, that opened his eyes to how space could be made through
quick movement and passing.

> I thought it might be possible to translate some of the
> dynamic qualities of Real Madrid into Gaelic football.
> When we did beat Cavan so convincingly in 1959, I felt
> particularly fulfilled to read the next day in the Belfast
> Telegraph that: 'Down has brought a continental dimension
> to Gaelic football.'

While undreamed-of success was still a few years away, there were
still teething problems at an administrative and selection level
and it wasn't all plain sailing. Carr remembers the 1958 Ulster
final defeat to Derry and how their most experienced defender,
George Lavery, missed that game because of a mix-up in transport
arrangements that left Lavery stranded in Magherlin, 'where the
only things moving on a Sunday morning were the ducks'. Lavery

shrugged his shoulders and knew there was nothing for it but to go home and listen to the game on the radio.

1959 was an important year for Down GAA as it brought their first Ulster success, but also saw the appointment of Carr as team manager – the first formal recognition and appointment of a team manager in Gaelic football.

On the pitch, the Down team were quickly developing a formidable style of play that was proving itself against all-comers.

'In the 1960 campaign, when James McCartan came into the half-forward line, between Paddy Doherty and Sean O'Neill, the forward line was complete,' says Carr. 'James had his own natural football instincts; there was nothing more exhilarating than to see him emerge from deep in his own half in possession, knowing intuitively where to plant the ball for any of his forward colleagues, but particularly for O'Neill or Doherty, who with him formed what I called "a football trinity" – one mind in three bodies.'

'Any manager worth his salt can get a team to play in a certain way, whether it be free-flowing football, possession football or whatever,' explains Joe Lennon. 'He would have to design his tactics to suit the mobility of his team and if he can't do that easily he's not doing his job. That's why Jim McGuinness is doing it so well with Donegal, his tactics suit the ability of his team. The Down players would spend an awful lot of time improving their ability to kick accurately, working a lot on the kick-pass. The other thing, of course, is that we had very good free-takers with the likes of Paddy Doherty and Sean O'Neill. People think nowadays that you don't need much skill to stand on the twenty-yard line and kick the ball over the bar out of your hand.'

'What we had was possession, because we had no midfield,' Maurice Hayes highlights. 'Joe Lennon wouldn't want to hear this, of course, but we had no midfield. We reckoned if we got 40 per cent of the balls out of midfield, we would beat anything.

The thing was the scoring machine on our team was the half-forwards, either you got the ball over to them and back to them or into them. We set a certain standard back then, and Barney Carr has to take the credit for telling the players to go out and enjoy themselves.'

In terms of tactics, the talent and intelligence of the players meant it was very much a group buy-in. Once, when Barney Carr moved Joe Lennon back from midfield into the right-corner spot, he received a nineteen-page letter from Lennon detailing precisely why he should not have been moved.

Off days became a rarity for that Down team. The county's first Ulster win in 1959 was not just any win, but a fifteen-point hammering (2–16 to 0–7) of Cavan, the traditional Kings of Ulster. If ever there was a moment to mark the changing of the guard in the province, it was that seismic victory. The incredible Cavan dominance stretching back to 1915 was coming to an end and from having only two Ulster final appearances in their history (losing both, in 1940 and 1942), from 1958–1969, Down reached twelve consecutive Ulster deciders, winning seven and losing five.

However, the county couldn't follow up on its provincial success in 1959, losing to Galway in the All-Ireland semi-final.

Defeat, though, was only a temporary dent in their ambitions. League success followed in the 1959–1960 season, with Down beating Kerry in the semi-final along the way, a timely reminder of their superiority when the sides were to meet in the All-Ireland final later that year.

The county board also decided to enlist the help of former Meath All-Ireland-winning captain Peter McDermott, who had successfully helped the Down side that contested the 1946 All-Ireland junior championship final. McDermott was to become a noted coach, managing Meath to All-Ireland success in 1967, as well as being largely responsible for the development of the International Series against Australia, starting with Meath playing a number of games against Aussie Rules teams in 1968.

'Peter had no time for losers,' remembers corner-forward Brian Morgan. 'He told us that if we were not prepared to go out and give of our best – even our lives – then we might as well pull off the red-and-black jerseys. We had to prove that we were capable of winning an All-Ireland title.'

Firstly, though, the players had to retain their Ulster title, which they duly did. Then came the semi-final against Leinster champions Offaly. It was a game, Carr acknowledges, that Down were lucky to win after a dubious penalty was awarded to James McCartan in the last few minutes to earn a replay in which they had to endure tough 'squalls' against Offaly, as Carr described it, which had an effect on the forwards. Going in at half-time, Down were in danger of being knocked out at the semi-final stage for the second year in a row.

As it was, Down saw their way through and had reached the promised land – a first All-Ireland final with Kerry. And what a day Sunday, 25 September 1960 was. A record 87,768 crammed into Croke Park in a sea of green and gold, but mainly black and red to see Down capture the Sam Maguire.

'They beat us in April 1960 in the semi-final of the league in Croke Park,' remembered Tom Long, a member of the Kerry team. 'It was our first defeat in over twelve months and when we met them in the All-Ireland final, worse was to follow. They were the first side to bring the professional look to the game, even the way they dressed was different.'

Down had introduced tracksuits to the squad in the previous year. 'You would see fellows stripped with their coat over them,' says Carr. 'And I thought that's not good. It was only the subs that had tracksuits at first and then when the subs got them everybody wanted them.' In the process, Down were building up their myth and mystique around their preparation and professionalism.

'What Down brought in, in my estimation, was they were breaking the ball in the middle of the field,' says Weeshie Fogarty of Radio Kerry. 'This was a huge development, they actually brought in breaking the ball off Mick O'Connell and the other Kerry midfielders. Mick O'Connell would never break a ball in his life, that wasn't his game. O'Connell was such a stylish player fielding and kicking, but they had developed the breaking ball. I remember when there was a night for Mick O'Connell in the Great Southern Hotel in Killarney and I asked some of the Down players about it and they told me they brought in the breaking-ball tactic to counteract Mick O'Connell. The game was changing right there.'

'[Down] were a great footballing side,' Tom Long remembers. 'Like the team of Kerry's golden years, but they were spoilers and well-tutored in the art of fouling and breaking the ball at midfield. They had a wonderful half-forward line, as good as I have ever seen in football, probably the best in the history of the game.'

High praise indeed coming from a Kerryman.

Kerry people pointed to their team playing an injured John Dowling, the mistake of Johnny Culloty in letting the ball slip through his hands for the first goal and, of course, the absence of their seer, Dr Eamonn O'Sullivan.

'They had dropped the pilot,' says Hayes. 'However, I still believe that even if Dr Eamonn had been in charge, Down would still have won. One of the things we played on for that game was the fact that Dr Eamonn had a theory of zones and what we introduced into Gaelic football was mobility. Your full-back or half-back could move up with the ball and even make or get a score. In the late 1950s and early 1960s, there was a certain static quality about Kerry football.'

'As there is no copyright in Gaelic football,' wrote Carr, 'the Munster men have no redress.'

Down had shown the way.

However, for all the celebration and history-making with Down's first success, retaining the All-Ireland against Offaly the following year ranks as the team's best performance for Carr – 'the greatest football feat I have witnessed in over sixty years'. Another record crowd, this time topping 90,000, had Croke Park bursting to its seams in September 1961, but as with the sides' previous meeting, it was to be a tough, scrappy affair.

What stands out for Carr was the ability of the team to overcome adversity no matter what. Down left themselves a massive mountain to climb after they conceded two goals in the first five minutes. 'With such strokes of adversity most teams would have died, but they only served to bring out the best in the champions ... when these All-Ireland medals are presented to the Down men, they should be inscribed with the words "For valour", for no sporting decorations have been so hard earned.'

Down came back from the dreadful start to score three goals of their own, squeezing past Offaly by just a point, 3–6 to 2–8. From being no-hopers for so long, Down were league, Ulster and now All-Ireland champions for a second time. Success, though, creates its own problems, and overconfidence seeped into the camp and ultimately cost them a three-in-a-row. In the run-up to the 1962 Ulster final, only half the team presented themselves for training – it was a team 'not tuned for a final,' remembered Carr. Sure enough, Cavan were ready and waiting to pounce to regain their long-held possession of the Ulster title in a ten-point hammering of Down.

Down's remarkable few years of unparalleled national success had come to an end and, slowly but surely, the men who helped make it happen left the scene.

Barney Carr stayed on for another year and saw the county win back their Ulster crown, before losing to Dublin in an ill-tempered All-Ireland semi-final. After that, Carr decided his time in county management was up.

The following year, Maurice Hayes resigned from the county board and apart from another league and All-Ireland double in 1968, it was to be twenty-three years before Down lifted Sam Maguire again.

Down's dominance in Ulster may have been over, but their sudden explosion in the early 1960s had laid the foundations for the future blueprint for Gaelic football. However, despite what he had seen, one man still believed that the catch-and-kick and zonal marking could win games, and when Kerry reached the 1962 All-Ireland final against Roscommon with O'Sullivan in charge, they regained the All-Ireland.

But it was a false dawn. Football had moved on. A new Galway team – which took the best elements of quick ball and fluid movements to merge it with the skill and scoring of their forwards – was emerging. In Dr Eamonn O'Sullivan's last All-Ireland, time had caught up with the legendary trainer's philosophy, and Galway were convincing five-point winners. It was to be O'Sullivan's only defeat in nine finals, a legacy and record stretching back forty years. Kerry had lorded it over the Gaelic football landscape in that time, but since the 1960 defeat to Down, the county was being left behind as the game changed and embraced the modern and the new.

Chapter 2

Like moths about a light

While Down were building a revolution in Ulster that was to have a wider impact on Gaelic football, in Connacht, Galway, under the guidance of John 'Tull' Dunne, were in the midst of making their own piece of history.

The Tribesmen had reached and lost the 1959 All-Ireland final to Kerry, and after another defeat in 1963, this time to Dublin, many in Galway would have been forgiven for believing perennial heartache was to be a feature of their county's football season. Memories of the three All-Ireland final losses in a row from 1940–1942 (twice to Kerry and once to Dublin) were still raw for Galway's football men. However, the 1956 Sam Maguire success, the county's first in eighteen years, was the spark that inspired the three-in-a-row in the 1960s.

Down may have been capturing the wider public's attention, but Galway were quietly confident themselves heading into the early 1960s. Whether anyone could have expected the team to achieve a three-in-a-row from 1964–1966 is unlikely – the only counties aside from Kerry to achieve this in the previous fifty years were

Dublin, from 1921–1923, and Wexford, who managed a four-in-a-row from 1915–1918. Down's success was built on the planning and vision of Hayes and Carr, but Galway's All-Ireland domination came about through the single-mindedness of one man coupled with some of the most talented forwards the game has seen.

'That Galway team of the 1960s didn't just come together, they were built,' asserts Cyril Dunne, who was himself a member of the three All–Ireland-winning sides and whose father, John 'Tull', was Galway's manager/coach.

Similar to Roscommon's approach in the 1940s, after losing two consecutive Connacht finals, Galway decided to give youth its fling.

'We lost to Roscommon in 1961 and 1962,' recalls Dunne. 'But the 1962 defeat was the ending of the 1956 team – if you like, they were nearly all weeded out at that stage. So the likes of myself and John Keenan and Pat Donlon, Christie Tyrell, Johnny Geraghty and Enda Colleran, we were all from the 1960 All-Ireland-winning minor squad. It was a building process really.'

Like so many of the teams featured in this book, those who went on to win at senior level had previously tasted success at minor level. The key then was ensuring the right balance in the mix of young players and hardened, older players. When the teams achieved that balance, the result was invariably senior success.

Dunne grew up in a legendary GAA household in Ballinasloe. His father, John, had won All-Irelands with Galway juniors in 1930, with the seniors in 1934 and captained the latter to further success four years later in 1938. John Dunne had a lifetime of involvement with Galway GAA, including as secretary of the county board, before taking charge of the minors in 1952 and becoming involved with the seniors from 1954 – a connection that was to last right up to Galway's All-Ireland appearance in 1974 (their last for that decade) when they were beaten by the up-and-coming Dublin team.

John 'Tull' Dunne was a natural organiser and manager, meticulous in detail, who took on the role of county secretary from a young age.

'He recorded all the teams that were picked down those years,' recalls his son, Cyril. 'It's a great record to have and it shows the type of detail that would go into what they were doing. But the county had a barren period at the start of the 1950s when Galway football went down altogether. There was a shortage of money and there's even records of when they had no money to even buy a set of nets.'

Galway was at its lowest point and, to make matters worse, their archrivals Mayo were having their best period of All-Ireland success, winning two titles on the trot in 1950 and 1951. If anything, Mayo's success was an even greater spur to Dunne and others to put Galway football back on the map.

The signs of promise were there. In 1952, Frank Stockwell returned from his Louth sojourn to revive his partnership up front with Sean Purcell at club and county level, forming one of the greatest forward double acts in Gaelic football history. That year, the 'Terrible Twins', as they became known, were just beginning. It was also the same year that Galway's youthful talent began to show what it was capable of, capturing the county's first All-Ireland minor title with John Dunne as manager.

'At that stage, he was moving players around to where they might best fit the position,' explains Cyril Dunne. 'He was always looking to make the team, rather than make the individual.'

With players of the calibre of Stockwell and Purcell around, it wasn't long before the blend of youthful talent and older know-how combined for All-Ireland senior success. Firstly, though, provincial success had to be achieved. Roscommon had dominated in the 1940s, while Mayo had won four Connachts in a row from 1948–1951, culminating in double All-Ireland success. Along the way, Mayo gave Galway a hammering in the 1951 Connacht final, beating them by sixteen points on a scoreline of 4–13 to 2–03. Roscommon won the next two Connacht titles before, finally, in 1954, Galway's underage promise was fulfilled with a first provincial success for the Tribesmen since 1945. However, their nascent campaign came to an end in the semi-final against Kerry and it was to be another two years before they tasted another All-Ireland semi-final.

The great 1950–1951 Mayo side was coming to an end, though there was one last sting from them in capturing the 1955 Connacht crown. The following year, Galway announced their supremacy over their great rivals, crushing them by seventeen points, 5–13 to 2–5, with Purcell and Stockwell lording it over the Mayo defence and erasing, somewhat, their sixteen-point humiliation from five years previously. The torch in the west was being passed on. Galway duly captured their second Connacht title in three years with a facile thirteen-point win over Sligo. The All-Ireland semi-final victory over debutants Tyrone was a tough, tight affair, but Galway's experience saw them over the line in a tense, low-scoring encounter 0–8 to 0–6, with Sean Purcell's free-taking the standout performance on the day. This time there was no Kerry to face, instead Cork stood in the way of Galway's first All-Ireland title since 1938.

'I never anticipated such polished and almost classical football from this recently sprung Galway side,' wrote P.D. Mehigan in *Carbery's Annual* that year. Once again, Purcell and Stockwell were the star performers on the day, with Purcell achieving a then-record tally of 2–5, which was to stand for another twenty years (and still stands as the sixty-minute record). The link-play between Purcell and Stockwell and overall quality of the game between Galway and Cork was hailed by writers of the day.

'The game had just everything,' wrote John D. Hickey. 'The

splendour of the football was inspiring, if not awesome; the tenseness of the closing stages simply beggars description; there were individual displays to rank with the greatest I have seen.'

'When Galway won the All-Ireland in 1956, it was huge,' says Cyril Dunne. 'The effect on the whole county was incredible. There was only seven of the team who survived from the Mayo hammering in 1951 and it was important that change was introduced. But also importantly, winning changed the whole way football was viewed in the county. It had been eighteen years since the last All-Ireland but now Galway were champions again.'

Liam Sammon, who was to star on Galway's team from 1966, grew up idolising the 1956 team.

There has always been a self-belief about Galway football. It came especially from the 1956 team which had a huge influence on the next generation. They were a fabulous team to watch and that brought in a new generation of young players.

John Dunne's tactical nous also played a big part in that 1956 team's success, as reported by the *Cork Examiner*.

History has many instances of battles won and lost through strategy; to determine the weakness of an opposing force and exploit that weakness to the full is an art of war. But in the All-Ireland football final, we learned the full scope and meaning of the word. We witnessed a peaceful but masterly display of good tactics. For the entire game, the champions were without a full-forward. It was opposed to the fundamentals of Gaelic football, but the Cork defence crumbled before the genius of the moves as executed by Frank Stockwell and Sean Purcell.

Kevin Heffernan wasn't the only one acting as a roving forward in those days and it's worth noting that, at this time, Down, with their versatile mobile forward play, had yet to appear on the Ulster scene.

However, despite going on to dominate Connacht, winning five-in-a-row from 1956–1960, further All-Ireland success was to prove elusive for the Terrible Twins of Stockwell and Purcell, who retired in 1960 and 1961 respectively. They were never able to add to their one Sam Maguire success, scant reward for their skills, talents and service to Galway football down through the years.

1959 was their last opportunity at another All-Ireland title when they reached the final to face Kerry, but it was a disappointing encounter, with Sean Murphy the outstanding performer for Kerry in the middle of the park, helping the Kingdom to win by nine points, 3–7 to 1–4. However, by this time, Down were on the horizon and were ready to light up the Gaelic football world for the next few years.

But the success of the 1956 team bred a new generation of players coming through and Galway won a second All-Ireland minor in 1960, beating Cork by thirteen points in the final. After hanging up his boots, Frankie Stockwell joined John Dunne on the management team and took over the training of the seniors, with Brendan Nestor from Dunmore also helping out. It was to prove a lethal combination.

'What really made it then was that I remember going to the 1956, 1957, 1958 training sessions and there wasn't the same intensity in the training,' remembers Cyril Dunne. 'The lads would come in and they mightn't train and they would go home. When we came on to the scene in the early 1960s we had a huge panel, the players were all in much the same age group and they were all keen looking for places. My father also then changed the football at that stage. He cut out all the kicking up in the air and he made us keep the ball down. We had some very fast players, you see. And my father was more or less trying to counteract the high fielders and the good catchers and he felt I suppose we weren't big enough for that type of thing. We would practise the ground kicks – punting the ball out in front of you – and, in training, it would be get the ball, allowed one hop or one tip on your toe and then you had to get rid of it.

'In addition to making use of our speed, he also moved the players around. He got Enda Colleran into corner-back and moved John Donlon out to the wing. He brought Bosco McDermott, who was a midfielder, he brought him back to make a corner-back because we were short a corner-back. Bosco didn't really like it when he was put back there but he turned out to be as good a corner-back as any you could get. It was really all a building process.'

Age and experience – or lack of it – didn't matter either. As Cyril explains:

It was a policy, not stated in public, but between himself and Brendan Nestor and Frank Stockwell, that if they saw a player and thought he was good enough, well, his age didn't matter.

Working in Posts and Telegraphs meant that Dunne was able to keep tabs on promising players from every corner of the county and he was always to be seen pitch-side for minor, under-21, junior and senior matches of all kinds.

Success wasn't achieved overnight either. The Connacht final defeats in 1961 and 1962 against Roscommon brought the need for change to a head and were important learning curves for the still-youthful team, but the defeat of Leitrim by twelve points in the 1963 final signalled the arrival of this great Galway team, though they reached and lost the All-Ireland final against Dublin that year in a poor encounter that had fifty-two frees.

Galway were to catch up, though.

'Galway were well-drilled and stylish. Years before their time,' wrote Mick O'Dwyer in his autobiography, *Blessed and Obsessed*. And while Down's forward line of Doherty, McCartan and O'Neill were grabbing the headlines, John Dunne had other ideas for his up-and-coming Galway side.

'We were very conscious of what Down were doing all right,' says Cyril Dunne. 'They were doing a lot of soloing, carrying the ball a good lot and they were a team that were able to get goals. But my father always harped on to kick it over the bar. "If you take your points then the goals will come," he would say, and down the years while we weren't the greatest goal-scoring team, we got goals when we wanted them, but the policy was more like, put it over the bar if you are in position.'

'Galway had, well we like to think we had, a distinctive type of play,' explains Liam Sammon. 'It was a fast movement of the ball, get it up to the forwards as quickly as possible. Also there were quite a few players who had come up through St Jarlath's and UCG and that closeness and know-how was there to see – there was always a slickness about the type of play that came from that.'

The emphasis from Stockwell's training sessions was on kicking practice.

'We had kicking practice where someone would be on the twenty-one-yard line,' explains Dunne, 'and you would come running in, and he would throw you the ball and you would have to flick it over the bar or try and kick it with your left foot. There were training sessions where you weren't allowed to carry the ball or weren't allowed to solo, that was great. He was against soloing the ball when you didn't have to, when you could find a lad twenty or thirty yards away with a kick. He always said the ball goes faster than the man. I would love to see the players nowadays trying this, instead of all this hand-passing, you know. An awful lot of the passes were with the feet, my father had that in his mind, he always tried to instil that type of thing – to keep the ball moving, make use of our speed.'

'Get the ball away and ask yourself questions after,' was how former player Colie McDonagh remembers Dunne's philosophy on the game. 'He didn't want any dilly-dallying on the ball from the backs. He wanted the ball cleared quickly.'

'John Dunne had a type of mantra about how the game should be played,' remembers Sammon. 'He was in total control of what he wanted. But, in fairness, a lot of it would also be coming from the players, the players themselves would know how and what way to be playing. John was a good motivator more than anything else.'

'What was really important,' says Cyril Dunne, 'was that the training sessions were really enjoyable for us. The training at that time was more sprinting and walks: sprint, run, walk, sprint, run and play football, and then we used to play what they used to call a bit of ground football – we couldn't call it soccer of course! But we did practise it for control of the ball. The great thing was that Frank Stockwell would always be involved with the players and he'd know that night that you mightn't be at your best and he would keep you ten or fifteen minutes extra – how he knew it I never knew. Then when the training would be finished, I remember myself, Pat Donlon and a few others, we would have a race from one end of the field to the other and we would finish up with that. We wouldn't just stroll off and walk in, we would finish up with that.'

The dedication to their fitness and training, being willing to go the extra distance, was what mattered and is another feature of all successful teams down through the decades, probably best epitomised by the Kerry players such as Pat Spillane in the 1970s.

'The sessions weren't really hardship, you know,' says Dunne. 'We togged out, had our bit of whatever we had to do, then we went back to the dressing room after that, had a shower – though some fellas wouldn't have them, showers weren't that popular at the time – we would have a bottle of milk and a few sandwiches in the dressing room. That's what we'd have and we would have a chat about things and then we would go home, and that was it. It was really enjoyable, it really was.'

'The vast majority of our team at that time would come in fit and they would come in just to be together because there was a great camaraderie between the players on the team, coming together and to play,' says Sammon. 'You even had some players and it would be hard to stop them from training, they wanted to do so much. And then there were very, very few who actually drank, I think there was only one or two guys who took a drink. It was a very dedicated bunch of lads.'

Galway came back again in 1964, beat Meath in the semi-final and faced Kerry in the final again – a repeat of 1959. But this was a new, youthful Galway team and Kerry held no shadow over them. John Dunne's team ran out five-point winners, 0–15 to 0–10, and they had proven equal to the standing of their 1956 predecessors.

It was, according to the *Connacht Tribune*, 'an exhibition of avant-garde football which underscored the scribes' and Kerry's ridiculous obsession that mediocrity plus tradition can win All-Ireland titles in the 1960s'.

Cyril Dunne scored nine of Galway's fifteen points and, despite Mick O'Connell's heroics, scoring seven of Kerry's ten, there was nothing the Kingdom could do to match the quick, passing game of the Tribesmen.

Galway and Kerry were to face each other once more, in the following year's All-Ireland final which was not a memorable affair. Mick O'Connell was kept curtailed by Pat Donnellan throughout and, despite Kerry coming back to within one point midway through the second half, Galway weathered the storm and four points in five minutes helped ensure that, for the first time in their history, Galway retained the All-Ireland, winning 0–12 to 0–9. It was also – and still remains – the only time in Kerry's footballing history that they lost two consecutive All-Irelands. The fact that it was against Galway on both occasions merely reinforced the superiority of Galway's style of play and how Kerry's traditional philosophy of play had to change. Speed of movement and superior fitness from other counties was showing them up badly.

That second final defeat to Galway left a bitter taste in Kerry supporters' mouths, and they let the team and management know how they felt, booing them off at half-time and when, after receiving Sam Maguire, Galway captain Enda Colleran called for three cheers for Kerry, a chorus of boos rang out around the stadium.

'All credit to the champions,' wrote the *Connacht Tribune*. 'It was no fault of theirs that the football suffered in the quest for honours. The mantle of greatness undoubtedly rests where it belongs – with the Corribsiders – a team which has exploded for all time the myth of Kerry invincibility in the football arena.'

'After our first All-Ireland, when we got back to training, we said we would try and put two back-to-back,' remembers Cyril Dunne. 'And when we got the two All-Irelands, I remember saying, "Well look, lads, we'll see if we can make it three in a row."'

And make it they did, becoming the first team since Kerry's 1939–1941 success to achieve the treble, and only the fourth county overall to do it. But it was not all plain-sailing, and, like any team that succeeds at the top, they needed a bit of luck along the way.

Galway scraped past Mayo in the Connacht final by a mere point, with Liam Sammon pointing the winner in injury time, and, in the semi-final against Cork, the Munster team spurned numerous goal chances with the Tribesmen battling through by just two points. The third of their successes – against Meath – was another poor affair with Galway out of sight even by half-time, leading by eight points. The Leinster men cut into the lead in the second half but the result was never in doubt and Galway won by six points, 1–10 to 0–7.

Would a four-in-a-row have been possible for Galway? If they hadn't gone to America, many in the county believe so, but the National League final was played in the United States that year – which Galway won, beating Dublin by two points – and just five weeks later they faced Mayo in a Connacht semi-final. Whether the team was jet-lagged or merely coming to an end, Mayo brought Galway's five-year reign in Connacht to a halt, dumping John Dunne's men out by an eleven-point margin in Pearse Stadium, Tuam.

'As we went on a bit, my father started to bring a few players in,' says Cyril Dunne. 'But I think it would nearly have been better off if he had cleaned us all out and got in more. The thing was the players were nearly all going to go together, but my father tried not to do that because he brought in the likes of Coleen McDonagh and Jimmy Duggan, who was only out of Jarlath's in 1966.'

But unlike the 1959 clear-out, John Dunne's team of 1967 had won him three All-Irelands. Dropping players who have achieved so much for you, and given years of their lives to sacrifice for the county team, is not done easily.

John Dunne remained and the county recaptured Connacht the following year and won the provincial title in four of the next six years up to 1974. Slowly, the players from the treble years moved on. Despite the efforts to bring through more young players, and despite reaching three more All-Ireland finals in 1971, 1973 and 1974, Sam Maguire didn't come west across the Shannon for another quarter of a century until 1998 when it took a Mayo man, John O'Mahony, to oversee Galway's next success.

After a lifetime of involvement – as a player, captain, trainer, administrator, secretary and All-Ireland winner – John 'Tull'

Dunne stepped away from the job in 1980. He had been with the county for nearly sixty years, a servant and master to Galway and Gaelic football in every sense of the word.

'He had a magnificent posture right up to the end, you never saw Tull dropping his shoulders,' recalled the reporter Jim Carney in 2009. 'I saw pictures of him leading out teams in the 1930s in this commanding walking style, straight leg and powerful shoulders. So at Galway matches, even in later years, you saw this tall man coming with the hat. And it created an impression.'

The impression was a lasting one, with his legacy etched forever in the record books. Youth was given its fling in the 1960s and, in Galway, had proved it could win All-Irelands.

Chapter 3

The cult of professionalism

Galway are rightly lauded and admired for their historic treble – something only subsequently achieved by the great Kerry side of the 1970s – however, their place in history, in terms of influence, seems to have been more parochial. Galway teams were forever playing in the shadow of Enda Colleran, Mattie McDonagh, Cyril Dunne and co., only finally managing to emerge from the past with Sam Maguire successes in 1998 and 2001.

On the other hand, Down's success transcended the county, and even the sport itself. They brought with them the beginnings of the modern. From every level – organisation, planning, approach, preparation, training, technique, style and thinking – Down set themselves apart from anything that had gone before.

Organisation and player welfare were set in stone, continental soccer influences brought to bear and the players, most notably Joe Lennon, thought deeply and wrote about the game itself – from both a philosophical and coaching perspective. Perhaps if John Dunne had set down in words his thoughts and thinking on the game, we might be regarding him and Galway's approach in a more analytical light, but it was Lennon who became the pre-eminent thinker of the day on Gaelic football coaching.

In 1964, while still a player, and while Galway were in the midst of their three-in-a-row All-Ireland success, Down's Joe Lennon wrote *Coaching Gaelic Football for Champions*, and also launched the first national coaching courses in Gormanston College, County Meath, at which thirty counties were represented. For the first time, and on a national basis, other players and interested coaches were being schooled in techniques and drills to ensure higher standards of play and fitness. The leading managers of the future, including Mick O'Dwyer and Kevin Heffernan, attended these courses which had a profound impact on their thinking and development of the training and tactics of teams.

But the hierarchy of the GAA was not impressed, criticising this approach to the game and attempting to portray the likes of Lennon as elitist. GAA president Alf Murray labelled it a 'new cult' of 'professionalism of the worst kind'. Whether the GAA hierarchy objected because they were suspicious of players taking control of matters for themselves or because they wanted their own influence to come to bear on such developments is not clear, but, the courses proved hugely popular and continued without the GAA's imprimatur.

'There was still an awful lot of opposition in some quarters to coaching,' says Lennon. 'For men like Alf Murray, who was a teacher, to condemn coaching out of hand, it beggars belief. There was certainly a fear that it would turn everyone into a professional. Today, of course, they can't get enough coaches.'

Cynically, Lennon was referred to as 'the high-priest of coaching' by officialdom but, having studied and graduated with a degree in physical education from Loughborough University, Lennon wasn't to be deterred in his attempts to help educate his fellow players and coaches on correct training techniques and drills.

Physical education degrees were only available in Britain and

were a recent development in sports science with an emphasis on
fitness, coaching and physiology. Thanks to the 1947 Education
Act (Northern Ireland), which provided for free post-primary
education for children in the North, more and more kids, especially
Catholics, were getting an education and, as a consequence, more
people went to university.

Jim McKeever, Derry captain of the 1958 Ulster-title-winning
team, was one of the first from Northern Ireland to come up through
that system and to go on and study physical education at college,
as he says:

*The idea of Loughborough was pretty new for the people
in Ireland anyway, and Northern Ireland in particular.
They had started building secondary schools in Northern
Ireland and they had to devise a programme which
included PE, but then they realised they hadn't got any
specialists in PE, so they started giving scholarships to
one or two people to go over and study at Loughborough.
The lecturers in Loughborough, some of them had various
kinds of degrees from Cambridge and other universities,
and they themselves had gone and taken physical
education qualifications. There were some specialists in
soccer, some specialists in gymnastics, some specialists in
athletics, so each of them specialised in their own subject
and took it very seriously. They analysed the activities bio-
mechanically and what the physical requirements were,
and all that was new and very interesting. Looking back
on it now, it wasn't rocket science.*

*The great thing about it was there were plenty of guys
from all over England, a few from Scotland, and a few
from other parts of the world, including an Egyptian guy
we were friendly with. They had come I suppose because*

*England had started this earlier than most other European
countries. Although the Danes and Germans were ahead of
them. There was an English rugby international there and
there were English amateur international soccer players,
there were plenty of national athletes, and meeting those
guys was even more eye-opening than the actual courses.*

When he went in 1952, McKeever was probably the first Gaelic
footballer to study physical education at Loughborough, but even
looking back on it all he still doesn't think of the teaching as being
that revolutionary. 'The revolutionary thing was actually deciding
to take sport seriously and have a career in it,' he says.

Nonetheless, the year in Leicestershire opened his eyes to other
ideas, other sports and the science behind the thinking – which
would stand him in good stead for both his inter-county playing
career and the remarkable thirty-five years he was to spend at St
Mary's College in Belfast in charge of their sports department.

'Loughborough was helpful in making me think with more
scientific knowledge,' he agrees. 'Looking back I wasn't
consciously aware of bringing that knowledge into the game, it
probably influenced how I thought and so on, but I think it was
just being part of the activity that you learn, you learn as you learn
to ride a bicycle. Nobody told me how to do it, but I fell off a few
times and then realised instinctively and did things to keep me on
it – that's not special. We have an ability to learn things without
actually analysing them scientifically and I think we did a lot of
that.'

For someone who didn't grow up in McKeever's time, listening
to his modest, gentle manner, it is easy to underestimate just how
highly regarded he was in the game at the time, including being
described by Kerry's Mick O'Connell as the best catcher of a ball
he had ever played against.

For someone of McKeever's talent, the game wasn't complicated, it was about simply doing things that made sense.

For your opponent, you tried to know what kind of guy he was – big, small, fast – and that helped you to adjust, to prepare and not have to discover it in the first fifteen minutes. The tactic would have been: how do you as a player cope with him? How should you handle this? You may even have switched positions if you found there was somebody else who could handle him better and could move into that position. That to me is not rocket science, just common sense. We always did that, even in our college-playing days.

Jim McKeever's exploits with Derry, in helping them to win their first Ulster title in 1958, will always be remembered, but it's his coaching methods with St Mary's that had an even wider influence and lasting legacy.

'Good coaching is like good teaching,' McKeever believes. 'Coaching is not about imposing your ideas on people, but making them think for themselves and learn to know what happens. That's why Down became so successful.'

In Ulster, the roots of coaching came through Jim McKeever at St Mary's College in Belfast and a whole host of future inter-county and college managers came under his influence, learning from him and, in turn, spreading their gospel of the game around the province. For McKeever though, throughout all those years, the principles of the game remained the same.

I'm a bit of a sceptic about modern tactics and modern ideas. At the end of my thirty-five years, I honestly don't think I was coaching any differently than I was at the beginning. The game was still the same. You still had to read the

player's ability, try and encourage him to develop what he
was good at and to maybe work on things and weaknesses
that were costly. You would maybe have certain suggestions
about whether he's moving about or not, or whether he's
not playing the ball early. You were trying to suggest and
build things into him that you think will improve his game.
You should actually encourage and teach and talk to them
and persuade them, so that they can think for themselves
and then have the skills to operate how the thing should be
done.

If McKeever was the first to actually study sport and coaching in
the scientific sense and bring it into a Gaelic football setting, it
was Down's Joe Lennon who took the science and thinking behind
physical education to a wider GAA playing and coaching audience
via his books and courses. As he says, 'I was always conscious
of starting with Gaelic football and saying, "Well what's the best
thing we can do here for Gaelic football?"' The success of his
coaching courses from 1964 proved that there was an appetite and
hunger within the Gaelic football community for more knowledge
– despite what officialdom might disparagingly say.

Lennon wrote about a 'new look' that had emerged in Gaelic
football which was 'based more on skill than brawn and which was
found to be eminently more satisfying to players and spectators
alike'. He went on to describe how:

The new fast integrated team movements characterised by
precise passing as opposed to the long, high kick are very
enjoyable to watch. The realisation that this new facet of
the game could be so artistic and thrilling had magnetic
effects. The popularity increased.

Echoing Dick Fitzgerald from fifty years previously, Lennon highlighted the science to the sport, but also, most importantly, hoped his book would inspire other coaching literature to appear.

I am alarmed at the proportion of the time we spend talking about and playing the games as opposed to thinking about the games and what can be done to improve them ... It is my hope that this book might prompt some other Gaels to devote some scientific thought to the game and perhaps encourage some others to write about the game.

The role and importance of physical education in the lives of the citizens was obvious from that period, with governments in the UK and Ireland actively funding and promoting its expansion through schools, something that Lennon was a keen advocate of.

'Modern educational thought has given a good deal of countenance to specialisation in almost all fields,' he said. In the field of Gaelic football, there was a need therefore to 'replace physical training with physical education'.

In the field of physical education, we have become accustomed to the specialists. They have pushed the frontiers of achievement along and widened our whole horizon. In Gaelic football, we can do the same. As other sports experimented and specialised and improved so too can we.

With chapters on tactics, training, scoring, drills, and a breakdown of the techniques and skills needed in Gaelic football, Lennon's thorough and forensic detailing of the game was a breakthrough in terms of the canon of coaching literature, giving a practical, hands-on guide to Gaelic football managers and trainers.

'We should bring some scientific thought to bear on every aspect of the game,' he wrote. 'It is only by keeping the game up with the progress of social, educational and scientific reform that we can hope to make it acceptable to the age in which we live.'

His thoughts on coaching and player involvement in the coaching of teams were also ahead of their time, espousing a two-way conversation between management and players, highlighting the need for 'players to think for themselves' – a technique that Kevin Heffernan was to use with such incredible effect ten years later.

Lennon's philosophy and coaching of the game was based on the premise of possession.

Possession is nine-tenths of the game ... risking possession for distance kicking is quite undesirable. The guiding principle should be to maintain possession as long as possible.

And in a direct riposte to the traditionalists of the catch-and-kick philosophy, he criticised 'the tendency to kick and hope ... players seem satisfied if they catch and kick on. If the ball does not reach a team-mate or if an opponent gets it, the fault is seldom attributed to the kicker.'

Ultimately, he said, coaching is 'directed at the complete exploitation of the arts and skills within the framework of the rules', and it was this calculating approach to the game that was to see counties in future years test that to its fullest.

Five years later, Joe Lennon brought out a second book, *Fitness for Gaelic Football*, and it was obvious just how far the game had come since the beginning of the decade.

'Now in 1969, it is true to say that the overwhelming weight of opinion is behind coaching and the few remaining advocates of traditional training methods are rarely if ever heard,' he wrote.

Having established sound fitness and training practices and

principles over the intervening years, Lennon presciently pointed to the mind and 'mental fitness' as playing a key role for Gaelic footballers.

Fitness for Gaelic Football was another scientific explanation and detailing of principles and techniques to be used with chapters on defence and attack. The key principles for play, according to Lennon, are:

- accuracy
- anticipation
- determination
- depth and balance
- mobility
- recovery
- safety
- speed
- superior numbers.

These varied in priority according to position on the field, but, ultimately, what it came down to was still the fact that 'possession is the law' – 'the more passes the more likelihood of an error costing possession,' he wrote.

As a precursor to what Dave Weldrick at Thomond College in Limerick was to preach in the 1970s and which was to be developed even further by Ulster teams in the 1990s and beyond, Lennon highlighted the need for defending to begin with the forwards. 'All players on the team that has lost possession are defenders,' he wrote. It was to be a principle that would be developed into the swarming-style in the 2000s and would become a standard coaching tactic in the years afterwards.

'I think the next decade will produce the best football we have ever seen. It is an exciting prospect,' Lennon wrote in his conclusion in 1969, and they were sage words. In the years to come, it was to be Dublin and Kerry that would dominate the Gaelic football landscape, creating their own history, taking Down's levels of preparation to new levels and bringing the game to an entirely new audience and standard of play.

Travelling home from one of Lennon's coaching courses at Gormanston in March 1975 was Mickey Ned O'Sullivan, who was just back from completing his own PE degree at Strawberry Hill in London. Beside him in the car was Mick O'Dwyer, who had been training the Waterville footballers, having brought them to three county finals. They had just seen Joe Lennon and Kevin Heffernan detailing the best coaching methods and habits, setting out how to do entire training sessions and, despite O'Dwyer's previous reticence, O'Sullivan knew it had piqued his interest.

'Would you train the Kerry team?' O'Sullivan asked him, knowing the county board were looking for someone to take over.

'No, I wouldn't,' replied O'Dwyer. 'I don't have the time. I'm too busy.'

But the drive from Meath to Kerry was a long one, and O'Sullivan didn't give up. By the time they reached Kenmare, O'Dwyer's opposition to the idea was softening.

'I rang the county board chairman, Gerald McKenna,' recalls O'Sullivan. 'And I said, "Micko will do it, but you will have to go back to him." So the following day, the chairman spoke to him and he accepted.'

Kerry had a new manager.

Gaelic football and the GAA was about to change forever.

Part II

Fitness Fanatics

'The task of the leader is to get his people from where they are to where they have not been.'

Henry Kissinger, former US Secretary of State

Chapter 4

'There is a place down there called Croker waiting'

If you are sitting in front of 82,000 people and everything has gone wrong in every part of the field, there is nothing in the manual that tells you what to do next if you are a manager. You have to have instincts, you have to know. Kevin had instincts and he knew what he wanted.

These were the words of Tony Hanahoe, former Dublin captain and player-manager, speaking about his manager, the quintessential Dublin GAA man Kevin Heffernan, just weeks before Heffernan passed away in January 2013.

In interviews over the years, Heffernan has given great insight on reviving Dublin GAA in the 1970s. His words are a reminder of his keen brain and how he turned a moribund team around to become All-Ireland champions and serial finalists in just two short years. As with all great sportsmen in their field, asking them to explain their magic can be a futile experience, with explanations about simplicity usually the mantra. For us mere mortals, trying to unlock their brains can be as impossible to understand as if it was spoken in another language.

Heffernan's success with the Dubs in the 1970s saw them reach six All-Irelands in a row from 1974–1979 (winning three, in 1974, 1976 and 1977), a feat only achieved by Wexford (1913–1918) and by Kerry – and not by the O'Dwyer team but in the 2000s from 2004–2009. When asked about his role and involvement in the process – which also helped create the greatest rivalry the GAA has ever seen, and helped to build the foundations for the modern game in the capital – his answer was simple:

> *It was very much an accident of birth really. It was just a case of getting a good team together at the right time. Generally, it emanates primarily through two or three gifted guys and they have an influence which spreads to the rest.*

When Heffernan took the reins after the 1973 season, things had been as bad as anyone could remember. Westmeath had dumped Dublin out of Leinster in 1967, then Longford, Laois and Louth in subsequent years.

'Kevin genuinely made a serious effort from 1970 to build a team,' remembers Hanahoe. 'And it was a transition period at that stage, trying to blend some of the remaining older players with newer players, but it wasn't as successful as he anticipated.'

Crashing out to Louth certainly wasn't part of the plan and, as Hanahoe describes it, '1973 was a period when a lot of people, including Kevin Heffernan and myself, had a lot of serious thinking to do about what we were going to do.'

Luckily for Dublin GAA, the county board were also sick of the barren, wasted years and wanted a resurgence in Dublin's fortunes for the greater good of the game in the county if nothing else. Dublin chairman Jimmy Gray saw fit to agree to Kevin Heffernan's appointment, but for Heffernan, the role came with one important change – there wasn't to be a convoluted club selector system, there were to be three men to lead the Dublin changes and no more.

'Nobody had ever heard of a manager back then,' recollected Heffernan. 'There was a selection committee and they were usually five guys. And it was the usual inter-club rivalries and who you know and all this shite. Bitterness and rancour and old scores being settled. It was depressing.'

In scenes reminiscent of Down GAA's turn-around fifteen years previously, Jimmy Gray forced through long-required and much-needed change.

'Fortunately, Jimmy Gray took the bull by the horns and said we are not going to have it like this any more. He was pissed off and it couldn't get any worse,' said Heffernan. 'So he appointed myself, Donal Colfer and Lorcan Redmond. The gas thing about it was I didn't actually know Lorcan and I didn't know Donal at all, yet we were twelve years together and we never had an argument and we never had a vote on what team we would pick. We would debate it and discuss it and we would start afresh and start from a different point of view and we continued for hours and hours until we were agreed. We never, not once, had an argument.'

And why Heffernan?

'It was probably because I was a mouth – "Jaysus that f–ing Heffernan" – I would always have had an opinion,' he remarked, only half-joking. 'But Donal, Lorcan and myself, we became as close as we are to this day. It was a remarkable association. We would start off from different points of view but there was never an acrimonious point of view, it was always one that very clearly recognised the value of each other's view and the fact that there was a legitimacy about it. I remember we started off late one night and said there is no way we can win on Sunday because we can't win centre field. That was the opening comment and then we spent hours and hours and eventually we came up with a combination that would upset the opposition and change our structures and our setup and it worked.'

From Tony Hanahoe's perspective, Heffernan was the only one with the kudos and gravitas who could take Dublin to the next level.

He was the one who had the experience and he also had the confidence, allied with that was the co-operative people at an administrative level and the very suitable persona on the management team with him. So then it was a question of getting the players together and the right type of players together, i.e. the ones who would blend into an overall team effort as opposed to an individual ability/brilliance. Players who were prepared to do the work, were prepared to work as a team, who were prepared to take instructions and they were prepared above all to give the commitment.

And extraordinary questions of commitment – levels never seen before – were sought for the 1974 season.

'Dublin had become so poor and the results over a few years had been so appalling that one had to start somewhere,' remembered Heffernan. 'The obvious place to start was fitness because if you could develop fitness and a team could win simply because it was fitter than others, then you had some basis for saying you are not that bad. Then you have a future and it is something to hang optimism on – you cannot just keep telling fellas they are good enough unless you are going to prove that they have some angle to it that is giving them an advantage or an edge. So we did a thing that was quite un-normal in the 1970s, believe me, and that was we started to train the team in the winter. Now, there might have been a genuflection of sorts made towards winter training by others but nobody really trained. We were training a lot.'

The Down teams in the 1960s had begun serious training at the start of the year to give themselves an edge; this time Heffernan brought things back even further.

We started from October and went right through. And nobody – that was the theory – nobody played football on a Saturday before a Sunday match because there was a view that came out of the Ark that you should be hungry for the ball. As if suddenly you saw it and you were going to eat it! So we trained two nights a week – heavy stuff in the winter and we played football on a Saturday.

The idea was to get as fit – and eventually we had to preach the gospel as we didn't know how long it was going to take, it might take fifty minutes or forty-five minutes or forty minutes – but you are eventually going to be running when these other fellas are feeling the drag. Eventually, that began to happen and as soon as we started to win, fellas got really interested – they began to listen and began to observe and began to take on board the messages. Once we started to win, it was then possible to start putting some sort of tactical plan together. Now that we were fit, we were starting to play with a tactical plan, which in turn was seen to be working, which in turn was increasing confidence and optimism. And which in turn was giving us a result. That was the key – starting from a jumble where nobody was confident and nobody believed anything, to giving them something, something to give confidence, something that people can hold on to and say well if we do that we have some chance. That is where the fitness started but that was only a starting point.

After years of wandering rudderless and bereft, the Dubs under Heffernan had a plan. However, grand aims of All-Irelands and days out in Croke Park weren't even considered or on the horizon. It was as simple as the hoary old sporting cliché of 'one game at a time'.

'We were playing every match as it came because we had won nothing,' says Hanahoe. 'And there seemed to be a certain psychological barrier on breaking through in the Leinster championship. The first match we played against Wexford was played as a preliminary before the replay of the National League final between Roscommon and Kerry, and it was like the Mickey Mouse show before the main event. It just cheered up the audience because there were so many mistakes being made.

'We moved up and played Louth in the next round and that in itself was even a formidable challenge – looking at Dublin through your eyes now at this stage, you have no idea what it was like from there at that time, looking at what we were looking at. Our weapon was a slowly growing self-belief. The next match, which was a significant match, we played Offaly at Croke Park, that was a formidable win because it was a very tight game and we won by one point and Offaly had been All-Ireland champions two years before. That Offaly victory gave us a disproportionate amount of confidence in ourselves. Here we had beaten an All-Ireland team of two years ago with household names, suddenly we realised we had gone up a few rungs on the ladder and at this point if we were capable of beating these guys who were we not capable of beating?

'By the time of the Leinster final against Meath, we were growing in a big way. I remember looking down the field that day and saying to myself, we are not going to lose this match, it may take ten minutes, it may take fifty minutes, it may take sixty-one minutes, but we are not going to lose, and we didn't.

'Instead of the usual 2,000 people attending the games, you suddenly had 50,000 people. The flash-in-the-pan comments were beginning to grow very hollow and our attitude was, keep underestimating us, it's good for us. If you look at the teams we had beaten and we had come in from nowhere, suddenly we were there. I remember being down in the Four Courts one day and I met a Kerry policeman who I knew was interested in football. I remember saying something about this year's All-Ireland final and he said, "Yes, I don't think you fellas are going to be in it." It was that much of a joke. But then Kerry started to change their training regime to what we were doing, moving to concentrate on the main ingredients of stamina, speed and skill.'

Cast aside in the 1974 Munster championship to Cork, Kerry were sitting up and taking note and began plotting their comeback for the following year. Meanwhile, Dublin faced the reigning All-Ireland champions, Cork, in the All-Ireland semi-final and nobody gave them a chance. 'A puppy dog biting at the ankles of a hound' was how one newspaper report compared the match-up, while another did a player by player comparison between the teams and gave it Cork 15, Dublin 0.

'It was an unbelievable day,' remembers Hanahoe. 'We just shot out of the starting gate like a bolting horse and all of a sudden the game was over and I would say that Cork totally underestimated us and then once they had lost the initiative they couldn't get back into the game. Even in the final, Galway underestimated us. No one could actually believe that this was happening. How many times could they underestimate us? The final against Galway wasn't a brilliant game by any means.'

Nobody cared about spectacle, not least the thousands thronged on the Hill. Dublin were All-Ireland champions for the first time in eleven years. A city had been woken up to the thrills and spills of Gaelic football once again. Heffo's Army was born.

'My memory of it was that the soccer teams like Rovers weren't doing very well at the time and it was into that vacuum that we suddenly arrived,' recalled Heffernan. 'I think there are a couple of things that appealed: we came out of the blue – nobody expected it – and we started to play a decent type of football. The guys on the Hill were looking for something to do on a Sunday afternoon; it was as if we were telling them, "Remember there is a place down there called Croker waiting", and they started to arrive again in an amazing surge of enthusiasm. It was reminiscent of Shankly's Army and all that, you know.

'But it was a huge thing and it was only subsequent to that it was curtailed because the guards got worried as there was so many people coming – there was so many banners, so many poles and they tried stopping them bringing the banners. I remember the first time I saw a banner – "Kerry for the Holidays, Dublin for the Sam". When you see that the first time, it is something different, there was just a tremendous atmosphere and colour. I remember going to matches in Tullamore and Portlaoise in the late 1960s and coming out and saying, "That was terrible. Why would I bother?" Now, we were putting on a show and people were happy to come and have something to be enthusiastic about.'

The Dublin team that announced itself to Gaelic football was a complete mix of personalities, talents, skillsets and ages. In a remarkable piece written for *Magill* magazine fifteen years after the Dubs' breakthrough success, sports journalist David Walsh revisited Heffo's team, each of them as successful and determined off the pitch as they were on it. It is the trait in all great teams: what makes great players ultimately comes from within and is reflected in mostly everything they turn their attention to. Kevin Heffernan wanted a team of intelligent, dedicated footballers that ultimately turned out to be, in addition to one of the greatest Gaelic football teams to grace Croke Park, also a team of doctors, engineers, a solicitor and an economist, executives and entrepreneurs, a schoolteacher and a publican.

'In our dealings with the players, we adopted an open approach,' Heffernan told Walsh back in 1989. 'We believed we should be able to justify, in front of all of the players, our decisions as selectors, our tactics, and we also wanted to be able to discuss the performances of individuals. I did not want strong dummies. At that time, intelligent guys were available and that is a very rare happening in sport. My contribution was to get the best out of them. Loyalty to each other was a hugely important factor in our approach.'

Sometimes, Heffernan found players for his plan by sheer luck. Returning from the first game of the championship having beaten Wexford, but in a disappointing display, Heffernan was dismissive of the players' performance and their lack of a free-taker when his wife's friend's seven-year-old son, Terry, chimed in with the suggestion of Jimmy Keaveney. 'I go to all Vincent's games with my dad and Jimmy never misses a free.' That evening, Heffernan rang Keaveney to see if he would be interested in coming on board. Thus, the final piece in the jigsaw was solved thanks to a seven-year-old's suggestion.

Tony Hanahoe, the team's future leader, was encouraged to come back and, when he saw what Heffernan was planning, he knew that Dublin GAA had found their answer. Heffernan was methodical in his approach to everything from the training to diet to tactics and even sports medicine. In many ways, with his expansive skillset, he was the modern version of Dr Eamonn O'Sullivan.

Dr Pat O'Neill remarked that even in relation to sports medicine, Heffernan's knowledge was ahead of the rest. 'All of the stuff that I have come across in the best books, stuff about the science of training, is stuff that I have experienced at first hand with Kevin.'

'I was carried away by the things that I found,' said Brian Mullins, who was studying physical education at the time in the recently opened Thomond College in Limerick. 'Training was so thorough, so professional. Since then, I despise any effort that is lower. Since then, it is harder for me to accept mediocrity. In my view, players are either in or they're not. The guys I played with then never funked it.'

The team would spend hours on the training ground, hours in team discussions and hours before the video recorder. Heffernan encouraged a group ethic of self-analysis and open and honest criticism. Thursdays were the nights for the team discussions and after expounding his thoughts, he would turn to certain players, putting them on the spot, asking, 'Right, what about you? What do you think?'

'We had a lot of self-analysis,' says Hanahoe. 'So by the time we got on the road, there weren't too many places to hide. If you weren't being honest with yourself, somebody else would be honest for you. In the group sessions, they were very honest, they tightened up a lot of areas that needed to be looked at. It was also a growing process for management and for the team, insofar as they now had a certain level with one another; suddenly as the confidence grew and the success grew you got more powerful personalities coming out of this whole thing. I suppose when you reach a certain zenith you nearly didn't need to tell them, they knew before you knew that they weren't doing it, so they were highly focused, determined individuals on that team.'

Kevin Moran, who was to go on to achieve success and fame as a soccer player with Manchester United and Ireland, reckoned Heffernan would have made a top-class manager in English soccer such was his ability in the dressing room.

Heffernan also introduced video analysis to prove his points, just in case anyone decided to dispute what he was saying. Tiarnan McBride was hired to tape their games and opponents' weaknesses, but, more importantly, the Dublin team's own shortcomings were highlighted and worked on.

But Heffernan could also be cold and ruthless; not every player on the All-Ireland-winning teams speaks of a warmth or closeness with him. While others felt his motivational approach, based on putting the fear of God into the players, could overstep the line. 'Which one of you will be the Judas out there today?' he coldly asked the team in the dressing room before the 1975 final.

In 1974, out of nowhere, and within just a year of taking charge, Dublin were All-Ireland champions and had announced themselves to the Gaelic football world. There was a brash new kid in town carrying with it an urban swagger that brought a whole new audience to the GAA.

The question now was who would answer Heffernan's challenge?

Chapter 5

Character is fate

When Dr Eamonn O'Sullivan stepped away from Kerry football after five decades, ending on a losing note to Galway in 1964, the warning signs for the county were already apparent. Gaelic football was modernising. Down and Galway had broken free of the shackles of restrictive zonal tactics, utilising movement and speed to work around opponents. Kerry football was in crisis and had to change. Either adapt or die.

For Kerry football, a crisis is not winning the Munster championship – not winning for two years in a row is unthinkable. When Cork beat them back-to-back in 1966 and 1967, the Kingdom knew things were bad and that something had to be done. The Kerry County Board turned to another Kerry legend, Jackie Lyne. Lyne's ten years on the team (1944–1954), as centre-back then corner-forward, along with his two All-Ireland medals in 1946 and 1953, gave him the credentials and reputation, but re-establishing Kerry football was not going to be easy.

Weeshie Fogarty played under Lyne when he took over their club team, Killarney Legion.

*It was the first experience I had of training under Jackie
Lyne. And we won the local championship – we hadn't
won it since the 1950s and, after that, Jackie was being
spoken about. Jackie would have talked in the local papers
criticising Kerry so eventually the county board went to him
and said, 'Look rather than criticise them would you train
them?'*

Coming off the back of two Munster final defeats to Cork, Lyne
didn't seek to instigate wholesale change or a playing revolution.

'He had trained under Dr Eamonn since he started playing in
the 1940s,' explains Fogarty. 'He held on to a lot of Dr Eamonn's
tactics about punching the ball in the circle and simple stuff, such
as no cones in training. But he started tweaking things, and he was
the first person I heard telling the late Eamonn O'Donoghue the
wing-forward to come back and collect the kickouts.

'Then, later on, Liam Higgins was brought onto the panel.
Higgins was big, strong and bony, he was a big country footballer,
great to get possession. Jackie Lyne brought him in to full-forward
and I remember hearing him say, "Liam, you have one job to do
now, catch the ball, come out and pass it to the man coming in."
And if you look at any of the old films, Liam Higgins comes out,
passes the ball and lays it off to Mick Gleeson, Brendan Lynch
or Eamonn O'Donoghue coming in, so, in actual fact, he was the
first Kieran Donaghy and precursor of the Bomber. There was also
Tom Prendergast who was playing corner-forward in 1968 against
Down, completely out of position, and Jackie Lyne brought him
back to wing-back and he got Footballer of the Year in 1970, so
Jackie had learned so much even from 1968. He was changing
things, trying to bring the game forward, maybe only a little at a
time, but it was a start.'

When Lyne took over in 1968, Kerry hadn't won an All-Ireland in six years, their worst run since the 1914–1924 period when the War of Independence and Civil War struck at the heart of the country. Kerry football still depended on its past, however, and in a Past Players versus Present game in Killarney, the era of Mick O'Connell, Mick O'Dwyer and Seamus Murphy still proved itself better than the current players.

Lyne persuaded these older players to come out of retirement, and they were instrumental in restoring Kerry's pre-eminence. To get themselves ready for the coming season, training sessions were held seven nights a week and Lyne's influence was almost immediate. The Kingdom won back Munster in a high-scoring 1–21 to 3–08 win over Cork but were beaten in the 1968 All-Ireland final by Down, thanks to two early goals from Sean O'Neill and John Murphy. It was to be the last of that great Down team's success, but Kerry were only getting started.

They captured the league title the following year – their first in five years – and followed it up with a long-hungered All-Ireland, beating Offaly 0–10 to 0–7, led once more by Mick O'Connell's feats in the middle of the park. Was it a case that order was being restored and the old ways winning out once more?

At the start of the 1970s, change was in the air in more ways than one. The contentious ban on the playing of 'foreign games' was finally removed at a special GAA Congress in 1971, while the year before, with one eye on the game as a spectacle, twenty minutes was added to provincial finals, All-Ireland semis and finals. Eighty-minute games now also meant an increased focus on fitness and the physical aspects of the game.

The 'old guard' of Kerry still outshone most others in the country, firstly with a thirteen-point victory over Cork in the 1970 Munster final followed by another All-Ireland final, this time against Meath. Meath had been All-Ireland winners three years previously under the guidance of Peter McDermott, whose management talents had also been called upon by Down GAA, and the 1970 final was being portrayed as old-school Kerry against the panache and swagger of Meath. Old-school won out in the end 2–19 to 0–18, with Kerry leading from the fourth minute of the game.

But this Kerry All-Ireland victory was far from rooted in old thinking. Despite Jackie Lyne's riposte that the win was 'our answer to the Gormanston professors and their blackboard tactics', Kerry had integrated into their approach many of the facets of mobile forward play. The programme notes remarked that:

> ... plenty of traditional Kerry style, yet plenty of the best in the modern game incorporated into a basically sound pattern. It is the integrated work of the forwards which has given Kerry a new dimension. Most of the six could easily be outmatched individually from the lists of Kerry forwards past: but when they use their talents in combination, they are exciting to watch and direct in their intention.

Kerry had retained the All-Ireland for the first time in nearly thirty years by integrating many of the new principles of play that had beaten them in the decade before.

Hopes of building another dynasty under Lyne were to be short-lived, however. A Munster final defeat to Cork in 1971 by eleven points signalled the end of the road for Jackie Lyne.

'I remember some fella asking Jackie, "How long will you stay with it?"' recalls Weeshie Fogarty. '"I'll stay with Kerry until we're beaten," he said, and when they were beaten in 1971 in the Munster final, he packed it in. But I often wonder if Jackie hadn't taken over Kerry at the time and hadn't brought back Mick O'Connell and Johnny Culloty, what state would Kerry football have been in? They were badly caught for players at the time.'

Two of Kerry's greatest players, Mick O'Connell and Mick

O'Dwyer, upon whom so much rested in winning the 1969 and 1970 All-Irelands, were in their thirties, they didn't have many more playing miles on the clock and would retire within a few seasons.

A new breed of young talent was needed and never was it more evident than in the 1972 All-Ireland when Kerry suffered their heaviest final defeat in the replay, 1–19 to 0–13, at the hands of Offaly.

Another Kerry legend, Johnny Culloty, cast his hat into the ring to take over from Lyne and proved to be another important link, one that was crucial in introducing youth to the team and giving them the taste of victory in the National League. Whereas it's easy to paint Mick O'Dwyer's eventual arrival as Kerry manager as the beginning of it all, many highlight Johnny Culloty's role in bringing through the next batch of players that were then at O'Dwyer's disposal when he took over.

The biggest stumble for Culloty, however, was getting rid of former team-mates. Captain of the 1969 All-Ireland-winning side, Culloty had shared the pitch and the dressing room with O'Connell and O'Dwyer going back to their early days on the Kerry senior side in the 1950s. He had only recently retired himself in 1971, having appeared in nine All-Irelands, winning five of them, and was now back just a year later succeeding Jackie Lyne.

'Jackie Lyne kind of mentioned my name,' remembers Culloty. 'I don't know how, I just fell into the job, that kind of way. I enjoyed it, but compared to playing there is no comparison.'

'The mistake he made was training fellas he had played with,' says Weeshie Fogarty. 'But people forget how stuck Kerry were for players back in 1968 when Jackie Lyne took over. That year, they were picking the Kerry team in the Park Hotel and the selectors were in conflict, they did not know what to do. At that time, you would gather outside the hotel and there would be huge crowds waiting for the team to be announced. But the selectors and management came out and walked straight through the crowd saying nothing; they walked up to Johnny Culloty's house down the road, knocked at his door and said, "Johnny will you came out of retirement and play next Sunday against Longford in the All-Ireland semi-final?" That's how bad it was.'

Despite guiding Kerry to three league titles to make it four-in-a-row for the Kingdom, All-Ireland success was what the county craved most, and defeat in Munster at the hands of Cork in 1973 and 1974 meant that Culloty's job was on the line. The seven-point loss to Cork in 1974 saw his three years come to an end.

But his place in Kerry's future years of success must not be forgotten, says Fogarty.

> Under the guidance of Johnny Culloty, the seeds of that great side had already been sown. On that 1974 team beaten by Cork, he included Paudie O'Mahony, Paidí Ó Sé, John O'Keeffe, Ger O'Keeffe, Paudie Lynch, Mickey O'Sullivan, Ger Power, John Egan, Jackie Walsh and Mikey Sheehy. The Killarney Legion man had laid the most firm of foundations.

For Culloty, the difference with this group of players coming through was their interest and dedication to physical education, especially with the opening up of Thomond College, Ireland's first college to focus on sports science.

> You had Pat Spillane, Jimmy Deenihan, Ogie Moran, Mickey Ned O'Sullivan, John O'Keeffe ... they were all very much into the fitness thing and when O'Dwyer came along, he proved to be very successful with them.

That 1974 Munster final loss to Cork was the last game in a Kerry jersey for the great Mick O'Connell and while the new blood was starting to come through, the team was now rudderless and in need of a manager who could take on the might of what Kevin Heffernan and Dublin were starting to achieve. The mantle had been thrown down to the Kingdom from their rivals from the Pale and, if Kerry's footballing legacy was to be preserved for future years, they had to answer it fast.

At the same time, and coming back from Strawberry Hill in London with a sports science degree, was a young Kenmare man, Mickey Ned O'Sullivan, who had a head full of ideas about physical education and its application to Gaelic football.

> *I was rubbing shoulders with the likes of Dave Bedford, the 5,000- and 10,000-metre record holder, you would have soccer players, international rugby players, all in the same class and we would be interacting and learning from them. You would be going to matches and you would be seeing them in the gym, you would be watching and learning all the time. I was eighteen and I was like a sponge to see all this.*

With his degree in hand, he knew Kerry was behind the times and needed to catch up.

> *I remember the first time I came back at Christmas and I went to the Kenmare AGM and they were asking for ideas, so I stood up and I said, 'We need a ball between two at every training session.' A guy behind me says, 'That's why Kerry football is f–ed up, when we were young we had one ball and we had to fight for it, now they all have a ball and no one fights for it.' That was the end of the motion anyway. It was difficult but then change did come slowly. I remember when Mick O'Dwyer took over. He came to me*

and he said, 'Any suggestions?' 'I'll make out a training session for you,' I told him. So I made it out, explained it to him and when it was over he asked, 'How was that?' 'Not hard enough,' I told him and that was the last time he ever asked me. From there on, the intensity improved and he was the same then with any session for the next few years. But in saying that, there were five or six PE teachers on that team and none of them would open their mouths about it because it was successful.

Coaching is a profession and a science. The same principles about opening up and closing down space that we were studying in Strawberry Hill are only starting to be applied now. Down started the coaching approach in the 1960s, but then Heffernan and O'Dwyer came along and f–ed it all up, because they were so successful with physical fitness. It was put down then that the only way forward was getting players so fit. That lasted for twenty years and it was to the detriment of coaching.

Strong words from the man who captained Kerry during Mick O'Dwyer's first year in charge. But then Mickey Ned O'Sullivan shares a similar sports science background with the likes of Joe Lennon and Jim McGuinness. The game is one to be approached and studied from a questioning, analytical standpoint. But as we all look back on the 'golden age' of Gaelic football when Dublin and Kerry's rivalry transfixed the entire country when O'Dwyer's Kerry team became the greatest of all time, O'Sullivan's comments strike at the heart of the development of the game. Because Croke Park was full, the media and public lapped it up, great players were on show and dynasties were created – how could it not have been anything but brilliant?

O'Sullivan begs to differ.

*Recently I came across the 1980 Kerry–Roscommon final
and there was some diabolical stuff. I said to myself any
club team now would beat them and I have no doubt about
it; we have a staple diet of the golden years and all you see
are goals and it looks good, though it was anything but.*

O'Sullivan also dismisses talk of the Kerry team of the 1970s–1980s
as being the greatest of all time, arguing that they wouldn't even
be beating the Tyrones and the Armaghs that have come through
in the 2000s.

*I don't think they would compete against the Donegals at the
moment – any team even over the past decade could beat
them. Look, the players from the 1970s were probably more
skilful, and they did have a lot of skill. In the 1960s, there
was no coaching but as kids they would go to the football
field in threes and fours and they kicked and they kicked all
day and they had a high degree of skill. Not because they
were coached, but because they did it themselves.*

*But the standard of play in the 1970s was very naive.
At that time, there was no defending as we know it today
because we didn't understand defending. It was purely man
for man. Part of the reason for the success back then was
that you had the cult of the manager coming on board.
You had strong characters on either team and presentable
characters and suddenly you had the ingredients. Now that
had nothing to do with the game.*

And that's the thing about O'Dwyer. For all the knowledge and
science that was in abundance, he could still do it his own way and
be successful no matter what.

What can you say about Micko? 'Charismatic', 'driven',

'determined' are the words that come first from other people's mouths when asked to describe the man.

'I tell you he had charisma, he was a leader,' says Weeshie Fogarty, who played with him. 'You should have seen him playing and the determination – he'd play with two broken legs.'

Stepping into the breach in 1975, O'Dwyer's reputation as one of Kerry's greatest players had already been cemented. He made his debut as a minor in 1954 aged seventeen and was the first person from Waterville to represent Kerry at any level. Two years later, he made the seniors and starred for them for eighteen remarkable years, playing in nine All-Irelands and winning four, as well as collecting a host of Munster and league titles.

Football was his life and nothing stopped him in pursuit of that. The game wasn't handed down to him from his family, though – 'My father wasn't a football man at all, beagle hunting, fishing, shooting, they were his games' – and it wasn't a sport that Waterville had a tradition of either. 'The cable company in Waterville had about 200 English people who were employed here,' remembers O'Dwyer. 'They had tennis and soccer and golf, it was an area mostly for the rich English within Waterville so Gaelic football wasn't big.'

It was to be the influence of his teachers that imparted a love of the game on him.

There were a couple of great teachers in St Finin's who encouraged us to play football. Throw your bag in the corner, get the football and go play kick, every single day of the week. When I would be down on the field, I would be trying to imitate Jackie Lyne, John Cronin or Paddy Sheehy. They were the heroes. That is where you honed all the skills, the catching, the kicking. A lot of that seems to be neglected today. I suppose when young fellows come in from school

today, what do they do, they sit behind a computer, spend
hours on end studying – in my day it didn't matter a damn,
football was more important than the books.

Single-mindedness. Another of O'Dwyer's traits. Tunnel vision
if you want to call it that. Know what you want and go after it,
no matter what. It included 100-mile round trips to Killarney for
training, picking up Mick O'Connell as his friend and team-mate
rowed out from Valentia, arriving home late into the night. The
thrill of the game, the winning was what sustained him – a life led
by one passion, Gaelic football.

He won his first All-Ireland medals as a half-back in 1959 and
1962 but then made his name in the half-forward line, losing to
Galway in 1964 and 1965, before he broke both his legs in 1966.
At thirty years of age, and with All-Ireland medals and a successful
career already achieved, many would have bowed out, but Micko
was only gone for two years before he came back as a corner-
forward for the 1968 final defeat to Down. Incredibly, he played
for another six years, becoming the top scorer in the championship
for three seasons, from 1969–1971. He collected a third All-Ireland
in 1969, as well as the Footballer of the Year award. A fourth and
final All-Ireland came the following year, before one last final
appearance in 1972, where Kerry lost to Offaly in a replay. Two
years later, O'Dwyer hung up his boots.

He wasn't finished, though.

Towards the end of his playing career, he began coaching the
Waterville club side, and the first sparks of his managerial genius
started to shine through.

'We [Killarney] met them in three finals,' remembers Weeshie
Fogarty. 'And we beat them in three finals because we were an
amalgamation of fourteen clubs. But they got to three county
championship finals, which was incredible because somebody

said at that time that their pick was so small that if you stood in the middle of Waterville and blew a whistle, you would have your whole team together. In one of those finals, we had thirteen fellas who played with Kerry, and yet they ran us to two points – he was the man who had that determination and he brought that into Kerry. That was an amazing achievement with Waterville and was probably as impressive as anything he subsequently achieved with Kerry.'

Taking over in 1975, O'Dwyer knew that he had a talented bunch of young players coming through. His focus was to match Dublin's fitness levels and beat them skillwise.

> I said to myself that if I can get a young team now I will have it for a number of years. I knew I had a good team. I got them exceptionally fit and they were wonderful footballers then as well. With fitness will come skill – if you get them exceptionally fit, then you work on their skills, they will get skilful. Distance stuff, game stamina, get them really fit and then play football. Games of football every chance you get, morning, noon and night. If you are playing football regularly and kicking the ball, and you see I have a system, no solo, no hop and make them play the ball in training. What we did at the period was we played an amount of football, backs and forwards and all that, there was no need for any systems at all because every fella on the field, they worked it out in training.

Former players have remarked that O'Dwyer's tactics could be written down on the back of a beer mat but, in many ways, O'Dwyer was a link to the past, of keeping the game simple, an emphasis on catch-and-kick, but he also held the keys to Kerry's future, recognising that they had to take on Dublin on their fitness strengths. Mickey Ned O'Sullivan is correct that after the years of progressive, studious approach to the game as developed by Down, the 1970s were retrograde in terms of an overemphasis on physical fitness, but that was the gauntlet being thrown down at the time by Dublin, and O'Dwyer could only match it.

Having eight or nine guys on the panel who had all studied for physical education degrees meant that their whole approach and lifestyle revolved around the game. These were players who looked after themselves fitness-wise, and who would stay back for hours after training practising and honing their techniques. Like Dublin, and so many other successful teams that emerge, the dynamic of the group becomes self-fulfilling, once it is organised and led by a manager of character, determination and inspiration.

Perhaps we'll win an All-Ireland in three years, were O'Dwyer's thoughts upon taking over but he didn't have to wait that long. Success for this Kerry team came much more quickly, although reports in *The Kerryman* after a league defeat earlier in the year were to be way off the mark. 'I don't think anybody in their right senses should say that the Kerry team as presently constituted is going to win an All-Ireland this year or in the immediate future,' wrote the journalist, yet this was a team made up of minor and under-21 All-Ireland winners from 1970 and 1973 who had an average age of just twenty-three years.

'In the run-up to the 1975 Munster Championship,' O'Dwyer recalled in his autobiography, 'we trained like no team had ever trained before. It was crazy stuff but they were young enough to take it and, anyway, I believed it was the right thing to do because Dublin had raised the fitness bar and I knew if we were to match them we would have to be better prepared.'

O'Dwyer had learned the importance of stamina training from no less than Sir Matt Busby, the legendary Manchester United manager who, in the 1950s, built the Busby Babes to take on Europe.

'I was great friends with the United scout in Dublin, Billy Behan,' explains O'Dwyer. 'When I was a player, he made arrangements for me to go over to see Manchester United training – off-season training – so I took advantage of it and I learned quite a bit over there. There was Matt Busby, Duncan Edwards, Tommy Taylor and Liam Whelan. It was amazing the stuff they were doing, there was a lot of distance running at that time. Stamina training more than anything in the off-season, but they don't agree with that now in Gaelic football, because they say it is out-dated, they have other methods now.'

When O'Dwyer took over, he held twenty-seven training sessions in a row.

'His big thing was the wire to wire,' explains Weeshie Fogarty. 'He'd line up three or four fellas and their hands would be on the wire above the Fitzgerald Stadium. When he blew the whistle, they would have to sprint from the wire across the whole length of the field, touch the wire and come back – flat out. They were doing that constantly and he would put the slow fellas in with the fast fellas so they would have to keep up.'

This was a team that had the discipline and mental strength to take whatever was thrown at them and it had been bred into them from a young age. Mickey Ned O'Sullivan took over the training of the under-21s in 1974, which had the likes of John O'Keeffe, Jimmy Deenihan, Paudie Lynch and Páidí Ó Sé in it. Nine of the 1975 team were on the under-21s that also won an All-Ireland the same year.

'We had an incredible talent in the under-21s,' says O'Sullivan. 'We developed a style at that time called the 'three Ss' – space, shout and support – and you didn't have to tell these guys a second time. A lot of the lads delved into other sports as well at that time and we began to play superb football. The thing about O'Dwyer in the seniors then, he had great discipline and he brought the fitness to a very high level and that steeled us mentally because you were going to pass the physical barrier every evening and you became very strong mentally from that. They were very young players and you wouldn't normally get that until later in life, in football terms, but he developed that early with them.'

That Kerry team was a unique bunch in that they were the first generation of Gaelic footballers to experience the nascent studies in physical education in Ireland first hand. While Jim McKeever paved the way going to Loughborough in the UK in the 1950s and Joe Lennon and Mickey Ned O'Sullivan followed in his footsteps, also studying in the UK at Strawberry Hill, Ireland's first National College of Physical Education (NCPE, later Thomond College) was founded at the start of the 1970s in Limerick, and eventually developed to become the University of Limerick.

Sports science at university level was only starting out in Ireland, and was light years behind the British, Europeans and Americans in terms of knowledge and infrastructure. But the first head of the college was Dr John Kane, a former Department Head at Strawberry Hill, so at least the state was determined the NCPE was going to start off on the right foot.

Another one early to the college staff was Dave Weldrick, who had studied physical education at Strawberry Hill and completed a Master's at the Western Kentucky University in the United States. A former soccer and Gaelic footballer of note at underage level in Dublin, nine months of office work in the civil service taught him that he had to be working in his real passion of physical education, and he has spent a lifetime coaching and teaching at the Limerick college.

The demand for places on the PE courses outstripped supply and it was quickly one of the most popular on the CAO, proving that the sports-mad Irish nation also wanted to study sports science. Being the first of its kind, the college attracted many of Gaelic football's elite and, under Dave Weldrick's stewardship stellar names, such as Brian Mullins, Johnny Tobin and Pat Spillane, were playing for him. With so many All-Ireland winners in the dressing room, it was no wonder that the college team, just like UCD at the start of the decade, won an All-Ireland club championship in 1978. But more importantly, Mullins and Spillane credited Weldrick's coaching and teaching as having a profound impact on their game and careers. As Weldrick says:

I remember the one principle I always used to outline, especially when we started the campaign, was I asked them, 'Do you want to win it?' Everyone said, 'Yes, yes.' I then said, 'More importantly, are you prepared to give it the commitment it takes?', and I outlined the commitment that would be needed. It had to be a 24/7 commitment, in terms of what they did off the pitch as well as what was done on the pitch, keeping in good shape and travelling long distances to be available for games and all of that which is far more difficult because, during the summer months, third-level students are going to the four corners of the world. So it was all about commitment. But, in fairness, they said yes and Spillane was absolutely dedicated and committed to it. He was only relatively a wet behind the ears young fella at the time, but he was fiercely determined and ambitious.

Tactically, Weldrick was following in Joe Lennon's footsteps and was preaching a philosophy and style of play that many of the Ulster counties would start to practise twenty-five years later.

When we lost the ball, our first line of defence was the full-forward line. I didn't expect to see three of my front guys, or any of my front guys, standing with their hands on their hips. We pressurised from the front. We talked about three thirds of the pitch, the defensive, the midfield and the front, we pressurised and if the ball was in the top third with the opposition we put them under pressure to get it back. Why should we wait until they came into our defensive third before we started putting them under pressure? It's too late.

When we defended, we closed down space and particularly the space of the opposition and particularly the space of the opposing player on the ball, so that he felt under maximum pressure when they had possession. When we attacked we had to create space and particularly space for our player on the ball so that he felt like they had the space to basically do damage to the opposition, either in passing or scoring.

The essence of the plan must be simplicity. The guys are under an enormous amount of stress from the opposition, competing, the stress to win, etc. and complicated tactical plans will go out the window and that's not the players' fault, that's the coach's fault. Plus, quickness – quick thinking, quick playing, quick movement – must be at the heart of it all. But it also doesn't mean rushing or hurrying or feeling under pressure in possession, we don't want that either.

Weldrick was also a proponent of playing the percentage possession game which was to become such a dominant style of Gaelic football in the 2000s. 'I would advocate don't put possession at risk if there is nothing on ahead of you, don't hesitate to pass it back and support from behind, it's something we would advocate and then the player supporting from behind has the opportunity because they will have the space when they get it quickly to play the ball forward.'

Even the tactic of stopping player momentum by not ceding

ground, as developed by Armagh under Joe Kernan in the 2000s, was advocated by Weldrick in Limerick in the 1970s.

'I did my Football Association coaching badge with a great guy called Mike Holiday,' he explained. 'Mike was a brilliant soccer coach and he taught me so much, but I always remember him telling me that my tackling in soccer was like the lion diving for the piece of raw meat and being held. "You don't do that," he said, "that's the way you trap the lion." I remember thinking at the time, what's he talking about? Then I realised he was right, the principle being delay and restraint in one on one.

'If you are coming at me with the ball – in soccer, basketball, Gaelic football, it doesn't matter – I'm going to slow you down. How do I not slow you down? I dive into the tackle and maybe foul you, and giving away frees in Gaelic football is merely putting points on the board for the opposition. We used to work in channels in every coaching session on how to defend technically and tactically in a one on one. We set up a thirty-metre channel, ten yards wide and you would have the ball and your job was to get past me and step over the endline. My job as a defender in a one on one was to stop you legitimately or, better still, dispossess you. My ultimate objective is to dispossess you and regain possession of the ball.'

With players like Spillane coming out of this hotbed of sports science and training under Dave Weldrick at the NCPE, it is little wonder that the young Kerry team were able and willing to train like demons for Mick O'Dwyer. For many of them, they were living and breathing sport every day of their lives.

In the six weeks between the All-Ireland semi-final and final, the Kerry players trained five nights a week, to which Heffernan responded by training Dublin six times in the week before the final. The Dublin manager even brought in Simon Deignan, a referee and chairman of the committee which had recommended the recent reintroduction of the hand-pass, to give the players a demonstration on how it was to be done properly in the eyes of the officials. Nothing was left to chance.

That 1975 season seemed destined to build to a crescendo between Dublin and Kerry, the ultimate test of the two fittest, fastest setups in the country, led by two county legends looking to outwit the other. All other counties seemed irrelevant in their wake. In Leinster, Dublin hammered Wexford 4–17 to 3–10, beat Louth 3–14 to 4–07 and destroyed Kildare 3–13 to 0–08 before beating Derry 3–13 to 3–08 in the semi-final and reach their second All-Ireland in a row, a feat not achieved by the county since the 1920s. Kerry, meanwhile, handed out a ten-point thrashing to Cork in the Munster final before annihilating Sligo in the All-Ireland semi, 3–13 to 0–5.

Kerry, however, were still the underdogs. Dublin were seen as the all-conquering city masters, hyped by the media, the Hill and the county. O'Dwyer played along, portraying Kerry as the young, wide-eyed innocents. However, within three minutes of the throw-in, the youthful Kerry side announced their arrival with a John Egan goal. O'Dwyer has described how he thought the Dublin team were vulnerable to conceding goals, having let in three against Wexford, four against Louth, and three to Derry; 'pace and constant movement' was his mantra to his forwards. Ger O'Driscoll scored another goal in the second half and Kerry were on their way, running out 2–12 to 0–11 winners. Kerry were All-Ireland champions with an average age of just twenty-three – the youngest winning team in their history.

Not only that, but it seemed as if, finally, Kerry were able to leave the shackles of the proscriptive catch-and-kick philosophy behind them – not ditch it altogether, but incorporate a style that was more inclusive of modern facets of play. 'Where each player's skill was fitted into the pattern rather than the other way around,'

O'Dwyer subsequently wrote. 'Catch-and-kick had served Kerry well but the game was moving on and if we didn't adapt we would have been left behind.'

'When Kerry came up and beat us we were a bit over-trained,' admits Tony Hanahoe. 'And we underestimated Kerry's determination. They came with a young team full of speed and they got an early goal that settled them and suddenly we ended up losing.'

Afterwards, Mick O'Dwyer claimed this Kerry team was the greatest of all time but then back-tracked, saying he meant they *could* be the greatest Kerry team of all time. Either way, this group of players led by the charismatic O'Dwyer knew they were on the cusp of something big. Just how big, only time would tell – but time was one thing these players had on their side.

Chapter 6

'You have to be positive about your own way'

When the 1976 season dawned, it was like a battle of wits between two grand masters as Heffernan and O'Dwyer studied ways and means to improve their own setup while spotting chinks in the other's armour. Dublin's weakness in defence had been shown up and, as Heffernan remarked in David Walsh's *Magill* piece, 'After 1975, we knew we needed a new half-back line. We had to dredge up three.' Heffernan, Donal Colfer and Lorcan Redmond tried to see as many games as possible and kept hearing good reports about a Good Counsel player by the name of Kevin Moran.

Moran was his own man, a UCD student with the long curls and a motorbike who was also a talented soccer player. He had exactly the qualities Heffernan was looking for – talent married with toughness and intelligence. Heffernan was always a man of dedication and hard work, but losing the 1975 final to Kerry had brought back all the painful memories of losing to them as a player. Would Kerry always have the upper hand on him and Dublin? They were the opposition that ate into him, and he was going to stop at nothing to prove that he could get one over on them.

Dublin started 1976 well, winning the league title, beating Derry in the final, and then retaining Leinster with a two-point win over Meath, albeit luckily when Colm O'Rourke missed a penalty for Meath. Their semi-final against Galway was a poor, scrappy affair with sixty-seven frees and five bookings, but Dublin came through 1–8 to 0–8. Once again, they were to face Kerry in the final. In Munster, Kerry had won a tight, high-scoring final replay over Cork 3–20 to 2–19 that had to be settled in extra time, before thrashing Derry in the All-Ireland semi-final, 5–14 to 1–10. 26 September 1976 was to be Dublin versus Kerry, Heffernan versus O'Dwyer – mark two.

In preparing for the final, Heffernan was worried about how easily Kerry could score goals – something that had beaten Dublin the year before – given that O'Dwyer's team had put five past Derry in the semi-final. But Heffernan studied the games and thought he'd found the answer: 'They were using their corner-forwards to draw the opposing team's corner-backs away from goal and then getting somebody into the space created.'

Kevin Moran was central to Heffernan's plans, and he directed him to ignore his man and cover in behind the Dublin full-back line. Ever the student, Moran wanted to see the tape and evidence of his manager's rationale himself. 'We sat down with Kevin,' Heffernan told *Magill* in 1989, 'and spent a couple of hours going through the video with him and eventually he was satisfied.'

Around 73,000 gathered in Croker to see city versus country, Heffo's Army versus. O'Dwyer's Men, Dublin versus the Kingdom. Heffernan had a lifetime of Gaelic football obsession to prove by beating Kerry. This time, it was Dublin who exploded out of the blocks with the famous image of Kevin Moran careering through the Kerry defence, taking a pass from Bernard Brogan only to shoot narrowly wide. But the tempo had been set and the marker laid down, and Dublin sealed a famous victory, winning 3–08 to 0–10 and keeping Kerry goalless. Dublin had regained the All-Ireland and, between the Masters, it was Heffernan 1, O'Dwyer 1. 'I've waited twenty-one years for this,' declared Kevin Heffernan in the aftermath, as the pain of the 1955 defeat was finally washed away.

Had Heffernan anything more to achieve? In his own words, he hadn't. 'I had done what I set out to do and felt no further reason to stay on,' and so, just two weeks later, he called a special team meeting in the Gresham Hotel on O'Connell Street and announced he was stepping down. 'There was a fear of staleness and a need for a new voice,' said Heffernan years afterwards, while some claimed Heffernan saw the team was coming to an end and didn't want to sully his reputation. With Kerry vanquished, Heffernan was suddenly gone.

However, what he had built wasn't gone. The foundations were strong, with a system that was understood and a group of players who were on the same wavelength and had two All-Irelands to prove their greatness. Into the breach stepped Tony Hanahoe, the glue who held them all together, the man the players trusted and whose selflessness on the pitch made things happen for others. His role was to draw the opposing centre half-back away from the zone that the centre-back normally patrolled and which meant taking himself out of the game to create space for the wing-forwards and midfielders to attack into. It was Hanahoe who enabled the others to flourish and it seemed natural that he became their leader off the pitch now as well.

'All I was doing was working and playing and training,' says Hanahoe. 'Plus I was a professional lawyer at this time too. I got a lot of co-operation from the two other members of the management team who stayed on so there was continuity there and the players gave me great support – they felt it was preferable to have an insider rather than an outsider. In the end, I didn't get any time to think about it. It just happened like that. Kevin didn't give anybody notice, he gave me a little more notice that he was going to go and he just went.'

One of Hanahoe's proudest achievements was overseeing a smooth transition after Heffernan's departure, so much so that Dublin went on to win another All-Ireland – beating Armagh by twelve points in the 1977 final and beating Kerry in the semi-final in a clash described by many as the greatest football game ever played (of the televised era up to that point anyway). Their third meeting in three years, the semi-final ebbed and flowed, two teams going full belt, scores given and taken from one end of the field to the next. And, twice, Hanahoe was the right man in the right place at the right time, giving the perfect pass to David Hickey and Bernard Brogan, who went on to score goals, sealing the Dublin win 3–12 to 1–13. The final was, in many respects, an anticlimax (though not for Armagh, who were in only their second All-Ireland), with most observers of the opinion that the real final had already been played. Dublin and Kerry were so far above the rest of the country that whoever won between them would inevitably lift the Sam Maguire.

'One long, gorgeous summer,' recounted Dr Pat O'Neill of those months. 'Training seemed easy and pleasurable. The city had this atmosphere that I hadn't noticed before. Dublin was humming. There seemed to be money around as well. Plenty of money for all the activities. It started turning a bit. It just evolved so slowly and happily.'

'I thought the semi-final win was the apex,' says Hanahoe. 'Given that we were two points down with seven minutes to go. During that time, it was always between the two of us, always the first team, it was like a boxing match, the first team to make a serious mistake nearly always lost the game. It was that crucial, both psychological and physical. So in 1977, with seven minutes to go and Kerry with a two-point lead, everybody was watching the clock. As a player you're not watching the clock, but I mean suddenly to end up winning by five … They don't like talking about it in Kerry. They never talk about it.'

'In my view, there were five footballers on the team,' remembered Robbie Kelleher in an article written by David Walsh in *Magill* magazine in 1989. 'Paddy Cullen, Kevin Moran, Brian Mullins, Dave Hickey and Jimmy Keaveney. And of that five, Hickey never fully realised his potential. The rest of us were not footballers but we milked what we had to the fullest. The team was a great complement of talents.'

The question was, how much longer could this Dublin team that Heffernan had built keep going? A third were over thirty and a tantalising offer from Manchester United meant that Kevin Moran had gone to ply his trade and gain stardom in the English First Division. The team had one more achievement in mind: the three-in-a-row.

'That was the encore, we had won the two previous years and 1978 was to be the third in a row,' recalled Pat O'Neill for David Walsh. 'I think we were getting a bit arrogant then, particularly in defence, but it was incredibly easy to play football in that team. We understood so well what we should be doing. It was a pity that we did not win, because I would have willingly retired then as would Cullen, O'Driscoll, Hanahoe, Doherty and Keaveney. It was our shit-or-bust game and, as the Americans would say, we got shit on.'

Yet things were going well. Another Leinster victory, a league title and a fifth All-Ireland final beckoned. But then, in the middle of the summer, Heffernan decided he wanted back in.

'In retrospect, some people said it was a weak decision,' recalls Tony Hanahoe. 'On my part, I felt I had to let him back – I felt he was involved for so long that he was entitled to get back in. However, the defining of the roles for that period wasn't the best.'

It was to be the beginning of the end. Dublin's star was in its descent while finally, after the initial breakthrough success and two frustrating years of being bested, O'Dwyer's Kerry finally fulfilled their potential. A convincing and one-sided seventeen-point victory, 5–11 to 0–9, pretty much summed up where the two counties stood. Dublin had their half-decade of glory years, Kerry would soon have theirs.

Characteristically, for Dublin and Heffernan, they found it hard to give up the fight – especially when the beating had just been handed down by their archrivals. 'Just one more crack at it' became the mantra but, despite reaching a record sixth successive All-Ireland final appearance in 1979, Dublin were once more well and truly beaten by Kerry on a scoreline of 3–13 to 1–8.

Should Heffernan have stepped down this time? Or should he have come back in the first place? He was to stay on – with Hanahoe assisting him in a selector and co-management role – into the early 1980s as the duo sought to build a second successful Dublin team. And that team did reach successive All-Ireland finals from 1983–1985, beating Galway in 1983 before falling once more to Kerry in the two later years. Players of the ilk of Keaveney, Moran, Hickey and Doyle were gone. The era was over – even Heffernan had changed his style.

'What Kevin Heffernan did with the 1983 team was deserving of the highest praise,' remembered Tommy Drumm, who played under Heffernan, in an interview for *Magill* magazine. 'During the 1970s, he gave the orders and the lads got on with it. Cold and clinical. That was not going to work with the 1983 team and Kevin changed his style. He cajoled them. He spoke with individuals outside of the group discussions and did many things completely differently to the methods he used in the 1970s. I would not have believed he had the capacity to change but I saw how he did.'

Heffernan's talent as a thinking footballer had made him stand out as a player in the 1950s when Dublin GAA was reinvigorated due, in no small part, to St Vincent's policy of playing locals only.

After years of country people continuing their GAA education with clubs in Dublin, the 'Gah' was often derided as 'bogball' by city natives for whom soccer had long had a greater impact, attracting weekly crowds of 20,000 for League of Ireland games. St Vincent's policy of nurturing only local talent was to pay rich dividends for the Marino club when it won its first Dublin championship title in 1949 before going on an unbeaten run for another seven years.

'The one important thing about the GAA and GAA clubs is the related place of origin,' Heffernan recounted. 'Place of belonging is an emotional grappling iron that is there all the time. If you get fifteen guys who come from a certain area, a certain school, a certain kind of general background – that has a uniting effect. It is something more than just the jersey you are wearing, it is associated with every facet of a certain way of living and becomes part and parcel of an emotional group. That will always give a stability that is very difficult to find anywhere else.'

Kevin Heffernan's ultimate achievement was how he re-energised Gaelic football in Dublin – both on and off the pitch. He turned the team into All-Ireland winners and irrigated the barren wasteland of the 'Gah' in the capital. He knew the city was merely slumbering and if the county team were successful, it could spark and revive interest in the capital once more. He succeeded in that and more.

'It was something to cheer about, in a place that hadn't had anything to cheer about in a long time,' said Dublin GAA chairman, Jimmy Gray.

But it was more than that: 'bogball' suddenly became sexy, shed its rural image and Gaelic football with an urban image was finally defined. The GAA in the modern, Dublin context had at last come of age. Today, whenever a Dublin team goes on an All-Ireland tilt, the county gets behind the team. The sky-blue jerseys sell out in quick fashion and from Leinster final onwards, Croke Park plays to full houses of Dubs – Heffo's Army lives on.

'He deserves his place in history for being a reformer and having the commitment to stick with it,' says Hanahoe. 'I was there as a young guy watching in 1958 when they won against Derry and to go from that to Dublin playing in front of about 2,000 people in 1974 before building it up into 60,000–70,000 people by the time we had finished, and that has continued right up until today, that is what he will be remembered for.'

The legacy of Heffernan will never be forgotten and it's unlikely that anyone will ever again have the same impact on Dublin GAA. Heffernan made the most of his time and that's all he would want from future generations to come.

'I remember in the 1970s people used to be telling me about the 1942 team,' Heffernan recalled. 'And I often remember saying to myself I wish they would f– off with their 1942 team. I don't care who they were, I never saw them, I don't want to see them.'

By sheer dint of talent and personality, one man's achievements can last long after he's gone and Dublin people will always be asking about Heffo's Dubs.

❖

The rumblings in Kerry weren't long coming. After O'Dwyer and his young team burst out of nowhere to capture the All-Ireland in 1975, the next two years were to be ones of frustration and unfulfilled promise. In the players' own words, most of them weren't ready for what ensued in the aftermath of their success. Pints being fed to them wherever they would go into the county – days, nights and weeks of celebrations, being feted in every town. They thought they had it made. O'Dwyer let them loose and said he'd see them sometime in the New Year.

'I was well aware of what was going on in the winter and spring of 1976,' O'Dwyer wrote, 'but what was I to do about it as there's no ear more closed than a first-time All-Ireland winner who doesn't want to be told?'

The contrast between himself and Heffernan couldn't have been any more stark. While both were tee-totallers, both allowed their players to let their hair down and enjoy themselves. Both men were respected by their players but whereas few were close to or knew the real Heffernan, O'Dwyer became like a father figure to his group of young men.

Perhaps they thought they had it made, that they could turn up for the championship the following year and continue where they left off; meanwhile, Heffernan was completely re-configuring his half-back line and finding a future star in Kevin Moran.

The Kerry team that faced Dublin in the 1976 final was the same starting fifteen as the previous year, but it soon became apparent that Heffernan's tinkering had worked. O'Dwyer, though, maintains that his mistake was in playing Jimmy Deenihan and Ger O'Keeffe who were both struggling with ankle injuries, but he was reluctant to break up the full-back line. Beating Derry by sixteen points in the semi-final gave them a false impression and Dublin were able to hold Kerry goalless for the first time that year.

'The message was clear,' said O'Dwyer. 'Dublin had learned their lesson in 1975, gone away, made the necessary corrections and cleaned us out. We had sat back and admired ourselves, ignoring the unquestionable reality that nothing remains static.'

The pressure was on O'Dwyer and Kerry for 1977. When they won Munster, they faced Dublin in the semi-final. O'Dwyer's answer was to revamp the Kerry midfield, bringing in the raw Jack O'Shea and partnering him with the dogged Páidí Ó Sé. Dublin didn't change their line-up from 1976, but Kerry's team still didn't have enough and, although they were ahead by two points with just seven minutes to go, Dublin ran out five-point winners. The knives were soon out for O'Dwyer, with many asking questions about his management skills.

Just as in previous years, Kerry GAA questioned itself severely when a period of two barren years was endured – Jackie Lyne and Johnny Culloty didn't last long when All-Irelands weren't forthcoming – and many wondered whether the success of 1975 was a flash in the pan. Kerry was always worried it was being overtaken by others.

O'Dwyer's ditching of the traditional catch-and-kick philosophy didn't help his cause either, and the rumblings against him, particularly from some of the old guard, were gathering pace. Luckily for O'Dwyer – and Kerry football – the man who appointed O'Dwyer in the first place, county chairman Gerald McKenna, survived a vote on his position and remained on as chairman in 1978. O'Dwyer was safe for now, but this time it was to be All-Ireland or bust.

The key to it all was the arrival of a big lump of a lad from Ballybunion called Eoin Liston.

'We were struggling in 1977, which was when we found the Bomber,' remembers O'Dwyer. 'We had to look for a big guy, someone who, if we were in trouble anywhere around the field, we could drive the ball in to. If you can get a couple of big men and plant them on the square and drive the ball at them, provided they can win the ball, you can win All-Irelands. The ball will travel faster than any man at the end of the day.'

Crude and simplistic it may have sounded, but what Bomber Liston gave the talented bunch of stars around him was an outlet and the chance for space to open up for them.

'You have to be willing to change,' explains O'Dwyer. 'You have to look at the other teams and see what they're doing, what's number one. I generally have a system of my own and I try that and if that doesn't work then you have to change. But you have to be positive about your own way, and if you are not positive about it, then you are going nowhere. If you are just thinking about the other team and trying to counteract them, you're not going to win.'

By miraculous coincidence, just as Liston got the Kerry call-up, he also got a job as a science teacher in Waterville, O'Dwyer's hometown. Every evening O'Dwyer would meet up with him and work on his fitness and skills.

'He came here for five years, and I had him in the field every single evening of the week kicking footballs.' Not only that, there'd be nine holes of golf to get around, some food, kicking practice and then finish up with a game of badminton. 'What went into practice proves what you can do,' remarks O'Dwyer, and the Kerry forward line reaped the dividends of the time spent working on Liston.

The 1978 final was Bomber's first All-Ireland. For the first twenty-five minutes, Dublin dominated, stroking the ball around and popping over point after point. Then came 'the goal', the most-talked about score in the history of the game. The whistle was blown as Dublin goalie Paddy Cullen tussled with Ger Power; most assumed it was a free out, but it wasn't. Robbie Kelleher unwittingly handed the ball to Mikey Sheehy, who with the referee Seamus Aldridge's back turned to play, gently stroked the ball over the fast-retreating Cullen and into the net for the most unlikely of goals. Kerry went in at the break two points to the good, and in the second half it began clicking together for them as Bomber Liston netted a hat-trick for himself. Kerry won by seventeen points. Dublin's three-in-a-row was over; Kerry had come back off the ropes and saved O'Dwyer from an uncertain future.

'[The Bomber] was a new weapon in our armoury,' wrote O'Dwyer. 'One that would help sink Dublin in the most dramatic fashion.'

'The Bomber made a massive difference because you had

penetration straightaway,' explains Mickey Ned O'Sullivan. 'Before that, it was support play. Defence, once they got back, they could kick you out, they could hit you hard, but once the Bomber came with the long ball and they could get it – he could use it or he could lay it off, he had great vision. Bomber was totally unselfish, Bomber was the link man.'

Any criticisms of Kerry's use of the hand-pass were silenced and a remarkable new era in Kerry football was beginning. As Dublin's dominance waned and Kerry's rose, the personalities of the two men who were dominating Gaelic football – the similarities and differences – were striking.

The obsession with the game, the single-minded determination, winning at all costs, the teetotal lifestyle. And yet so different.

Heffernan was the student and thinker of the game, the man who would spend hours with his selectors Donal Colfer and Lorcan Redmond dissecting the opposition, coming up with the right formula; he was the man who gave new meaning to self-analysis among the players, men who were prepared to take as much criticism from their team-mates as was required. Heffernan was a man who instilled fear and respect in equal measure; a man it was never easy to get the handle on. And then there was O'Dwyer. Equally determined, equally dedicated, but a man who was close to his players, not one for over-analysing situations or trying to reinvent the wheel. He knew enough to ensure that Kerry's style of play modernised and incorporated hand-passing into their approach, but kept one foot in the traditions of the past, emphasising stamina training and running the players into the ground.

It says a lot about the feeling the players had towards the man that among the five PE teachers in the squad not one dissented or raised an issue about the singular methods being applied. If O'Dwyer wanted them to run, then run they would. O'Dwyer had enough belief in Kerry football and this group of talented players that he didn't have to teach them that much. This, like Heffernan's Dubs, was a group that believed in self-improvement.

'I remember distinctly watching them training at the Fitzgerald Stadium,' says Weeshie Fogarty. 'And I remember Pat Spillane's trademark of kicking his points from up the field, a big loop kick, and when training had finished, I saw Spillane stay behind for one hour kicking that ball the same way as all the others, and Bomber Liston too, they would stay behind and they honed their skills relentlessly. But he had them like that of course because that's the way he was himself. O'Dwyer wasn't a classy player. He was tough and he got every ball that came to him, he was very strong. His kick, he could drive the ball the length of the field and he had fierce determination. What he instilled into the players was mind over matter.'

O'Dwyer's men didn't have nights like the analytical robustness in Parnell Park that Heffernan presided over; the Kerry squad instead attracted thousands to their training sessions in Killarney where the football on show was better than most other inter-county matches. Backs against forwards, football, football, football was O'Dwyer's means of getting the message across. Let them play ball. Talented, dedicated *and* intelligent footballers, that's what O'Dwyer and Heffernan both sought and found.

'The one thing about the Kerry footballers who have come through,' says Fogarty, 'is if any fella gets on the Kerry team, he is going to be 100 per cent dedicated. There is no time for a fella in Kerry if they are not giving it 100 per cent or else if you don't do it we will get someone else.'

Having dispatched Dublin in 1978 and 1979, the question now was, just how far could O'Dwyer's team go? The struggles of 1976 and 1977 were a distant memory. The Bomber Liston had been found and slotted in to the system, Jack O'Shea had solved the midfield dilemma to become of the game's greatest midfielders and the forward line of Spillane et al. was playing with a confidence that comes only with wins and intuitive second nature among themselves.

'I tell you it was the greatest team that ever played the game, what a marvellous side,' beams O'Dwyer with a fatherly pride as he sits in his Waterville pub thinking back thirty years. 'They were marvellous, every one of them, totally committed to the cause. They would be training on their own, they would be running the beach in Banna and they would be running hills and what-have-you. They were real professionals.'

Kerry saw off Roscommon in 1980 to establish their own three-in-a-row – not achieved in the county for forty years – but it was the semi-final against Offaly that was to be the championship highlight. Offaly had finally broken Dublin's stranglehold on Leinster, guided by the genius of Matt Connor, who was to break Mick O'Dwyer's own championship-scoring record with a total of 22–135, but they lost the semi-final 4–15 to 4–10. The game was a feast of hand-passing and goals par excellence, but the GAA decided to ban the hand-pass the following year.

Had the game become too riddled with hand-passing to the detriment of catch-and-kick? Dublin and Kerry's fast-movement style had put them far beyond the others; Offaly's rise in the early 1980s showed they too were adopting similar tactics, while Roscommon's rough-house style on Kerry in the 1980 final showed that the close tactical possession game could descend into an unseemly spectacle. Gaelic football was being compared to basketball and rugby, possession football was a 'nauseating' feature that was detracting from the game, it was being claimed, even in Kerry itself, which had done so well in adopting the new style under O'Dwyer's management. These were all arguments that would resurface twenty years later when Armagh and Tyrone reigned supreme.

The GAA decided to act and a special congress was set up in 1981 at which the use of the hand-pass was redefined as a 'visible striking movement'; as always, the lack of real clarity in the rule meant that interpretation by different referees was going to cause problems. For O'Dwyer, it meant a slowing up of the game and a detraction from the speed, flow and spectacle of Gaelic football.

Still, though, the 1981 final between Kerry and Offaly saw just thirty-one frees – the lowest since 1966 – but it was also to be the lowest-attended final since 1947 with just 61,000 showing up. Maybe the public had been put off by the affair offered in the previous year or maybe it was just *ennui* at yet another Kerry final appearance – but Kerry's win saw them create their own bit of history with the first four-in-a-row since the county's great 1929–1932 team, which had been regarded as the county's finest up to that point. Offaly weren't done yet, though, and as the talk during 1982 focused on Kerry's attempt at an unprecedented five-in-a-row, the Leinster champions were happy to let the spotlight shine on O'Dwyer's men.

Much has been written about the famous last-minute goal by Offaly's Seamus Darby that saw them make footballing history by denying Kerry's destiny of five-in-a-row. Was Kerry's Tommy Doyle pushed? Did he misjudge the ball? It all depends on which colours you're wearing. Ultimately, what goes down in the record books is that Kerry were denied Gaelic footballing history and yet Mick O'Dwyer's stance all these years later is not one of what-ifs but instead he points to the fact that the team went on to achieve another three-in-a-row from 1984–1986, something he believes wouldn't have happened if they had won in 1982.

The following year, Kerry relinquished their grip on Munster after nine years, losing to another last-minute goal, this time to Cork, meaning that the incredible and historic Kerry bandwagon shuddered to a halt. Just as Dublin were doing in the east of the country, rebuilding under Heffernan for another tilt, O'Dwyer was forced to consider his hand.

He started a formal, collective winter training regime starting in October – something that Heffernan had done eleven years previously – and brought in new players alongside the existing medal contingent. But perhaps the biggest achievement of O'Dwyer's man-management skills was in convincing players who had already won five All-Irelands that the appetite for more was still there.

The wear and tear of being on the road for so long was inevitable, but with the likes of Liston, Spillane and Jack O'Shea, an incredible will to keep going was still in evidence. A three-in-a-row followed, with two defeats over declining Dublin teams that were to herald the final goodbye to the Hill for Kevin Heffernan.

But the writing was on the wall. O'Dwyer's men had played in ten All-Ireland finals, winning eight, a record of consistency and success that has not been beaten – and is unlikely to ever be. The spell was finally broken when Cork took Kerry to a replay in the 1987 Munster final and then beat them on their own patch in Killarney, with Kerry scoring just 1–5. O'Dwyer described how the team were flat, no longer able to recharge when things were down for them and, for once, neither the players nor management had an answer.

O'Dwyer struggled on, not wanting to throw in the towel, believing that things could be turned around, but Cork, under the expert guidance of Billy Morgan, were now dominating, retaining Munster and then completing their first three-in-a-row in the province. A three-point defeat in 1989 and O'Dwyer finally knew enough was enough.

There has been criticism of O'Dwyer for staying around too long, of not dropping the old guard and bringing in fresh talent but, in his eyes, those players had achieved so much for him, put their bodies on the line for so long, and it could never be him that called time on their careers. Instead, time was called on O'Dwyer.

'Oh I knew it was the end, I knew it was time for me to go,' he says. 'It was a case of start the building work again and it would mean dropping all the fellas who were there and picking a new team, that wouldn't have been easy. Even if it was that bad, I wouldn't drop them. They gave everything to the team and the county and the bond that was between those players, it amazed me. If I started to drop them, we would be bad friends, because we are only human after all.'

'The biggest problem was O'Dwyer,' says Mickey Ned O'Sullivan. 'I was selector with O'Dwyer from 1984 to 1987 and we had a bit of a disagreement and I said, "Mick, we are beaten, we have to shelve the lads now, they have been good, but they have to go" – but he wouldn't. Loyalty has to go out the window, you have to have a conveyor belt of talent and I said, "Mick, I can't continue because I think we are going down the wrong road now." We agreed to differ and there was no problem, we are still the best of friends, but I just could not continue, he still had them for about two or three years, the same lads, and we lost a lot of players as a result of that. Had we brought them in that time we wouldn't have had that eleven years of barrenness that was about to happen.'

The remarkable thing, as O'Dwyer stepped away from Kerry football after fifteen years at the helm, was that he wasn't finished. He had notions of going out on his newly built boat and seeing to his lobster pots, but it would never have been enough for him. Just two years later, he was to begin another chapter in his management career, leading teams outside of Kerry. The Kildare years proved his exceptional man-management skills, leading them to a Leinster title and a first All-Ireland final appearance in over sixty years. Then there was Laois, which he guided to a first Leinster title in fifty-seven years. Five years at Wicklow proved that his appetite for the game hadn't diminished in any way and during his stint there, when Wicklow faced Fermanagh in the qualifiers, he achieved the remarkable feat of having faced every county as a manager, another achievement that will surely not be surpassed.

Aged seventy-seven, Mick O'Dwyer's most recent role was with the Clare football team. A quarter of a century after he left Kerry, he was back in Munster helping to revive football in a hurling stronghold.

'It is not about what I am going to do in the present day, though I am hoping that I will be able to improve the team there, but the most important thing is to the future, the youngsters, getting them to play,' he said during his time there.

As always with O'Dwyer, it was about the game; nothing more and nothing less. It's a game that has given him an incredible life. His wife used to say that if he had put as much time and dedication into the running of the hotel and garage in Waterville, he'd have had an empire and they'd have been a wealthy family. But money had no hold over O'Dwyer. His life's ambition was about the game. One thing. A simple philosophy really. Knowing what that is and following it wherever it may lead you.

'I can't understand all those people who are driven after money,' he said. 'It's crazy, because at the end of the day you can only go through this planet once and if you are not going through it and enjoying it then what are you going to do?'

Pat Spillane was privileged enough to have played under both Heffernan and O'Dwyer and after all the All-Irelands, the tactics, the techniques, the stories and the myths, he stripped their essence down to one simple truth.

'The two most competitive divils ever put on this earth I'd say. They'd have different ways of handling people but would be able to see right through you from the time you shook hands and said hello.'

Part III

Men for the Hard Road

'Be a yardstick of quality. Some people aren't used to
an environment where excellence is expected.'

Steve Jobs

Chapter 7

The accidental manager

I got involved in management by accident. I was looking to play football but I was only a pathetic junior footballer.

Eugene McGee is as direct and straightforward as you could ask for. A long-time columnist and journalist with forthright views on Gaelic football and the GAA, his knowledge and experience encompasses both the college and the county scene followed by the view on the other side of the fence with the pen and notepad. But in a lifetime of dedication to the GAA, he is probably best remembered for managing the Offaly team that ended Kerry's five-in-a-row dream in the 1982 All-Ireland final.

For a guy who says he couldn't make it as a player, it was the ultimate achievement, denying the game's greatest side. Heffernan and O'Dwyer were All-Ireland legends, men whose stature was already guaranteed before they became managers. For McGee it was different and his reputation had to be earned another way.

It started when I was in UCD because, at that time, there was only one football team in all the college and the captain traditionally went around the team, he was in charge. Then higher education began to expand slowly, Freshers' teams started and then other teams started as well, so suddenly you had three or four teams in the college and the idea that the senior captain would run the team was out of the question.

I just drifted into helping the captain and then basically got involved in being in charge of the team because most captains didn't particularly want the job anyway, so that's how I started. My first involvement would have been in the 1960s. UCD were better even than Dublin; they were in the Sigerson, they had won the Dublin championship in 1963 and 1965 – I was involved with the one in 1965 – so I basically started my apprenticeship from there.

It was into an expanded educational environment that Eugene McGee first arrived at UCD in the mid-1960s. The sixth of seven siblings ('I was second last in a family of seven, so the others were more or else looked after'), he studied agriculture at first but got out when he discovered that physics and chemistry were on the agenda.

Not only was UCD responsible for nurturing his love of Gaelic football, it was also to introduce him to his other great passion – journalism.

The 1970s also saw an increased interest in studying sports at third-level, including the establishment of Thomond College in Limerick, and UCD was at the forefront of these developments when it established its first sports scholarships (in soccer), led by the future Director of Sport, Dr Tony O'Neill.

While the GAA and third-level Gaelic games have had an uneasy relationship down through the years, there is no doubt that the training and development of hurling and Gaelic football in the colleges was integral to the improvement of the game at inter-county level.

Just as physical fitness and preparation was becoming more and more intensive at inter-county level, so, too, the demands being placed on Sigerson players rose and regimes of four or five months were being introduced. McGee led the way in introducing strict training regimes and was the first to start sessions at 7 a.m., a trait that was to be brought back into vogue by Dublin and Donegal in 2010.

'UCD had been in the doldrums,' explains McGee. 'They hadn't won the Sigerson in about six years and I wanted to create an element of sacrifice above and beyond the norm. Guys had to get up at half six on a winter's morning and get out of bed and train in the dark. That was unheard of, but I felt something extra was needed to jolt them and the morning training gave it that extra element.

'At that time, students didn't go home at the weekends, so it was very easy to manage them,' he says with characteristic humility. 'Most of them were there seven days a week anyway and there was no club football down the country in the winter time. It is not like it is now, hanging on until the championships are over, it really was a captive audience for them and it gave them a focal point.'

Alcohol was banned two months before the start of the competition and special pre-match drinks of diluted orange and glucose tablets were given to give the players 'a kick'. But going that extra mile was to pay dividends and, despite the outbreak of foot-and-mouth cancelling the tournament in the winter of 1967, UCD ended their barren Sigerson spell in January 1968.

Eugene McGee had got the management bug and it was to take over his life for the next twenty years.

He was also trying to read up as much as he could on

management and sports psychology, and had to source information
and books from the United States.

> *I remember getting these sports injury books from America*
> *and also sports psychology books. I still have them,* Sweet
> Spot in Time *– I can remember that one – and there were*
> *several others. Part of my training for the HDip for teaching*
> *was psychology and that's why so many of the teachers in*
> *the GAA are fairly good at managing, they have an element*
> *of psychology in their training and they understand the*
> *principle of psychology anyway.*

It wasn't the science it is today, but things were changing. People
were coming back having studied PE and new ideas and new
thinking were changing the way the game was being approached
and thought about.

'Things were developing certainly,' agrees McGee. 'Whereas
before it was the captain who was motivating the guys in the
dressing room, as fellas got more sophisticated and other sports
got more scientific, a better system of training was needed and
organisation and preparing for matches began to be taken very
seriously. Then, when you moved into the 1970s, of course, it
began to change at county level also.'

The effect of McGee's influence, the seriousness with which
the side prepared for competition, and the pick of rising inter-
county stars meant that UCD enjoyed unprecedented influence in
the 1970s, winning six Sigersons in seven years from 1973–1979.
They were also to contest five Dublin championship finals in a row
from 1972–1976, meeting St Vincent's every time and winning
two (1973 and 1974).

Indeed, there was a rising antagonism between McGee and
Heffernan, each prowling the sidelines, Heffernan affronted by the

rise of UCD, consisting as it did of many country stars who were studying in Dublin.

'Needless to say they resented the students and usually they tried to kick the shit out of them,' says McGee. 'One of the dirtiest matches I ever had was the Dublin club final, it was shocking; we won it anyway, but the referees were usually afraid of St Vincent's. It was hard taking them on – they were all-powerful at that time.'

Heffernan wasn't to have it all his own way, however; UCD were the first Dublin side to capture the All-Ireland club championship, winning it two years in succession, in 1974 and 1975, with Vincent's following quickly in their wake, winning it in 1976.

UCD were also able to exploit the rule allowing for evening students to play in county competitions, and so the likes of Damien O'Donovan from Kildare and Jackie Walsh from Kerry joined their ranks.

'There were always three or four players coming from there and they were useful because they were a bit older than the normal students, they were about two or three years older, so that was a big factor winning the All-Ireland championships,' says McGee.

From being a complete unknown, McGee's reputation in management circles rose considerably. In 1975, UCD were Sigerson, Dublin, Leinster and All-Ireland champions. This may have been achieved with a host of inter-county stars – even their bench would be filled with them – but McGee's no-nonsense organisational style meant he was able to control the personalities in the dressing room.

Inter-county management seemed the next logical step, but McGee dismisses the idea that he had any notions of taking things any further at the time.

I had absolutely no ambition to get into inter-county at all.
I had long since graduated out of college and done different

jobs in Dublin, ending in journalism which was my focus. People say to me, sure you took the long-term view starting off in UCD, but that's not true at all.

Then out of the blue, Fr Sean Heaney, Offaly's chairman, rang me and asked if I would be interested in training the Offaly football team – 'training' was the word he used. I hadn't really thought about it, it wasn't on my radar at all.

Why me? I suspect it was Kevin Kilmurray, he had been on the Offaly team that had won All-Irelands in 1971 and 1972 and had also been on the UCD team that won the two All-Irelands. I suspect that they were in dire straits, they were gradually beginning to go through every member of the team, the usual stuff that happens with a manager and trainer and one was worse than the other.

But McGee was different. Having made the breakthrough in 1971 winning their first All-Ireland senior title and following it up with a second the following year, Offaly knew they could pit themselves against the best once more. By 1976, they just needed somebody with the managerial talent and modern know-how to move the county on. As McGee explains:

Offaly were in transition, of course. Ironically, I had written an article in the Sunday Press *just the year before about the demise of Offaly and the end of an era. Offaly had been relegated on a bitterly cold day in March against Mayo and they were very poor. I wrote one of my better pieces, I have to say, I even had a bit of poetry at the end of it. Then, just a year later and I'm manager of the team!*

But I had no knowledge of Offaly whatsoever. My first game with Offaly we were playing Limerick down in Askeaton which was about as low as you could go at that time, bearing in mind that, five years previously, they had won the two All-Irelands. It didn't help either that I was handed four selectors, none of whom I had ever met, so that wasn't a big help. They were there not to rock any boats, because nobody in Offaly had ever heard of this guy McGee. I was only about thirty-two at the time and literally nobody knew who I was because not many people were interested in third-level football.

While Offaly had achieved remarkable success just five years previously, McGee knew it was time to sweep out the old and bring in the new and he already had one eye on the talented youth coming through.

What encouraged me to take the job was being at the Leinster final; Dublin were playing Offaly in the minor match and I said I would look at them and I remember ticking off five or six players on the minor team. They were only beaten by a point and I thought to myself, these guys seem to have a lot to offer and it encouraged me at any rate that there was something going on there. I was thinking it would be a minimum of three years before you could do anything with a new team.

There was also talented under-21s that came through – Tomás Connor, Gerry Carr, Vincent Henry and I got off to a great start in my first year when we won the Leinster under-21 championship, beating Kildare. I insisted on managing the under-21s. I didn't want any conflict because I knew they would be the basis of my new team, they had to be because any of the 1971, 1972 team were beyond twenty-five years of age and maybe hitting thirty, they were only a stop-gap measure really.

I remember we had 20,000 at the 1977 under-21 final in
Portlaoise – they were as mad about football at that time
as they are now – but then we lost in the All-Ireland semi-
final replay. The following year, we got to the Leinster final
again and lost by one point. The following year, we won the
Leinster final, so we won two Leinster under-21s in three
years; that was a great start. Winning in that first year saved
me. I had won something and there was a future there.

I moved very gradually because the previous manager
of the winning team was Fr Tom Gilhooly who had a great
affinity with the players and that was the important thing.
They had a great set of players but they were a dirty team as
well. Now, it was also a great advantage to me afterwards
because all my time there people would say, from other
counties, if there was a draw coming up they would say,
'Jesus, not f–ing Offaly, anybody but Offaly.' People hated
playing us. But winning the Leinster title with the under-21s
meant there was something to go forward with.

McGee had been proved right, there were talented players coming
through the Offaly ranks, and he had also proved to himself that he
could manage successfully outside of the normal stellar cast at UCD.
But he knew wholesale change could not come immediately; any
sports science notions and ideas of 7 a.m. training sessions would
have to be put on hold while some of the old guard was still there.

In 1977, Dublin were at their peak, having won their third All-
Ireland in four years. They had been utterly dominant in Leinster
too, winning their fourth provincial crown on the trot, dominating
the way Offaly had done at the start of the decade. The question
now was whether or not McGee could get the Offaly team to match
Heffo's Dubs, who were being touted as one of the greatest sides to
grace Croke Park. Heffernan and Dublin held no fear for McGee.

He had tussled with the St Vincent's brigade for nearly a decade in his time with UCD in the Dublin championship, but he still knew he faced a mammoth task.

'The last person that Dublin would have wanted to be in charge of Offaly was that "f–ing McGee", because they hated me with a passion, really hated me,' he says. 'The first time I met the players was on a Saturday afternoon. I told them, first of all we are going to have to try and beat Dublin, that could take you a long time and then when we do beat them, Kerry would be there behind it, so we were facing what seemed to be the impossible because the Offaly lads were only starting out.'

While the under-21s had won Leinster and the seniors had won promotion back to Division One, all eyes were on their opening game in the Leinster championship against Wexford. It wasn't what McGee had planned – they shipped four goals in a poor performance and their summer was over before it had even got started. An opening Division One encounter against Kerry in Tralee later that year saw them on the end of a ten-point hiding. He knew he had to start bringing in the core from the under-21s if they were to make any inroads.

McGee was studying the game, looking to see how he could best exploit what was at his disposal. Kerry were using Bomber Liston as an outlet and lay-off man to enable the fast hand-passing of an exceptional forward line; Dublin were using runners pulling into the corners to create space in the middle. Offaly needed to find their own way. Instead of launching balls long into the square, McGee decided Offaly should avoid that route altogether.

We had a prearranged signal, the ball would be chipped in front of the thirteen or fifteen and the player would know it was coming twenty-five yards in front of him so he would run and get it. That was revolutionary at the time. You were

*supposed to kick the ball into the top of the square and the
full-forward, someone like Sean Lowry or whoever was
there, was going to catch it.*

*By doing a few things like that, the players began to
believe in me, and that was crucial, because after all I
was never famous, never a county footballer. For donkey's
years, all managers would have been former players. Here
was I with no playing experience to my name trying to show
them new ways to play the game.*

There were stirrings of movement in the right direction. Despite
losing to Dublin in the 1978 Leinster semi-final in Portlaoise,
Offaly were definitely on the up. It was McGee's first match-up
with Dublin, though he knew the players and their methods inside
out from his UCD days. Offaly were even leading at half-time and,
as McGee walked by the Dublin players, he could see they were
complaining and whining. Offaly had begun to get inside their
heads. Kevin Moran, who had been flown back from Manchester
to see out the Dubs' campaign, was sprung on for the second half
and Dublin came through to win the game.

'That was the first sign of life that the fans saw,' remembers
McGee. 'They were very happy leaving Portlaoise that day, they
saw they had something going for them.'

The following year, McGee's Offaly went a step farther, this
time meeting Dublin in the Leinster final. Dublin were going for a
record-equalling sixth provincial title in a row while Offaly were
back in a Leinster final for the first time since the last of their three-
in-a-row in 1973.

'We blew that game,' says McGee ruefully. 'Dublin got a goal in
the last second from Bernard Brogan and they won by two points.
Jimmy Keaveney got sent off so we had an extra man in the second
half and we still didn't win it, it was a very low-scoring game.'

Three years into the job and the knives were beginning to be sharpened for McGee. For a county that had only won its first All-Ireland nine years previously, expectations were nevertheless high. They were sick of playing second fiddle to Dublin. McGee admits he was lucky not to be sacked in the wake of that 1979 final defeat, but the under-21s had won another provincial crown and once again some of the pressure abated. 'I was hanging in there,' he says.

They were getting closer, however, and as the fortunes of the team began to pick up, so too did the arrival of new talent, willing to go the distance for the cause. Matt Connor came in 1979, Liam Curram and John Guinan followed soon after, and the pieces of the jigsaw were starting to come together for McGee. By the start of the 1980s, Dublin's dominance had waned, Kerry now had the upper hand and Leinster was there for the taking. This time Offaly didn't mess up, thanks in no small part to the genius of Matt Connor, who was to score twenty-two goals and 135 points that year, eclipsing Mick O'Dwyer's own ten-year record. Connor went on to be the leading scorer in the country for five years and in the 1980 Leinster final against Dublin scored an incredible 1–7 of his side's 1–10, as Offaly finally dethroned Dublin by two points.

Victory for McGee over his old Dublin rivals, Heffernan and the rest of the Vincent's brigade, was sweet and the breakthrough that he badly needed.

> When we won Leinster, there were two things. We had put Dublin out of the way for a couple of years which brought us into the reckoning and I knew at that stage that Kerry would be gradually eroded, maybe only slightly, but they couldn't go on forever. In 1980, though, they were still bloody strong. They weren't just winning, they were beating the living shit out of everybody, including Offaly. Our semi-final against them was 4–15 to 4–10, which is a joke because they should have won by fifteen points.

I knew we would have no trouble facing up to Kerry because Offaly were never overawed by Kerry having beaten them in a replay, which is very rare, so that was a big thing to have. As well as that, I had the insight on a lot of Kerry's setup because I knew Ogie Moran, John O'Keeffe, Jackie Walsh who was always a sub there; I knew a good few of them. That was a big plus for me. We never had any fears about playing Kerry and that was a great help for a start.

Despite that semi-final defeat, things were starting to click for Offaly. After years of playing catch-up, McGee felt they were now getting to the level where they could compete at the highest standard. Key to that had been firstly bringing the fitness up to scratch and so McGee hired PE manager Tom Donoghue, who was a teacher in the Probation School at Tullamore.

'There was a big twenty-five-acre field outside the old GAA ground which was very, very steep,' remembers McGee. 'For two winters in a row, we did very, very severe stamina training up that hill, under the guidance of Tom Donoghue, and it was definitely a key factor in the success of the team. We were always trailing behind in fitness because Dublin and Kerry had the residual effect. Each year when you do a massive training session, you retain maybe 50 per cent, so therefore you are starting at a higher base each subsequent year, so Offaly were behind all the time, and that's why we increased the level of the fitness and brought a bit of science into it. We used to do gym training at night as well as circuit training in the winter time.'

Despite developments in sports science, some of it still remained very rudimentary, with one particular fad at the time being the steak dinner before the match.

'A steak on the rocks, maybe with a small bit of salad, that was about it,' says McGee. 'If we trained, we had a steak every night after training right up to the 1982 All-Ireland final in a small hotel in Tullamore.'

McGee even changed the training base to a small pitch out the road in Ballyconlon where they could get away from the public attention. This proved very successful, bringing the team closer together, placing it within the county's local rural context and helping to build the identity of the team and so give the players something extra to fight for. Then there was the time he and a few of the backroom staff visited Arsenal's training ground during winter to find out about their training and physio techniques.

Always looking for new ideas and improvements, in the spring of 1982, McGee introduced the first sun-training break when the team headed off to Spain for two weeks for a holiday and workout. The players trained twice a day and then could enjoy themselves in the evening with wives or girlfriends. They went into the hard part of the season in the summer time, a unified and happy group of players that was gelling together.

It was the little things that counted and these eventually add up to be greater than the sum of their parts. There were the personal lines that McGee would write out for them on the Wednesday before match day, positive affirmations that they could reflect on in the build-up to the game.

In 1981, Offaly retained Leinster and this time they did reach the All-Ireland final, but once again Kerry were waiting. Luck was not on their side either, with two of their key midfielders, Tomás Connor and Johnny Mooney, sustaining injuries.

The minute I got the phone call to say that Mooney had fallen and broken his shoulder, I knew that was it. Mooney

> *would have been our number one midfielder and Tomás*
> *Connor was the other. Connor had been injured in the*
> *previous match in the shoulder and the first ball that came*
> *for him, he was flattened, that's the name of the game, so*
> *he was a dead duck. We were playing then with two hands*
> *behind our back.*

Offaly lost by seven points, outclassed by Kerry, 1–12 to 0–8. In the aftermath, criticism still abounded within Offaly, but McGee knew the pieces were coming together, they just needed a bit of luck the following season.

The 1982 season, of course, was all about Kerry's bid for the historic five-in-a-row. Nothing else mattered, and nobody else could stop them, it seemed. Songs were released about it; the radio phone-ins in Kerry were wondering would Killarney or Tralee be the first to host Sam Maguire. Everyone seemed to be forgetting about one thing – Offaly. Led by Eugene McGee, they were quietly plotting and quietly confident. Offaly duly completed their three-in-a-row in Leinster, a nine-point win over Dublin, illustrating just how far the pendulum had swung away from the Dubs in the province. They scrambled through against Galway in the All-Ireland semi – a game McGee says they should have lost – but things were starting to go their way.

Driving home from training on the Tuesday before the All-Ireland final, McGee had the radio on listening out for word on the Kerry team.

'It was about 10.15 in the evening,' he remembers vividly. 'The Kerry team was announced and it came up: centre half-forward Sean Walsh and left half-forward Ogie Moran. I stopped the car, got out and let out a big cheer. To me, that was the missing link because I knew that Lowry would have major troubles: Lowry was six foot two inches, Ogie Moran was five foot eight inches, and was very fast and nippy, he was going to cause us problems but less so out on the wing. I was hoping against hope that he wouldn't be centre-forward.'

McGee was very precise about his team selections and match-ups against the opposition, and with Moran moving out of the centre-forward berth, it was playing right into McGee's hands.

The main thing was that we were able to pick people who could play key roles. Like Liam O'Connor, who would have been a very unglamorous player. He was a six-foot-four full-back, the old style, but all wire and iron, he would persecute you with every part of his body and he began to learn how to cope with Bomber Liston and that was a huge, huge plus. Liston was nearly impossible to mark, he had destroyed Dublin with three goals in 1978 and every other year as well. But in 1981 and 1982, we partially culled him anyway. It was impossible to stop him altogether.

The biggest thing for me was we had decided after the 1981 final that we would probably be playing Kerry again, that's the way football was, we gambled on that, and we planned on that. In the 1981 final, Tim Kennelly got man of the match, he was marking Gerry Carroll and he destroyed him and blew him out of the water; we knew that couldn't be allowed to happen again and we were limited, so we decided to take a drastic step with Richie Connor who was our normal centre-back moving into the centre-forwards.

We made that decision pre-Christmas, but we didn't do much about it until later on; I don't think he ever played centre-forward for us in private or in public at all. But we were happy enough that he had the strength and the power; he was a good footballer and good distributor of the ball, especially with giving short passes – either foot or hand. I

was a firm believer in studying each player and seeing how
you could exploit them, and I mean they still do that today.
They have the advantage of DVDs today which we didn't
have, though we brought in our own video.

From the starting fifteen in the previous year's final, only five players remained in the same position. McGee wasn't afraid to change things around. The abolition of the scored hand-pass rule the year before also played into their hands – suddenly Kerry's most potent weapon had been blunted.

'Kerry used to score a minimum of five or six goals in every match, a minimum, it was extraordinary, and then their four goals in the semi-final in 1980 against us re-emphasised that but the rule changed and the hand-pass scores were banned. That was a help. The biggest change was that the forwards got no goals in 1981 against us; I built on that straightaway, even afterwards in the dressing room after the match I told them, "We've got within shouting distance of them now, we have covered their forward line, they got no goals", and in 1982 they got no goals either.'

Offaly knew they were close, and driving home that Tuesday night they were even closer. But still nobody gave them a prayer, which suited them just fine.

'We used to play Kerry in challenge matches on open pitches a lot because my policy was the more we play them, the better,' says McGee. 'Eventually we would reach the stage where we would be playing in the All-Ireland final sometime and the more you play them, the better. We played two matches behind closed doors in the two weeks before the final. We played Down and Roscommon because there were certain things we wanted to try out and we beat them by an enormous margin. James McCartan senior was the manager of Down at that time, he just came over at the end of the match and said, "I would be amazed if you didn't win the

All-Ireland." We had played brilliantly in those two matches, everything worked perfectly – Richie Connor worked perfectly, the whole team were brilliant, Matt Connor was demonstrating all his stuff, we were in great form mentally.'

In the final training sessions of the week, McGee had the players play the last ten minutes of their practice sessions in complete silence. No shouting, no calling for the ball. 'With the wall of noise in Croke Park on the day, you won't be able to hear yourselves,' McGee told them. Getting them used to the silence was preparing them for when it was only their body movements and eyes that would act as their signals. The little things all added up.

Plus they had plenty of ammunition to get stuck into Kerry and McGee made sure he made the most of it. He was turning the mind games up a notch in readiness.

When I heard the song about Kerry's five-in-a-row, I used it in the training session the next day. It was a glorious opportunity, talk about putting the team up on the dressing-room door, it wasn't a patch on it, to hear this song. It had never happened before a match to have a song like that and then there was also the big story in The Kerryman *front page about the row about whether the cup would go to Killarney or Tralee first. That was the lead story in the paper. It was manna from heaven for me as a manager to present that to the players.*

Acres of print have been written about that famous day, most notably by Michael Foley in his book *Kings of September*. It was the day when Kerry had Gaelic football history in their grasp only to see it snatched from them in the dying minutes by Seamus Darby, the last link to Offaly's previous All-Ireland success in 1972. After nearly ten years in the wilderness, Darby was recalled for the Leinster final before being sprung from the bench in the dying moments of the All-Ireland.

Two points down with two minutes to go, the instructions from McGee were clear: 'Stay forward and go for goal.' A high, lobbing ball dropped into the Kerry defence. Inexplicably, Kerry's Tommy Doyle misjudged the flight of the ball and missed it, enabling Darby to catch the ball, turn and bury a shot into the back of the net.

There was time briefly for one last desperate Kerry attack but it came to nothing. The final whistle went and, amazingly, and in the most dramatic of circumstances, Offaly had beaten Kerry. Croke Park erupted. Kerry players were shell-shocked, unable to believe what had happened. But all that mattered was the final scoreline: Offaly 1–15, Kerry 0–17. Seamus Darby was the goal-scoring hero and Eugene McGee had masterminded a shock of gigantic proportions against arguably the greatest side that Gaelic football had seen.

'It was definitely the pinnacle of my career,' he says. 'In the GAA, it was only the second time that there was a chance for someone to win five-in-a-row, and there will probably never be another one, it's not very often you're actually involved in something so historic. As well as that, it was a very good game – that's what I get most satisfaction out of. Paddy Downey wrote the following day that it was the best final he had seen for twenty-five years and there wasn't a better one since, I would say.'

It was just one of those moments, never to be repeated and seemingly written in the stars. Written in the stars after six years of patiently building a team from scratch, ignoring the rumbling criticisms, tweaking things, adding here and there, making small advances each year, and using a potent mix of man-management, psychological and tactical skills.

It was as if McGee's entire coaching life had been building to that one game. From his years at UCD getting to know Kerry players such as Ogie Moran and John O'Keeffe, to developing the under-

21s and youth players in the Offaly setup, to taking on board the new advances in sports sciences and to trying to outwit O'Dwyer with tactical changes, it all culminated in perfect symmetry with that last kick at goal from Seamus Darby. Nothing could ever come close to replicating it.

The following season ended disappointingly with defeat to Dublin in the 1983 Leinster final. The foot had been taken off the pedal and McGee had begun taking his tactical experiments to even further heights. The secret, of course, is knowing when to stop.

'I was trying to maybe use some new experimental moves, some new tactics, but anyway we lost,' he says matter-of-factly. 'Then 1984 was the centenary year and I had to stay on for that though I had no real interest and Dublin beat us again in the semi-final.'

McGee knew his time was up and moved on, his place in Offaly and Gaelic football history assured.

He spent a few years with Cavan, across the border from his hometown in Longford and, ironically, one of his last games with Cavan was seeing their under-21s lose the All-Ireland final – to Offaly, by a point. Youth was still having its say and the foundations he had put in place in the Leinster county were still going strong.

One of McGee's proudest achievements was winning the county championship with Newtowncashel in his native Longford. The seniors had never won a championship match but McGee's managerial touch was proved again when he turned them into county champions.

To this day, I never found out why they asked me because I didn't know anyone there, I knew nobody in Newtowncashel. I had to look it up on the map to find the bloody place. They were a typical country club, they had got a lot of talent but needed somebody to organise them. And when I came

*along it just took off. I don't know why. I just gave it a bit of
organisation.*

*For instance, there were four sets of brothers on that
team and there were always mini-rows in these clubs – like
a lot of clubs. There would be somebody coming out with
something, f–ing around, then somebody would walk away
for a few weeks, so I got rid of all that immediately. I said
I will do it but it will be on my terms, in other words you
can f– off, like, and that's exactly what happened. But they
were a wonderful set of dedicated young men, fantastic
to deal with. Ironically, I missed the county final as I was
still managing Offaly at the time and the Offaly under-21s
were playing Down in Newry the same day. At that time
you couldn't get a phone and I didn't hear the result of the
match until seven o'clock in the evening. I couldn't believe
it that they had won and the joy they got from doing that.*

The crossover between business and management was never more
apparent for McGee than when he took over the *Longford Leader*,
where he found that the necessary skillsets between the dressing
room and boardroom were easily transferable. He lists organisation
as being most important, followed by man-management, 'but the
ability to instil discipline without getting abrasive – that's the
biggest test really'.

That's why Pat Gilroy was so successful with Dublin because
he knew how to allocate duties and how to insist that they are
implemented properly. He didn't ask them to do unreasonable or
impossible things, that's all part of it.'

Some would say that what McGee asked of the Offaly team that
had been relegated to Division Two – to look up, first to Leinster,
to Dublin and an All-Ireland final and beating Kerry – was an
impossible task. But sometimes the impossible can be achieved.

Chapter 8

'You might be able to play, but can you compete?'

Longevity and success. These are what first come to mind when looking back on the incredible managerial career of Seán Boylan. He led Meath for twenty-two years – a tenure unlikely to be equalled in GAA management terms – and brought them from also-rans to All-Ireland winners. Not only that, but he rebuilt the team, brought in new players and won the All-Ireland again. Not many managers can claim success having built up two different teams.

To sum up Seán Boylan only in the context of Gaelic football is to do him and his achievements an injustice. When you speak to his former players, they speak of him in such respected tones, of someone who was more than their manager, someone who was there as they also went through life's ups and downs.

'He was a brilliant man-manager. He worked with individuals in a remarkable way in terms of the hours he spent with them, he didn't shy away from spending five or six hours in a player's home,' explains Liam Hayes, the midfielder and man of the match in Meath's first All-Ireland triumph under Boylan in 1987. 'He would become a friend as well as a manager. He got very, very close to all his players. He got to know them intimately and was very clued in to where everybody was. That was Seán's real genius as a manager.'

The bond and the closeness was what Mick O'Dwyer had with his young Kerry players, but whereas O'Dwyer brought a single-minded obsession about Gaelic football and nothing else, Boylan brought an interest in nature and the human spirit to his management philosophy. A fifth-generation herbalist, people from all over Ireland come to visit his clinic outside Dunboyne for remedies and help with problems that conventional medicine hasn't been able to cure. He is a firm believer in what nature can help solve in life and it is a spirit that blankets his personality. A diminutive figure, he greets you with a warmth and friendliness that speaks of someone at peace with himself and the world around him. But it's also marked with a strong-willed mentality to succeed at whatever he is putting his mind to at that very moment.

He is not someone you can put in a box easily. O'Dwyer and Heffernan, they were football men wanting to win a game at all costs. Everything else came second. With Boylan, although winning mattered, you get the sense that it was about the approach to winning, the place you were in as a person to make it happen that mattered as much.

'Seán would have more belief in nature, more belief in water and more belief in air,' says Liam Hayes. 'When Seán would bring us to Dalgan Park he would tell us, "Smell that air, lads, take that air into your lungs, this is good air out here." He would be a man very much in harmony with nature and with the power of nature and the team would have come to understand it and knew that living by Seán's rules and ways was good for them.'

Part of the secret to his success was that he was also not afraid to try new things, introduce new concepts and ideas to the training and development of his players. Without any preconceived notions of the way things must be, Boylan brought a unique mindset, an all-encompassing holistic approach to the game of Gaelic football – a natural successor in many ways to that other trainer of legendary longevity, Kerry's Dr Eamonn O'Sullivan.

Like so many of these master-stroke appointments, it very nearly didn't happen. Boylan was a hurler first and foremost, had played junior and senior with Meath for over twenty years and in his last year ended up as player-manager. However, when a row between clubs and county over players reared its ugly head, he upped sticks and left them to it – this wasn't how he wanted to run things. The hurlers' loss was football's gain.

In 1983, it had been sixteen years since Meath's last All-Ireland success. There had been another final appearance in 1970 when they lost to Kerry and even a National League title in 1975, but, since then, Dublin and Offaly had come to dominate Leinster. Meath reached four Leinster finals in five years from 1973 to 1977 but lost each time to either Dublin or Offaly; their four-point loss to Dublin in 1977 was the final kick and they had lost their way since, not even reaching the provincial final. But Meath had always had talented players coming through and it was a county that believed strongly in itself. It had a rich past going back to league success in 1933 before the All-Ireland breakthrough in 1949 that saw them beat Cavan and reaching the finals in 1951 and 1952 before claiming a second Sam Maguire in 1954 when they beat Kerry.

Having lost its way since then, when the Meath County Board approached Boylan about taking over the footballers, it seemed a last, desperate throw of the dice to put a former hurler and team masseur in charge.

When they asked me, I told them I had to think about it. I spoke to Dr Brian Smith, the county board chairman and

who had lifted Sam Maguire in 1949, and decided at about 2
a.m. that I would take over the reins. 'But only until you get
somebody else,' I told him. That's exactly how it happened.
I had no ambition in the world to do it.

I remember on the first day being back in the Imperial
Hotel after seeing the team play and thinking these are great
lads, but they've no idea what fitness is. I was sitting at the
table with Colm Coyle, Liam Hayes and Finian Murtagh
and these were the three young lads who had come up the
ranks. I knew lots of these lads, I had seen them playing for
their clubs and teams and playing with Meath, they were
good players but they weren't able to sustain it. To sustain
something, you have to realise that half the training you
do is to absorb the tension and the stresses that go along
with competition; hundreds can play, but not hundreds can
compete.

Having spoken to the players, seen them playing and got a sense
of their desire to succeed, Boylan was on board. Success didn't
come overnight, however. There was an O'Byrne Cup win but that
was followed by an eleven-point defeat to Galway in the league. In
1984, Meath proved their standing by winning the GAA Centenary
Cup and that same year in the 1984 championship, they reached
the Leinster final, the county's first in seven years. Despite being
quietly confident against Dublin, Heffo's men came through by
four points with Meath's Pádraig Lyons missing a penalty early
on. Then there was the ten-point hammering at the hands of Laois
the following year, and the team were shell-shocked. One step
forwards, two steps back it seemed. 'Sure what could you expect
from having a hurler in charge?' the rumbles around Meath went.

'A few weeks after that loss, one night six of the players came
to see me – the senior players such as Colm O'Rourke, Gerry

McEntee, Liam Hayes, Mick Lyons,' says Boylan. 'And the lads said to me, "Listen will you put your shyness in your arse pocket." You mightn't believe it because of the profile that I would have, but I'd be of a shy disposition – I'd much prefer to listen than to talk. But from then on, we talked openly and though it meant they were going to say things to me I mightn't like to hear, likewise I was free to say what I had to say as well.'

Other important changes were implemented too. Boylan sought – and received – his own selectors with Meath finally scrapping the outdated system of having half a dozen selectors – something Dublin chairman Jimmy Gray had done away with in the capital twelve years earlier. With Pat Reynolds and Tony Brennan alongside him, 1986 was going to be make or break for Boylan and his players.

'It was the defining year,' agrees Colm O'Rourke, one of the game's greatest forwards and who had been at the coalface for the Royal County since the 1970s. 'A few of us had been playing a long time, so it was getting close to the point that we had to be able to do something otherwise our careers were going to just spin out of control and we would have forced early retirements. We hadn't won a Leinster title at all at that stage, in our time. If we didn't win the Leinster final in 1986 the chances are that there would have been further changes and maybe Seán mightn't even have been in charge. So that actually was the most important year of all.'

Defeat to Laois in 1985 proved to be not so shocking after all when the Leinster county surprised the Gaelic football world by winning their first National League title the following year. For Meath, however, their sights were fixed firmly on capturing a first Leinster title in sixteen years.

'Even though our performances early on in 1986 weren't particularly special, at least people were fairly confident that there was a better method about it,' says O'Rourke. 'There was a greater unity of purpose and it really took the Leinster final win to effect that but I think we all felt it even in training that year.'

'Seán was in the process of actually building a team,' explains Hayes. 'It was like a three-piece jigsaw – there were three different parts to that team that he was fitting together. There was the core part of half a dozen older players who had been around for seven or eight years. The largest part of their career possibly was over, they were in their late twenties, they were very mature and were really big players. Then there was a second group which included myself who were slightly younger and newer to the team, we were a good solid group. But he really needed to get the third piece and it was a group of young players whom he found and brought in and who were absolutely crucial people. There was Robbie O'Malley, Bernie Flynn and Brian Stafford; Robbie turned out to be the best corner-back in the country at the time and Bernie was one of the most talented forwards.

'The most fortunate thing that happened was that Seán found Brian Stafford and he literally put our free conversion rate from 70 per cent up into the 90 per cent – that gave us about two points per game. When the really big games started, it was crucial. The biggest example of all was the four-game series against Dublin in 1991 when Dublin dominated us on each of the four occasions and in each match, every single match, when Dublin were maybe four or five points up, we would get a free down the other end and Brian Stafford would put it over the bar. That kept us alive more than anything else in those games. It was a lifeline and without a first-class free taker we wouldn't have had that lifeline.

'It was Seán who found Stafford, and worked very hard to find him. He'd never played minor or under-21 for Meath, he was a very shy character and didn't want to come in and Seán literally found him. So, when you look at all the great abilities of managers, Seán Boylan also had that aspect of actually physically building a team.'

Just as O'Dwyer found the likes of Liston, and Heffernan went scouting for his half-back line in 1976, the talented managers knew what pieces they were looking for, found them, and made sure they fit into where they were supposed to go.

'Between 1985 and 1986 there were seven lads brought in,' says Boylan. 'And they were involved in the Leinster final the following year. Earlier in the season, we met Dublin in the quarter-final of the league in Croke Park and I remember coming off the field that day and Brian Mullins putting the arm around me saying, "Seán, you can win the league, we'll win the championship." We went in at half-time, Dublin were six points ahead, and the quietest man of the whole lot, Brian Stafford, said, "That's it, for f– sake, lads, these fellas are no use." And he started hauling the ball around the dressing room. Despite Dublin being six points ahead, our lads were still confident in themselves. I knew that day we'd win the championship.'

Having a talented and hungry group of players under the guidance of someone of Boylan's calibre who was also taking training sessions to new heights – and it wasn't textbook stuff that would be studied in university – meant that Meath were getting close to a winning formula.

'We would have been conditioned with Seán right from the very beginning,' explains Hayes. 'He did things instinctively and he built his own coaching sessions. Everything from Seán, even from the stretching that we would do before matches, wouldn't be found in fitness books by and large. Seán was a man in massive physical shape – he said he would never ask us to do anything he couldn't do himself. He could bend and stretch his body in the most amazing ways, even as a forty-year-old when he took over the team. The physical preparation of our team was something that was unique to us, unique to Seán Boylan.'

1986 was to be the last year for Dublin under the managerial

genius of Kevin Heffernan. Like Heffernan, Boylan introduced his
own methods that kept Meath one step ahead of the pack.

> We did an awful lot of work, but it was varied from Tara
> Hill to the beach at Bettystown and the dunes and so on.
> But it was all at different times of the year and no training
> sessions would ever be longer than the length of a match.
> In the county here, you were dealing with different types
> of soils and we had muck that would pull the legs out of
> you. That can be fine, there can be a place for that, but if
> you're going to be playing football in a few days' time, you
> can't do that. So you had to vary that, you had to go where
> you would be on top of the ground, but that meant having
> footwear right.
>
> In terms of mental preparation, I wanted to get people to
> take ownership, that no matter what you do in life, you have
> to take ownership of it. The thing I talked about with regard
> to making excuses is, if you start doing it, it becomes easy.
> If you want to play it, you want to play it. Being anxious,
> being nervous, that's all part and parcel of people's make-
> up. It's how you deal with that. I was also very lucky with
> my selectors, they were great men who had great knowledge
> of the game. Did I know all about it? Not a clue. I just knew
> that these lads were good footballers.

Meath faced Dublin in that make-or-break Leinster final in 1986.
Two years earlier Dublin had seen them off by four points; the Dubs
had made the previous three All-Irelands but were creaking and
coming to the end. Besides, this was a different Meath team with
different structures in place and a new-found confidence and belief
in themselves. One last throw of the dice for them. All or nothing.

'It was the last session before we played Dublin in the Leinster final,' remembers Boylan. 'I was saying a few words and a dear, old friend of mine, Frankie Byrne, who had won the All-Ireland with Meath in 1949 and 1954, and would come down to watch the training … Frankie was a great thinker of the game, a great tactician, and he stood up and said, "Lads do you mind if I say something? Seán, do you mind?" "Fire ahead, Frankie," I said to him. "Lads, look, we get all the glory," he said, looking around at each of them. "We brought back the first All-Ireland, but I just wanted to say we wouldn't have kept the ball if it had been kicked out to you." In other words, Frankie was telling them just how good they were. The next night the lads were talking and saying Frankie's words meant an awful lot.'

The breakthrough came. They beat Dublin by two points, 0–9 to 0–7, and the ghosts of past defeats were banished. In the semi-final, Meath faced Kerry who were on the brink of a three-in-a-row, and though Kerry ran out seven-point winners, it was a tight contest with Kerry struggling to see off Meath. Kerry duly won their third All-Ireland on the trot, and the eighth in ten years under O'Dwyer, but Meath knew they weren't that far off. They had finally won in Leinster, the next target was Sam Maguire.

Winning All-Irelands is anything but simple, but for Liam Hayes and the rest of the Meath team, Seán Boylan's approach and tactics were all about simplicity itself.

'We had one of the simplest approaches of any of the All-Ireland-winning teams over the past twenty years. I'd say ours was maybe the simplest game plan ever,' explains Hayes. 'That was to get the ball; whether it was a defender or whether it was one of us in the middle of the field, our objective was to get the ball into the full-forward line as fast as possible. Normally, we did that with a diagonal ball, so if I got the ball on the right wing in the middle of the field I was going to hit a fifty- or sixty-yard pass into space in the top left-hand corner.

'The basis of our philosophy was that we had the best full-forward line in the country and if we got sufficient balls, fast enough, into them in space then we would win matches. When you look at the really great teams over the past twenty years – and I'm not saying we were really great – but the really great teams have three geniuses in the full-forward line. I always say we had two and a half. O'Rourke was the greatest footballer I've ever played with or against, Brian Stafford was just exceptional and Bernie was exceptional but he was the half, he was half a genius, the other two were fully fledged geniuses.

'If you have three geniuses in your full-forward line, no matter what style of game you are playing, your number one aim is get that ball, probably by the foot, into that line as quickly as possible. If you don't have three geniuses, you're going to adapt your play. If you have two, you're going to adapt your play, if you've one, you're going to adapt your play, and if you've none, you're definitely going to adapt your play. You have to build the team with the realisation that every team does not have equal full-forward lines. Full-forward lines win and lose games and they win and lose All-Irelands and that's been proven since the start of time.'

Even geniuses don't stand out a mile, especially if they're playing junior club football, and part of Boylan's exceptional insight and broad-thinking was the fact that he wasn't afraid to scour intermediate and junior divisions for the type of player he was looking for.

'During the summer, I'd see five or six matches a week then maybe two or three on a Sunday,' he recalls. 'I remember in 1985, it was the night Denis Taylor won the snooker, that morning I went to a match down in Castlebar, Sligo were playing Trinity, in something like the Trench Cup, and I went down to see a player and I ended up getting another one. I went down to see Ciarán Carr and Joe Carr and I ended up getting Declan Mullen. I came back from there to a match in Meath where St Michael's and Mark O'Connor's team were playing and left there to go to Navan for another game, and I left there to go where Summerhill were playing O'Mahony's and Mick Lyons was playing full-forward for his club. I went from there to a Meath under-21's game against Roscommon and from there I went to Tony Brennan's house to pick a team with Tony and Pat Reynolds. That was the day! Now, people would say, it's an awful step up from junior to intermediate and intermediate to senior, and it *is* massive. But there were guys like Robbie O'Malley and Bernard Flynn whom I didn't want to get bad habits from their clubs so I brought them in when they were just eighteen so they would be learning the system. I brought them in with a view of two years ahead, but Robbie made it after three months, and Bernie after eight.'

With the squad in place and a system of play that the players bought into, confidence after 1986 was growing. What was needed now was that extra edge, that 1 per cent that could make all the difference.

'What you had to do was get the agility of mind and body, to get that to be able to ride the punches as the saying goes and to play the type of game that was really suitable to us,' says Boylan. 'We had a squad of players who could play great football for maybe ten minutes, but to stay going for another five or ten minutes after that, both mentally and physically, that's what you had to get into them. At that stage, we were doing Tuesday, Thursday, Saturday, Sunday and we had to do it just to get where we were, because some of those lads were so physically strong what you had to do was so much stretching to loosen them up.'

'We did a lot work at the beach, we did all sorts of unusual things and he was fantastic at keeping the team fresh, mentally and physically,' remembers Colm O'Rourke. 'Even though we did a lot of hard training, he found different places to do it, he mixed it up and it never seemed as if it was drudgery. Then when it came to the big games, he would have you really jumping out of your skin, everybody would be bouncing. He seemed to be able to gauge a player's welfare very well just by looking at them. He had that talent of seeing in a person's general appearance and body language and their skin and eyes and things like that whether or not there was enough in the tank to perform on the day. Oftentimes, coming to games then we did very little, we larked about with the ball but on the day everybody felt a million dollars.'

For the 1987 season, the likes of O'Rourke, Lyons, McEntee and Hayes were in their prime while the younger guns of Stafford and Flynn were getting used to playing and winning at the higher altitude. For the first time in twenty years, the Royal County retained the Leinster title, and beating Dublin once more in the final made it all the sweeter. Having seen off Offaly's dominance in the early 1980s, Dublin were having to deal with a new, powerful Meath side and it was this rivalry that was to dominate Leinster for the next five seasons, culminating in the historic and breathtaking, four-game series between the two sides in 1991.

1987 started convincingly for Boylan's side, beating a Kerry team on the decline by eleven points in their league meeting. The hard yards had to be done in the early part of the season but come the business end the focus was on ball-work and perfecting their simple game plan. However, things were not all going according to plan: against Laois in the Leinster quarter-final, Meath conceded a goal to leave the teams level with twelve minutes to go. Meath dug deep, hardened bodies and minds not letting it unsettle them; Laois never took the lead in the final phase and Meath kicked over the points to come through as three-point winners. A six-point victory over Kildare in the semi-final meant they were meeting the old enemy, Dublin, once again.

'Like boxing, whoever was able to stay up and slog it out the longest was going to win,' said O'Rourke, and it was a tough and tense encounter in Croke Park. Both sides were reduced to fourteen men and despite grabbing an early goal, Dublin came back into it to lead at half-time. This time, though, for this Meath team there was to be no capitulation. Liam Hayes recalled how Meath had been used to dutifully succumbing to Dublin teams in the past, but now that subservience had passed. Meath were able to dig deeper, want it more, and were four-point victors, 1–13 to 0–12. For the first time in their history, they had beaten Dublin in two Leinster finals in a row and they had retained their Leinster title for the first time since 1967 – when Meath last won the All-Ireland. Their sights were now set firmly on emulating the 1967 team.

With the great Kerry team out of the way, it seemed as if the playing field had been levelled a bit more for everyone, and the four provinces battled to see who could come out on top. Under the expert guidance of Billy Morgan, and led by Larry Tompkins in the forward line, Cork had come out of Kerry's shadow at last and also wanted to finally climb the steps of Croke Park on the third Sunday in September. Cork's most recent All-Ireland had been in 1973 when Morgan was the goalkeeper, and the Rebel County hungered for it as much as Boylan's men.

They were to meet in the final that year. Meath beat Derry by seven points, 0–15 to 0–08, and Cork beat Galway in the other semi. It has been described as an unspectacular final between two hard-hitting teams and yet 68,000 turned up to see the spectacle – the same number that had been coming to Croke Park to see Dublin versus Kerry and Tyrone versus Kerry the previous three years. Attendances over the 70,000 mark were the exception rather than the rule in those days.

Cork were in their first final since their last success in 1973 and started off well. Midway through the first half, they were already four points up when Jimmy Kerrigan was through for what seemed a certain goal that would have put the Rebel County up by seven points and in a convincing lead. While Kerrigan was blamed for lacking conviction in his shot, it was the desperate last-gasp intervention from Meath full-back Mick Lyons, a player who had been toiling with Meath teams since 1979 and who had been revitalised since the arrival of Boylan, that managed to block the shot and take the sting out of it. The years of hard slog training, the mental conditioning by Boylan, the trust he placed in his players, all came together in that one moment as Lyons stretched out his hands to Kerrigan's goal-bound shot. Instead of facing a seven-point deficit, Meath were still in the game.

Going in at the break a point ahead, Meath had turned things around. The writing was on the wall for Cork, and Meath ratcheted up another eight points to Cork's three to win 1–14 to 0–11. Seán Boylan's team had won their county's fourth All-Ireland title and, after just four years in charge, the Meath team had gone from being perennial strugglers in Leinster to All-Ireland champions.

People question the quality of football being produced in the 1980s, comparing it to Kerry and Dublin in previous years, but Boylan says their football suited the players he had at his disposal.

That 1987 team, they were huge, big men. And we played a certain way to suit that. Bernie Flynn was the only one who was under six foot – although he thought he was seven foot tall, and was an extraordinarily confident player. And if you look at that Cork team, they were beaten in two All-Irelands, came back for one and two and that takes some doing. You look at the physical condition of both those teams at the time, it was absolutely immense.

We weren't specifically looking for physically big players – you would just see something in players. Take David Beggy. When he came in April 1986, he'd been playing

rugby in Navan. I always remember his first time in the
dressing room, we were playing Cavan and here Beggy
arrives on the motorbike, he had this amazing energy, was
completely fearless, high even on the Gaelic football scales,
but he was also a great thinker of the game. He mightn't
have the natural innate skills at the start, but they came. His
percentage of scoring from play was enormous and because
the angles that he took them from were so unorthodox, it
caused terror among defences. I remember saying, 'Lads, I
can't change him, I'm not going to take this style out of this
man, if he can cause uncertainty with opponents, it's up to
us to work round that.'

'Seán had a good football brain,' says Hayes. 'But his real strength lay in building individuals into their positions and understanding who would do the job for him. We never used tactical boards, we never used that sort of thing at all; we would talk about games, whereas nowadays everything is broken down on boards and everything is very much instructional to the players. In our day, it was more instinct and Seán put more belief in his players doing the right thing at the right time, rather than him telling them what was going to happen or telling them exactly what to do.'

Meath were the best team in the country and were all-dominant. They won the National League at the start of 1988, beating reigning champions Dublin after a replay. The sides met again in the Leinster championship final later in the year and no matter what Dublin tried, Meath were always one step better. But completing their first ever three-in-a-row in Leinster didn't come without its own luck and drama – in the dying seconds of the game, Dublin's Charlie Redmond fired a last-minute penalty over the bar when the three points were needed.

Likewise in Munster, Cork were making sure of their superiority over previously dominant opponents, but Kerry forced them all the way and Cork retained their Munster crown by one point, 1–14 to 0–16, a game notable for the newcomer Maurice Fitzgerald kicking ten of Kerry's points. Cork and Meath duly won their semi-finals and were set to meet in the All-Ireland final for the second year in a row.

There was no love lost between the two sides; two teams full of talented but also battle-hardened men, used to winning tight, attritional games in their province and beyond. There was nothing to separate them and again Meath were lucky to survive: just thirty seconds from the final whistle and trailing by a point, David Beggy was adjudged to have been fouled just fourteen yards out – Cork players will insist to this day he took a dive – and Brian Stafford converted for a last-gasp equaliser that they scarcely deserved. Once again, Cork's failure to take their scores was to prove crucial – they had fifteen wides to Meath's seven.

Not surprisingly, the replay had plenty of niggle and bite. Meath's Gerry McEntee was sent off after just six minutes for a blow on Niall Cahalane. Without even needing instruction from Boylan, P.J. Gillic moved into midfield in McEntee's place while the half-forward line dropped deep to crowd and contain Cork. When Cork moved forward, they found themselves facing eleven Meath men harassing them at every moment.

Midway through the second half, Bernard Flynn scored to put Meath in front for the first time, and last-gasp defending from Liam Hayes, Robbie O'Malley and Martin O'Connell helped see Meath over the finish line by a single point, 0–13 to 0–12, the lowest All-Ireland winning scoreline since Kerry's tough win over Roscommon in 1980. The battles between Meath and Cork from 1987 and 1988 were not glamorous, free-flowing affairs – a long way from the twenty-point scorelines of the Dublin–Kerry years.

Cork's Dinny Allen claimed that Meath 'gloried in intimidating

Cork and resorting to fouling to retain their title' (the Leinster side had men sent off in both the All-Ireland and league finals that year and yet had gone on to win both). Colm O'Rourke, in a controversial interview given to the *Sunday Tribune* afterwards, explained their tactics as 'controlled aggression'. The controversy over rough-house tactics went on for months but it didn't change the record books: Meath had won their second All-Ireland in a row.

With two All-Irelands under their belts, it would have been understandable if players such as Colm O'Rourke and Gerry McEntee, who were in their thirties and who had been on the road with Meath since 1975, had decided enough was enough after bowing out to Dublin in Leinster in 1989. But another part of Seán Boylan's success was his ability to ensure that players lasted long into their twilight years. His unique training methods, despite their unorthodoxy, had already proved successful. It was enough to convince both players to stay on the road and have another go in 1990. Besides, with rivals Cork as reigning All-Ireland champions, Meath felt they could dethrone the Rebel County and take back their All-Ireland. If those two sides were to win their provinces and meet again, it would promise to be a stormy All-Ireland series.

Chapter 9

'Second-class citizens'

Billy Morgan is quietly spoken but there's an intensity and steeliness there too. When you're running fifteen minutes late to interview probably the most influential figure there has been in Cork football, and you're met with the annoyed glare, you know apologies and offers of cups of coffee will count for nothing. It is only football and talk of Cork's place in the past, present and future of Gaelic football that will ease the tension. And as we talk, and Billy Morgan breaks down the game, you think of all he has achieved as a player and manager and realise if he had been born in Kerry, he would have been feted and revered even more. But then again, Kerry has always been the backdrop and shadow to Morgan's career.

From the early days when Cork's success was subsequently overshadowed by Mick O'Dwyer's record-breaking achievements, to his time as manager at the other end of that era when he oversaw Cork's return to prominence from the sideline, Morgan and his achievements with Cork must be defined aside from Kerry, for to do otherwise would be to do a great disservice to one of the game's great thinkers.

It was a mark of his resilience and determination that after the second consecutive All-Ireland final defeat at the hands of Meath, he as manager, and the players themselves, didn't throw in the towel and accept defeat. After all, they had finally surpassed probably the greatest Kerry side to grace the game and put them to bed in Munster – that in itself was a hugely significant achievement, but it was All-Irelands that they wanted.

In 1989, Cork were going for three-in-a-row in Munster, something the county had never achieved. The last time they had had it in their grasp was 1975. But that was when O'Dwyer's Kerry was just starting off; fourteen years later, 1989 was to be the Waterville man's last year in charge and there was to be no last sting in the tail. History had been made in Munster but it wasn't enough now. The semi-final against Dublin was another fractious affair with penalties, a sending-off and a broken jaw for Keith Barr but Cork once more came through the battle to win by four points and reach their third All-Ireland final in a row. This time it wouldn't be Meath they were facing but Mayo, who had been guided there by John O'Mahony in only his second year in charge.

Defeat just couldn't be countenanced for Morgan's team. 'The population of this county will drop by thirty-five if we are beaten by Mayo,' declared the Cork team doctor, Con Murphy, in the run-up to the final, and he probably wasn't far wrong.

Criticisms had abounded over the previous three years that they couldn't see out teams but, at the third time of asking, there was no way back for Mayo and Cork were 0–17 to 1–11 winners. Cork and Billy Morgan had finally done it. They had captured their first Sam Maguire since 1973 and had finally emerged as winners in their own right.

A year later, and Cork hammered Kerry in Munster by fifteen points, 2–23 to 1–11. 'Players didn't want to come back out after half-time,' recalled Kerry's Charlie Nelligan, and with O'Dwyer gone, their reliance on veterans Pat Spillane and Jack O'Shea showed just how much the Kingdom needed new blood. Reigning supreme, Cork reached their fourth All-Ireland final in a row, a feat last achieved by the great Dublin and Kerry sides of the previous decade and which was to put Cork's success for the time into context.

This time, Billy Morgan's men were facing a familiar foe: for the third time in four years it was to be Cork versus Meath and it was no surprise that the game produced sixty-nine frees in a stop-start final. Despite having Colm O'Neill sent off just before half-time, Morgan's smothering tactics worked. Meath just couldn't break Cork down and it was the Rebel County who ran out two-point winners. Just two weeks previously, the Cork hurlers had captured the Liam McCarthy Cup and now Teddy McCarthy, Cork's dual star, became the first GAA man to capture both hurling and football All-Irelands in the same year.

Retaining the title and beating Meath in the process had put any lingering ghosts from 1988 to bed, but, Morgan believes his Cork side was not given the credit for much of what they achieved. The problem, though, was that the game was being dominated by tough, hard battles that were getting most of the headlines.

Whether Cork were playing Dublin or Meath, the matches seemed to inevitably have an edge that bordered on the extreme. Sendings-off and yellow cards dominated games and Gaelic football's reputation was dragged down as a result. In Ulster, four players were sent off and six booked as Tyrone and Down faced each other; in the previous round, Tyrone footballer John Lynch was struck by an Armagh supporter; in Connacht, two were given their marching orders and another six booked after a replay in the provincial decider. Such were the recurring scenes on the football field, but Morgan defends his team as one that would grace any period.

'We had a great team and should be regarded alongside the best teams that won All-Irelands with some of the greatest players,' he says. 'After 1988, a rivalry developed between ourselves and Meath which people looked at and in fairness the 1990 final was a poor final, real dog eat dog. However, it shouldn't be overlooked that at the time the two teams were head and shoulders above the rest of the country, but coming off the back of the Dublin–Kerry rivalry and then the Ulster breakthrough in the 1990s, we were overlooked.'

Morgan was an expert at driving his men on, albeit in different ways.

'The first thing you look for is honesty with your players,' Morgan explains. 'Honesty in the hard work they put in and honesty of effort – not looking to hide. I knew players who were expert at just doing enough, trying to hide their real lack of effort, and you have to watch out for that. No matter what era, you'll get players who are easy to manage and those who are difficult and you have to treat them differently and speak to players individually. Some need a kick up the ass and others an arm around the shoulder. But what stood out with that team in the 1980s was their mental toughness.'

To get it in the first place, Morgan had to convince them they were good enough. Over and over. If they saw that he believed – really believed – then it would also come from within them. It was a ploy that Jim McGuinness was to repeat twenty years later when he took over Donegal and told them in that first year at every moment that they were going to win an Ulster title by season's end, no matter what.

'After being beaten twice, people said we would never win an All-Ireland, we were done,' remembers Morgan. 'Personally, I knew we were the best team in the country and it was a question of convincing the players and I did it by repeating it, keep repeating it, keep repeating it to them and get it across to them that I believed it, believed in them and they believed in themselves as well. We had a lot of leader types in the 1987–1991 team.'

Morgan stepped down from management of the Cork team in 1996 after ten years at the helm, overseeing the most successful period in the county's footballing history. He wasn't done with football, however, and he soon took over his club side, Nemo Rangers, with whom he had won All-Ireland club titles as a player in the 1970s. Bringing his same principles and managerial style to the game, Nemo won the county championship after a gap of six years before going on to win club county and provincial titles for the next three years, the first time it had been achieved in Munster for sixty years. In a cruel twist of fate, Nemo were to also reach three All-Irelands in a row, losing the first two but finally, just as Cork did in 1989, they won the title in 2003 at the third attempt, beating Crossmolina of Mayo by two points.

Later in 2003 he took charge of the Cork seniors again after seven years away from the county team. Physicality was still to the fore in the game, but this time there was a huge sports science element behind the methods used to make players bigger, faster and stronger, and why this was necessary. He was to come up against superb Tyrone and Kerry teams and tried to put Cork into the mix, but for him the no-risk, all-possession style just didn't sit right. The modern game was not for Billy Morgan.

'I don't like the modern game. I don't like watching it,' he says. 'I like watching Kerry and give Jim McGuinness his dues, fair play to him, Donegal's game has evolved; sure they defend in numbers but they also break forward in numbers. I remember watching Cork and Donegal in 2012, I was sitting in the corner of the Hogan Stand looking right down the pitch. There was space in the two corners and I thought time and again Donncha O'Connor and Colm O'Neill made good runs into the space but they weren't getting the ball. Cork were afraid to lose the ball and risk that pass.

You're going to have to start taking those risks but you just don't see it nowadays.'

For all his disdain of the no-risk coaching policies prevalent today, many aspects of the game were ones that he himself first espoused back when he was playing in the 1970s. An avid student of the game and sport in general, Morgan was in that wave of Irish students – along with Mickey Ned O'Sullivan and Dermot Earley – who got the opportunity to pursue their physical education studies at the renowned Strawberry Hill in London.

That's where I got all my ideas. I was teaching at the time and the Department of Education sent a number of graduates over to do the post-grad in PE. I was like a sponge over there getting ideas from different sports. I got an awful lot of ideas about training and tactics from the soccer I was playing. I also wrote a paper at the time about Gaelic football and formations. I remember writing about the need to change formations and not just have the static ones with the six backs, forwards and two midfielders.

My thinking was, if the opposition has a great midfielder is there nothing we can do about it? I wanted to change formations where you would have an extra midfielder to deal with that. There was a discussion of my ideas when I came back home but there was one fella who completely disagreed with it. He was a traditionalist who wouldn't counter any change to the six–two–six. That was the way it was always done and the way it should always be. But sure Dublin and Kerry introduced the formation changes when they came along a few years later.

Certain quarters of Gaelic football weren't ready to countenance any changes to the game or new ideas – despite the fact that Down had shown the way ten years earlier, and Kevin Heffernan was about to do the same with Dublin.

'When I came back from Strawberry Hill and started training Nemo in the early 1970s,' explains Morgan, 'my philosophy was always that we tried to create an extra man either defending or attacking. Get the team very fit so if we lose the ball, fellas track back and when we win it we go forward – the half-backs in particular push up and help the forwards. I wanted to always create an extra man so if they had two, we had three, if they had three, we had four, and it was all through sheer running and support play.'

In many ways, Morgan's philosophy and vision for the game was the precursor to how it would eventually evolve some thirty years later, but as Mickey Ned O'Sullivan has highlighted, coaching was to take a back seat in the intervening period as the O'Dwyer–Heffernan years put an emphasis on fitness.

'I'm all for the interchanging of players and positions that we're seeing nowadays,' says Morgan. 'I remember when I was managing, telling the players that if a half-back has the ball facing his own goal and is in a bit of trouble, I've no problem with the corner-back coming out and breaking the line to support him. I think the modern game has suffered in the natural skills of the game. Most of the ball in the middle is broken and I don't agree with that, fielding is suffering and kick-passing is going out of the game. But if you can kick accurately and quickly into the forward line, it is a way to beat the possession and swarming game.'

As a goalkeeper, Morgan was in the perfect position to be watching and studying the game as it happened, but despite coming back from London brimful of new ideas, Cork football was stuck in the past.

'I remember encouraging Jimmy Kerrigan to attack,' he recalls. 'But then I would hear the selectors on the line saying to Jimmy to "get back, get back". Backs were encouraged to stay defensive. Forwards were encouraged to stay up. That was the way it was.'

Cork won the 1973 All-Ireland with Morgan as captain, a first All-Ireland win for the county since 1945, but they were about to be overtaken by Dublin and then by Kerry. Cork's failure to evolve at the time meant they wouldn't win a Munster for another nine years and it would be twenty-six years before their next All-Ireland success.

'At the time we played a natural game,' Morgan explains. 'We had good ball winners and good natural footballers. Our game was about good, accurate kick-passing, something like the Mick O'Connell style of play. We had good forwards, and it was a direct style of play to get the ball into them. At the time, we had hammered Kerry, beaten Tyrone and beaten Galway by seven points. Unfortunately for us, Kevin Heffernan came along and took over the Dublin team, bringing a new level of fitness to Gaelic games.'

In the same year that Heffernan took over Dublin, Cork beat Kerry in the Munster final and were overwhelming favourites to beat Dublin in the All-Ireland final.

'When they played us that day, we expected to win,' says Morgan. 'I remember thinking with five minutes to go and we were a couple of points behind, if we're not careful here we could get beaten. They just ran us off the pitch. We underestimated Dublin. Heffo told them Dublin could always beat Cork and had always beaten them in championship games. But, in fact, it was actually the other way around but that was Heffernan, he had them convinced.'

That defeat to Dublin was to be a fateful day for Cork. Kerry were on the way up the following year and it was to be Dublin–Kerry that dominated the footballing landscape for the rest of the decade. By the time Mick O'Dwyer had left Kerry, Billy Morgan's playing days were behind him but it was inevitable that he would find himself heading towards management, although it would never replace the emotions and pleasure he had as a player.

'There is no substitute for playing and having direct involvement on the field. Playing with Cork we had some great players but really suffered because of mismanagement and I did swear to myself that if I ever got the opportunity in the future to manage, I would take it.'

His opportunity arose in 1986 just as Seán Boylan's Meath were emerging as a force in Leinster, and Morgan and Cork's battles against that team up to 1990 was to be the defining rivalry of the time.

John Allen, a future All-Ireland-winning manager with the Cork hurlers, also played football for the county from minor up to seniors and played under Billy Morgan in the early 1980s, seeing at first hand his style and techniques.

Billy was the first person I would have known who absolutely lived for the game, who knew everything about the players. I remember meeting him back in 1973 when I was a minor and even at that time, he knew who I was and I was so impressed that the captain of the Cork team of 1973 knew who I was even though I was a nobody. That told me that Billy Morgan's interest in football was all-encompassing and then, when I knew him later as a player, I could see that he never stopped thinking about it.

Billy Morgan was the ultimate player's player, because he believed in you whether you were good or bad, he was full of praise for fellas and full of confidence-building with everybody. He was one of the lads if you like but at the same time he was a qualified PE teacher, he had the qualifications and training.

While the Cork footballers had finally climbed out of the shadow of Kerry, Cork's footballing success was also to coincide with the county's hurlers winning the All-Ireland in 1990. With Cork GAA at its peak, in terms of stature and standing, there was, however, really only one sport that truly captured the hearts and minds of Cork people.

'The footballers I always felt were like second-class citizens,' admits Morgan. 'Football's tradition is in west Cork. The city is traditionally a hurling area and if you look at the county board, I suppose they always looked at having more chance of success with the hurlers than the footballers. We felt down through the years that they always got treated better. I remember at the last training session before the 2007 All-Ireland final, there was only a handful of spectators watching us. You would have expected the place to be packed and I remember feeling sorry for the players because they weren't getting the acknowledgement from the fans for what they were doing and had been achieving.

'If we'd had the likes of Seán Óg Ó hAilpín, John Gardiner, Tom Kenny with us on the football side – big, powerful men – we would have achieved more, but you can understand why they wanted to play with the hurlers, seeing at the time they had a better chance of an All-Ireland, but nowadays you know, there might be a better opportunity with the footballers.'

John Allen, who is in the unique position of having seen it from both camps as a dual player and then as county hurling manager, agrees with Morgan on the stature of football in the county.

'The hurling fans are extremely loyal, and the football fans are extremely loyal as well,' he says. 'But then when you look at the stats and Cork have played in twenty-four football finals and have lost seventeen of them and won only seven, it means that success was very sporadic and it was very hard to hold on to fans. How do you carry the fans along if you're not winning very often? There was definitely a divide in the 1980s where the footballers didn't get the same treatment in terms of training facilities and gear. I remember playing for the team back in the 1980s and we were locked out of the training ground because somebody had forgotten to book it and they wouldn't open it and we had to go away down to a common ground to Mahon to train on. There is no doubt that football was a second-class citizen.'

As John Allen says, Morgan, who had played the game himself and won All-Irelands at every level, was a players' man and knew what made them tick. For Morgan, winning All-Irelands had to be all about the players, without any corners being cut. It's one of the sadder aspects of Cork GAA over the early part of the 2000s that between player strikes and rows with the county board, there was never a unity of purpose from the top down as so evidenced in Kilkenny or as had been established in Down in the 1960s. In such an environment, and looking back on the near-misses, the what-ifs for Cork and Billy Morgan remain.

After over a quarter of a century of involvement with Cork football, in 2007, after a humiliating ten-point All-Ireland final defeat to Kerry, Billy Morgan stepped down. The footballing cycle had come full circle once more and Kerry were to dominate over Cork again; in the end, for Morgan, Kerry were still standing tall.

In the ensuing years, however, it wasn't to be as stark as the 1970s and 1980s; Cork did not disappear into the shadows. Conor Counihan, a former player under Morgan, took over and Cork won three of the next five Munsters. They were to suffer more All-Ireland heartbreak in 2009 with another final defeat to Kerry (albeit by four points this time) but, as before, Cork's mettle ensured they came back to contest their third final in four years and this time made it count, beating Down by a point, 0–16 to 0–15.

Conor Counihan's tenure has been a remarkably successful one, with, in addition to the Munster titles and All-Ireland success, the county also won three league titles in a row from 2010–2012. But as people once spoke about Morgan's teams, questioning if they had underachieved, so too people wonder if Counihan's Cork team should have achieved more than the one All-Ireland title to their name. The challenge for them now is to try and match what Dublin and Donegal have achieved in recent years.

But although Billy Morgan's sides sparred with and lost to Meath in the 1980s, those two final defeats didn't see him throw in the towel. Morgan had come too far with Cork football as a player and manager to give it up for the title of 'also-ran', and if anything was to sum up his attitude and approach to the game it was coming back the third time in 1989 and finally proving to himself, his players and the county that Cork footballers weren't second-class citizens and could stand proudly on their own achievements alongside all the other game's greats.

Chapter 10

'How are you going to face
the people of Meath?'

Despite losing their Leinster crown in 1989, Meath's defeat of
Laois in the 1990 Leinster semi-final showed just how far they had
come in the five years since the sides had last met. Bernard Flynn
scored 2–2 of their 4–14 to Laois' 0–6, resulting in a twenty-point
victory – a stark contrast to the ten-point loss Meath had suffered in
1985. By the start of the 1990s, Meath were two-time All-Ireland
winners under Boylan and still wanted a shot at a third.

It was Cork versus Meath for the third time in four years. There
was little give or take anywhere on the pitch but in contrast to Cork's
two previous defeats, they were able to curtail their wides and take
their chances – just seven wides as opposed to Meath's thirteen.

'Billy Morgan had chosen his team well,' said Seán Boylan.
'They totally smothered us and we could not break them down.'

Despite this defeat to Cork, incredibly, this Meath team reached
one more final the following year – also matching Cork's four final
appearances for this period – but it wasn't Down's All-Ireland
victory in 1991 that was to cause the most talking points from the

season, it was to be an historic four-game series against Dublin in the Leinster championship.

When the two sides met in the preliminary round of Leinster, knowing the encounters over the previous years, most expected a close, tight game. Nobody could have guessed that trying to separate these two teams would take four games, be attended by over 250,000 people and transfix a nation, raising the profile of Gaelic football once again, in the wake of Italia '90.

For the record, the first three games read: Meath 1–12, Dublin 1–12; Meath 1–11, Dublin 1–11 and Meath 2–11, Dublin 1–14. 'There are good reasons why we managed to cling to Dublin and finally beat them,' Liam Hayes wrote in his autobiography *Out of Our Skins*. 'We remained calm all through. We knew what it was like to beat Dublin. We hate losing to them.'

Gaelic football had never seen anything like this series, each side matching the other all the way through the games; it was both mentally and physically draining and no team or management had ever been through anything like this before. Typically, Boylan had prepared Meath in a new and unorthodox way that was a closely guarded secret.

'The more I thought about the stamina work I wanted to do with them, I decided I couldn't do it because there was a lot of mileage there,' recalls Boylan.

He had heard about the US athlete Joan Benoit who had won the marathon by using a buoyancy aid to train in water after a knee operation just six weeks before the Olympic Games. With the help of Sonia O'Sullivan, thirty buoyancy suits were sourced from the United States and shipped to Meath, where hardened footballers looked sceptically at Boylan as he explained what they were going to do. *Had he completely lost the plot this time?* they wondered.

'At times the players would laugh, and we would amuse ourselves by saying, "Jesus, he's totally lost his senses now,"' says

Hayes. 'But at the same time we understood he was the man who was helping us to achieve.'

Boylan was a firm believer in the regenerative power of water and he had used water constantly as a means of healing aching bodies and limbs.

'Regularly during the winter we would do a lot of training sessions on the beach,' remembers Hayes. 'And at the end of the training sessions we would go into the water and we would stay in the cold, freezing water for up to half an hour because Seán believed in the power of the sea water and the contents of the water in terms of helping the recovery of aches and strains.

'I remember I had a very bad ankle ligament injury one National League campaign and five or six Saturdays in a row, Seán would bring me over to Bettystown and we would, even in the spitting rain, both go into the water, and we'd stand there under umbrellas for half an hour, the water up to our waists. Seán would do those sort of things. When horses tread in water, they find it very forgiving and Seán had a universal appreciation of sport and men and animals, and things like that always worked. We were doing things that no other teams were doing.'

Even by Boylan's standards, the buoyancy aids were another leap of faith for the players and after the first night in the pool at Gormanston College, Gerry McEntee was worried about what would happen if the latest Boylan idea didn't come off.

'If we're beaten in the first round against Dublin,' he said, 'and people ask, "How did the training go?" and you answer, "We were swimming", how are you going to face the people of Meath?'

Colm O'Rourke was a believer, though.

'He was ahead of his time in that way, he was different and he had different ideas and sometimes people thought they were off the wall but they worked most of the time. Most people would have been afraid to do some of the things. The idea of training for the championship in buoyancy suits was fantastic, it was a brilliant method of conserving people like myself who had lots of injury problems and it got us fit. I was thirty-four at the time and there was no pounding, no damage to joints and we were feeling very well as a result of it.'

It wasn't until May, three weeks before the Dublin game, that Boylan brought the players out onto the training pitch.

'We knew we were rusty,' he remembered. 'But you never doubted the bunch of lads. You always felt they had that something, and the new lads that had come in were learning from the older ones.'

Three drawn games in and the results of the pool training were in evidence; the Meath players were able to last throughout the games and go toe-to-toe with the Dublin side. Before the fourth instalment and with the country talking of nothing else, Boylan decided he would take the entire squad with wives and girlfriends away for the weekend, something to break up the intensity and routine of what they had been going through.

'We'd been playing badly against Dublin,' Liam Hayes explained. 'We needed to take time away from them and view them from a distance.'

Settled in beside the shores of Loch Lomond in Scotland, the players were able to relax and kick back, train and stay up drinking in the bar. As Boylan recalled, he wanted to freshen things up and even on the training pitch, he was extolling them to throw the ball around again, to get back to positive play. 'Get rid of the negativity. Let's be positive, let's have a go at it,' he recalled years later in the *Irish Independent*.

Meath worked on a drill of moving the ball the length of the pitch.

'For forty minutes, we did nothing else but movement,' remembered Boylan. 'It was starting from the back, tight space, ball movement all the time. Forty minutes is a long time for that concentration.'

Meath returned rejuvenated but with twenty minutes left in the game, Dublin were in a commanding 0–12 to 0–6 lead. Then, slowly, Meath clawed back the lead to three points when with just eight minutes left in this epic series, Dublin were awarded a penalty. Score and surely there would be no way back even for this dogged Meath team. But Boylan called Liam Hayes over. 'Get the lads to start throwing the ball around like they did last Sunday,' he told him. 'If they score the penalty, we'll still beat them.'

Boylan never had to find out if his incredibly resilient team could have come back from six points down once more. As Dublin's Keith Barr ran up to the dead ball, Mick Lyons ran alongside him to put him off – grounds for a retake – but it worked as Barr's shot drifted wide. Meath were still in the game.

'Meath had the guts and the heart to carry it off when the crunch came. They never give in while there is half a chance to turn the tide,' wrote Paddy Downey in the match report for *The Irish Times*, and that half-chance did indeed come, with just sixty seconds left in the game.

Taking Boylan's lead and remembering their training drill from Scotland, the players decided to 'throw the ball around', moving the ball from defence. Gerry McEntee passed it on to Tommy Dowd, who made a powerful, probing run at the Dublin defence, who were all standing off. Colm O'Rourke received it in the right corner, passed it back to Dowd and finally Kevin Foley, who had tracked the movement all the way from the backline, ran through in space and buried the ball into the back of the net from the edge of the square.

Dublin were stunned. A seven-man move without any Dublin players touching the ball, starting from their own half, had resulted in an unexpected Meath goal. The sides were level and yet there was still time for one more twist. Still shell-shocked, Dublin's kickout was won by Meath and in possession and space, David Beggy, the man who Boylan had never tried to curtail, went past his marker to shoot the winning point.

'"Incredible," he said, stunned like the rest of 61,543 spectators when the final whistle sounded at Croke Park on Saturday,' wrote Paddy Downey in a match report in *The Irish Times*. 'And then, pointing to the pitch, the man on the upper deck of the Hogan Stand drew breath to add, as if struck by revelation: "That's what they coined the word for." So it seemed, and so it was – incredible. Meath, a beaten team, we thought, midway through the second half, were winners of the most amazing, enthralling, fantastic (pick any word you like) event in the whole history of Gaelic football. Dublin, who appeared to have won the third replay of this first-round Leinster Championship fixture when they led by three points as the hand of the clock moved up to the stroke of seventy minutes, left the sunlit field sicker than the sickest parrot that ever lived.'

If Boylan had never introduced the buoyancy aids, or trained the team in the pool all year, would they have come through the gruelling series? What if the Scotland trip had never materialised and the players never had the chance to relax and play positive football as their manager instructed with eight minutes to go? What if David Beggy's style and personality had never been incorporated into Meath's system? What if O'Rourke, Hayes and Lyons had called it a day years before? The what-ifs are the inches that matter, the small things, the differences that are questioned, but when push comes to shove at the crucial time, the what-ifs never need to be answered.

Meath went on to retain Leinster, beating Laois in the final, winning their fifth title in six years before reaching their fourth All-Ireland final in five years, but it was perhaps inevitable that time would finally catch up on them, in this, their longest season.

For once it wasn't Cork that was awaiting them but surprise Ulster champions Down, who were appearing in their first All-Ireland final since Joe Lennon lifted Sam Maguire in 1968. Confidence was never lacking for Down teams in Croke Park and they were not fazed by the game, despite facing the experience and toughness of this Meath team. Down built up an eleven-point lead before Meath tried to claw themselves back into the game once more. It was a bridge too far for Seán Boylan's men, even though they gradually reined in Down point by point to get within two. There were to be no last-gasp heroics this time. A record championship campaign of ten games had taken its toll.

Over the next three years, the old guard moved on and, with the team in transition, Meath failed to reach another Leinster final until 1994 when a one-point defeat to Dublin and a league title showed glimpses of what might lie ahead for the next generation of players coming through. One step forward and two steps back however and, in the 1995 Leinster final, Dublin handed them a ten-point hammering – the heaviest loss to Dublin since Kevin Heffernan gave Paddy O'Brien a trouncing in 1955. It was the final curtain for the last survivor of the 1987–1988 team. Thirty-seven-year-old Colm O'Rourke, one of the game's greatest forwards, retired from the game, twenty years after making his debut for Meath. He had seen it all, from the bad, barren days right through to Seán Boylan's arrival and All-Ireland glory. Most importantly for players like O'Rourke, who suffered greatly with injuries throughout their careers, it was Boylan's techniques that ensured their careers lasted twenty years. 'There is no doubt,' he says, 'if Seán wasn't training the team, I wouldn't have been playing as long, no doubt about that.'

By 1995, in the wake of the humiliating Dublin defeat, Meath had reached a new low, it seemed.

'I remember Gerry McEntee coming down to the county club that evening,' remembers Boylan. '"You've given a huge service to me, you've had great results, you've had great success," he said. "Seán, maybe it's time for you to step aside, you're going to get hurt." But I knew with the players coming through, Trevor Giles, Darren Fay, Ollie Murphy, Barry Callaghan, I knew these boys were something.'

Boylan's eye for what was required in players was still as good as ever and he proved his managerial genius by producing another All-Ireland-winning team within a year, from that same group that had been hammered by ten points by Dublin. It was an incredible turnaround, on a par with Heffo's Dublin All-Ireland win in 1974 and, once again, not knowing defeat was the hallmark of the Boylan side.

In 1996, they came back against Dublin with four unanswered points to capture their first Leinster title in five years and then in the semi-final against reigning champions Tyrone proved that they had lost none of their physicality either. Tyrone's creativity was smothered at every opportunity by hook or by crook and two Tyrone players had to play the second half with bandaged heads.

'When Meath put it up to us physically, we should have taken them on at their own game,' remarked the Tyrone player Ciarán McBride afterwards, but, either way, Meath had reached another All-Ireland final – Boylan's fifth in nine years.

Mayo were waiting for them as the Connacht champions sought to end their All-Ireland hoodoo stretching back to 1951 when they had beaten Meath in the final. Mindful of what Tyrone endured in the semi-final, Mayo fronted up to Meath and were six points in front in the second half before Meath once more clawed their way back to force a replay.

The replay was an equally unforgiving contest, with neither side giving an inch, resulting in a mass punch-up for nearly thirty seconds after which Colm Coyle and Liam McHale were both given their marching orders. In the aftermath, a further eight Meath and six Mayo players were suspended for their roles in the melee.

For the actual game, Meath again trailed for most of it but came back in the last ten minutes to take the lead for the first time and finally score the winning point in the seventieth minute to claim an unlikely win. That was Seán Boylan's teams – never giving in, always having the physical strength and fitness to keep going, and, most importantly, having the mental fortitude and belief that they could win, no matter what.

Having built an All–Ireland-winning team ten years previously, Boylan outshone even the likes of Mick O'Dwyer by achieving it again with an entirely new team. To do so in an amateur game where managers can only pick teams based on the players available in their county – as opposed to professional sports buying in talent – is all the more remarkable. After that initial success, the young team went off the boil as a resurgent Offaly under Tommy Lyons and Kildare under Mick O'Dwyer ensured that Leinster was becoming a competitive province outside of the big two of Dublin and Meath.

There was to be one more success though for Boylan's men at the end of the millennium, bouncing back again in the 1999 season. No team was dominating Leinster, although it was Meath's sixth Leinster final appearance in a row, equalling their own previous record from 1986–1991. Facing familiar opponents, this time it was a comfortable victory for the Royals, running out five-point winners over Dublin.

Boylan's sixth All-Ireland final was once more against Meath's old foe, Cork. This time, Billy Morgan wasn't in charge and they faced a new Cork team. Thankfully, this final had none of the pitched battles of the 1988–1990 finals and there were no sendings-off. Despite missing a penalty at the start of the second half and giving Cork the lead briefly, it was Meath who ran out three-point winners to give them their second title in four years. This team was nowhere near as dominant or as imposing as that of the O'Rourke-Lyons-Hayes era, but with the skills of Giles and Murphy they were at least gaining plaudits for their style of play. As Boylan himself admitted, 'We had a better image and I was pleased that the lads were belatedly getting credit for their achievements.'

Seán Boylan had been in charge of Meath for sixteen years – by far the longest tenure with one county in Gaelic football – and each time they looked down and out, his teams would come back to surprise the doubters – the 1996 and 1999 titles were remarkable, achieved as they were with different players and playing a different style. Two years later, Meath won their eighth and final Leinster title under Seán Boylan. Fittingly, it was a victory over Dublin, just as it had been for the first title seventeen years previously, the one that set the team and the manager on the road to success.

Then, in 2001, came a third All-Ireland appearance in six years and Meath were overwhelming favourites against Galway after handing Kerry one of their heaviest defeats – a fifteen-point hammering in which Kerry scored only 0–5 and just once in the entire second half.

The final saw the first 'back door' finalists, after the qualifiers system was introduced. It was the most radical change introduced to the game by the GAA, allowing beaten teams back into the All-Ireland series through qualifier games. It helped Galway in its year of introduction and they took the opportunity with both hands, after they had been beaten in Connacht. Facing Meath, they were into their third final in four years. But the sending-off of Nigel Nestor and the broken hand of Ollie Murphy left Meath severely depleted and Galway ran out convincing nine-point winners. It was to be the last All-Ireland final appearance for Seán Boylan.

Despite continuing for another four years, the footballing world had moved on and different counties were competing for provincial and national honours. Laois and Westmeath, inspired by two Kerry legends in Mick O'Dwyer and Páidí Ó Sé were shaking things up in Leinster, while All-Irelands were being divided up between Armagh and Tyrone, who had brought a new form of swarming-style football to the scene.

Finally, in 2005, after a Leinster quarter-final loss to Dublin, Seán Boylan bowed out. He had been at the helm of Meath football for a record twenty-two years. Eight Leinsters and four All-Irelands were testimony to his managerial achievements on the pitch; he had managed sides through three decades of change, from the tough, physical encounters of the 1980s to the more stylish 1990s play to the 2000s where an Ulster influence of defensive football came to the fore.

The game had changed beyond all compare since 1983 when he thought the county board were offering him the hurling manager's position. Sports science had since taken over, dieticians, statisticians and analysts were part of the backroom staff. Men and women with degrees, Master's degrees and PhDs were imparting their wisdom on training and techniques on the field of play now. But for Seán Boylan, most of what he knew and learned hadn't come from a book, it had come from life and nature around him.

Nearing the end of that epic four-game series against Dublin in 1991, Seán Boylan stood on the sideline; a hush had descended on Croke Park as Keith Barr placed the ball for his fateful penalty. Boylan looked on, belief in his team ever-present. Then a voice in a Dublin accent could be heard in the Hogan Stand behind him, 'Go way, ye bleedin' witch doctor!' In more ways than one, for Seán Boylan it was a compliment; for a man who had brought unorthodox and untried ideas to Gaelic football, he did things his own way and the players believed in him. His was a holistic way of looking at life that centred on everything he did, including Gaelic football management.

'I think, with any of the great managers, he's got to live in the players' head,' believes Liam Hayes. 'Sometimes the players would be fearful, sometimes they'd be excited, but they'd always know that he was there, like a spiritual presence, always. Even if he wasn't in their midst or in the same room as them they would feel him. Very few managers do that; very few managers can do that. But Seán was one.'

Part IV

Ulster Rising

'Face reality as it is, not as it was or as you wish it to be.'

Jack Welch, legendary chairman and CEO of General Electric

Chapter 11

Lighting the fuse

From the 1960s, Ulster coaching and influence has led the way. Beginning with Down's analytical and organisational approach that revolutionised the sport, followed by Joe Lennon's full-time courses and books, as well as the teaching and influence of Derry's Jim McKeever, the culture and science of GAA coaching has been led by men from the North.

John Morrison is another of those leading coaches and innovative thinkers. You'll learn more in an hour of conversation with him than in a lifetime with many others. But why exactly has Ulster created so many leading thinkers and coaches of the game? Not surprisingly, the Troubles are a starting point, a dark period that forced people to find light somewhere for themselves and, for many, it was through Gaelic football.

'For thirty years, it was horrible up here,' says Morrison. 'We literally had to fight for our lives as well as our sport, there were some nights you were stopped going to training. Training was maybe called off for weeks because you would have been intercepted on the way and shot at. It was dangerous. At that time, not politically but sporting-wise, clubs adapted, the GAA adapted up North. I believe the Troubles stopped in 1991, it certainly got easier after that. From 1991 to the mid-2000s, half of the All-Irelands were won by Ulster teams, and that had never happened before.'

The rising tide was helping to lift many boats in the province and, between 1991 and 1994, Sam Maguire was lifted in four successive years by three different Ulster champions. The first wave of Ulster influence came in the 1960s, the second to hit Croke Park's shore was started by Down's Pete McGrath.

Some people are thrust unexpectedly into coaching and management, having no inclination to get involved, and some are just born for it and find themselves gravitating to it even at a young age. Pete McGrath was still playing senior football when he got involved in coaching the club's under-16s. From there, his former coach at St Colman's College, Ray Morgan, asked him to get involved with the college team, while at the same time the county board asked him to look after the county under-16 side for an inter-county competition. Before he knew it, at the age of twenty-six, in terms of playing, training and coaching, football had become a full-time occupation, and it's something he's never let go of.

Unusually for the time, and with the vogue of sports science and PE graduates coming through the ranks in Ireland and the UK, McGrath was, in fact, a history and maths teacher who also helped out with PE. Having played and won an Ulster title with Down in the 1970s, McGrath's insights came not from textbooks but from experience on the field of play, similar to his mentor, Ray Morgan, who had played with Down in earlier days but proved himself a very successful coach at St Colman's and in club football, winning two All-Ireland club titles with Burren in the 1980s.

Surrounded by youth, and working in the hotbed of Gaelic football at St Colman's – which was second only to St Jarlath's in terms of Hogan Cup victories – it was only natural that McGrath's early management years were spent guiding young and talented footballers, keeping his coaching, in his own words, 'simple'. It is a philosophy that is echoed by all of the game's most successful managers and coaches down through the decades.

'I am not sure if one could survive in the current educational climate, teaching a subject that you are not a specialist in,' says McGrath. 'But in the 1970s, 1980s and indeed right through the 1990s, there was no issue. I was teaching PE and I always kept it very simple. There wouldn't have been the same proliferation of literature that you have now and indeed, let's be honest, the approach to training, even training in the county teams, wasn't as scientific as it would be today. I would have used my own experience having played inter-county football and trained under various managers and different trainers and obviously learned from them as I went along.'

The 'high priests' of coaching, such as Joe Lennon and Kevin Heffernan, were still preaching the gospel of 'proper training and coaching techniques' and it was from these sources that McGrath was able to pick up hints and tips.

When I was appointed Down minor manager in 1982, there was a coaching seminar organised by the Ulster Council which took place in the Four Seasons Hotel in Monaghan. And at that coaching seminar you had people like Joe Lennon, Sean O'Neill, Kevin Heffernan, Jim McKeever, and, to this day, I still have the notes that I took from the speakers because it was fascinating. People like Kevin Heffernan who had achieved so much and was still at the height of his powers, while Joe Lennon had managed Down the previous year to the Ulster senior title.

I suppose I would have been someone who was very

*interested in learning and listening. There was also the Old
Bushmills School of Sport in Coleraine and it would have
covered different sports — basketball, soccer, hockey, even
Gaelic football was included. Those were the ones that really
gave me a crash course in other people's ideas, in coaching
methods and what to look for in a good coaching session.
As well as that, working with Ray Morgan all through the
years was very enlightening as well, needless to say.*

*The big thing about Ray Morgan was his enthusiasm
and his ability. I thought he was always very sensible in
his approach to coaching the basics and keeping the thing
simple, getting people working hard. Generally speaking,
if you had a team that was working hard for each other
and physically fit and playing to their strengths, then you
were well on your way. And St Colman's had a very strong
tradition in football obviously going back to the 1940s
and 1950s, it was just a hotbed of Gaelic games and that
certainly had an influence on me as well in my love of Gaelic
football and coaching.*

Having managed the Down minors to All-Ireland success in 1987,
when the senior job became available, it seemed inevitable that
McGrath's name was on the list to take over. He was still only
thirty-six when he took charge of the seniors, but could point to a
ten-year career in coaching already that included MacRory, Hogan,
Ulster minor and All-Ireland minor titles.

*I was relatively young coming into county management.
But the advantage I had was that, at St Colman's, I would
have managed people like Greg Blaney, Ross Carr and also
at that time people like James McCartan were bound to
come into the senior team, so I had a knowledge of them. I*

had a knowledge of the minor teams since 1982 and there were other senior players who I would have managed at minor level, people like Paul Higgins who played on both All-Ireland-winning teams. It's not as though I was coming into an environment where I was managing people who I didn't know personally. But did I have all the answers? No. Because, at the end of the day, I was putting my toe in the water for the first time as far as inter-county senior football was concerned. But, in working in St Colman's and working with Down's minor teams for quite a few years, I certainly realised and appreciated the value of sound coaching, of coaching the skills in such a way that you were going to get people, no matter what their age, to improve their skill level and therefore by definition the skill level of any group collectively. So I was coming in with a fairly clear mind in terms of the type of coaching that I was going to do in the Down senior setup. I was coming in confident that if I could get my message across and get the players committed, enthused and believing, then I thought that there was going to be a decent chance of achieving some success.

Gaelic football had suffered damage to its reputation in the 1980s with sendings-off, dust-ups and low-scoring, physical encounters dominating. The emphasis on fitness was paramount, but Down, who prided themselves on their attractive footballing style, were getting left on the canvas and had not won an Ulster title since 1981 – the longest barren period since the breakthrough years of the 1960s. For McGrath, it was about getting the right mix of physical fitness and football skill.

As far as I was concerned, it was always a question of getting the right balance between the team. Of players

*who were physically fit and getting a team of players who
could catch the ball over their head, give good passes,
play well together, take scores, tackle properly, so it was
trying to get the right balance. But as far as tactics were
concerned, I came into the job knowing, as a lot of people
knew, that for many years Down teams had been soft targets
in the championship. The Tyrones and the Monaghans of
this world had roughed up Down in the 1980s and the one
thing I knew that had to happen was the Down team had to
become more physically imposing. We had to have players
on the team who were going to be able to handle themselves
and not be bullied or intimidated as had been happening.*

*Down were a good National League team, where people
maybe let them have the football a bit, but when it came to the
hard, cold light of championship football, then people were
found wanting. So my first, and I thought my most important,
task was to make the Down team physically more imposing,
get players who could look after themselves whenever the
opposition maybe tried to rough them up a bit. That was a
serious consideration going forward. I didn't go in with any
predetermined vision of the type of football that we were
going to play, but I knew enough about Down footballers
even at that time to realise that we had good forwards.*

*I knew the forwards would be there to play the football
– if you could get the ball to them – and that they were
prepared to take a bit of physicality and not be roughed up.
Even then, I would have appreciated the need, particularly
for people in the half-forward line, to be able to defend, to
tackle back and to win their own ball, particularly in the
air. That's how we ended up with people like Gary Mason
and Ross Carr, both of whom had actually had histories of
playing in defensive positions for Down. Then with people*

like James McCartan and Mickey Linden on the full-forward
line and you had Greg Blaney at centre-half, the tactic, and
our way of playing the game, was to get the best-quality
ball into the area where these guys could do damage.

Like all great coaches, McGrath had a clear idea of what he wanted,
how he could deal with the opposition, while also playing to his
own team's strengths. After that, it was going to be a case of seeing
just how determined and how much the players wanted to succeed.

A lot of it depends on where the players themselves
are coming from, and I think that the greatest power of
motivation comes from within a player. Certainly, managers
can paint pictures for players and we can encourage, say
things and we can lead, but I think that when it comes to
the really hard work and people needing to be very singled-
minded and very focused, I think that has to come from deep
inside a player.

Unlike many other counties, especially in Ulster, Down already
had a self-belief and self-confidence that they should be contesting
for All-Irelands, a trait that had come mainly from the legacy of the
1960s. As McGrath explains:

From the 1960s, people in Down felt like a privileged
species. We had been the first county that had taken the
cup across the border and nobody else looked remotely like
doing that. To do it three times in the 1960s, it certainly
created in the minds of Down people and Down footballers
a confidence and a sense of self-assurance that whenever
we got our minds right and got the chemistry right, we had
nothing to fear because people we knew had done it. That

is what tradition is all about in the sense that people that
you know, people from your own community, have done
this, therefore that type of mentality and confidence can get
through to you as well.

Now, there were definitely Down teams that suffered from
overly high expectations as well, particularly in the 1970s
and 1980s. If Down won a championship match and were
going reasonably well, people were talking, saying, 'This is
it, this is the second coming. There is going to be another
All-Ireland here.' In some instances, that was a millstone
around people's necks. But once you got the chemistry right
and you got players with confidence, then that confidence
that the 1960s team had, the tradition that they established
and the legacy they passed on, all of those things became
very positive.

Even so, an All-Ireland wasn't even on the horizon for McGrath. Ulster was the target and he declared publicly that they would do it within three years, anything else would be a failure. With the quality of Down footballers, if they got out of Ulster, then who knows what could happen, but first they had to navigate their own local waters.

The first year, they lost to eventual Ulster champions Tyrone, and in 1990 proved their resilience by coming back from an eight-point deficit in the last ten minutes to earn a replay against Armagh, which they subsequently lost. However, McGrath saw encouraging signs in those first two years. The players were getting battle-hardened and knowing what to expect; if they got the breakthrough in Ulster, they knew they would be flying. In 1991, the opener against Armagh was the usual tough, Ulster fare with eight players booked. However, Down had shown that they weren't afraid to front up, to take what was being meted out, and a Mickey Linden penalty saw them through.

Against Derry in the semi-final, there were another eight bookings as well as two sendings-off, with a free every minute and more wides than scores. A replay was the last thing anyone wanted but at least the football was of better fare. For Down's Mickey Linden, getting through those two games against Derry to reach their first Ulster final in five years was the turning point.

Both teams played fantastic football, but the scores, the support play, the commitment – all ingredients for a great football team were there. I think we knew then what the team was capable of.

Donegal were the reigning champions and Brian McEniff's side was not expected to be knocked off course, but Down surprised everyone outside the county by easily dispatching them by eight points, an early Greg Blaney goal setting them on their way.

Kerry awaited them in the All-Ireland semi-final, reviving memories of 1960, and, as before, the Kingdom held no fears for Down. In nearly a mirror scoreline of that historic 1960 final, Pete McGrath's men once again kept Kerry to just eight points and ran out seven-point winners, 2–9 to 0–8, Dan Breen's fiftieth-minute goal sealing the victory.

Down found themselves in their fourth All-Ireland final, the first since 1968. Down had a 100 per cent record in All-Ireland finals up to then and as media and fans alike recalled the days of Doherty, O'Neill and McCartan and all that they had achieved, for McGrath, there was no focus on the past, merely one more game to be overcome.

When we beat Donegal in the Ulster final, and given the quality football that the team played and the personnel that was there, I felt we had every opportunity of winning an

All-Ireland because I always knew, and it has been said in
Down more than once, that for a long time Down's problem
had been getting out of Ulster. Once we got out of Ulster,
sometimes what comes after is actually easier. So beating
Donegal and moving on to the All-Ireland, we knew that we
weren't just going to be cannon fodder for anyone.

But it was Meath that were waiting for them in the final, and while Down may have been used to the rough-house tactics of Ulster football, Meath were appearing in their fourth final in five years and comprised experienced, hardened men such as Mick Lyons, Colm O'Rourke and Liam Hayes.

'A fortnight before the All-Ireland final,' says McGrath, 'I remember having a long conversation with Sean O'Neill after training and he was telling me just what to expect and what the players should be prepared for. The one thing he did alert me to was to "be in no doubt, this Meath team will test our forward line, they will test their courage, they will test their ability to take both intimidation and provocation, physical and otherwise, and you've got to be ready for it".

'It really made me aware of what it was going to be like and we made sure that message was passed on to the players. I had great respect for that Meath team, they were a team that took the physicality of the game to the very wire. I have no problem with that because that's what the game is about. But what Sean said to me that night, the forward line knew exactly what they were going to be facing that day against Meath, and they were ready. To have people like Sean O'Neill coming to the training and saying those things, it was important for players to hear things like that, this man who had been through it and you feed off these things.'

The main talking point that year hadn't been about Down's emergence – although they were only the third Ulster team to make the All-Ireland final in the twenty-three years since Down's 1968 victory – but Meath's four-game series against Dublin in Leinster. Having come through that in such dramatic, last-minute circumstances, it seemed written in the stars that Meath would now go all the way. But it was to be one game too far for Seán Boylan's team and Down's confident swagger quickly got going as they raced into an eleven-point lead before Meath even knew what hit them. When Meath finally woke themselves up to get within two points, it was too late. After just two years in charge, Pete McGrath had overseen Down's rapid ascent and following in the footsteps of the 1960s heroes, they were once again All-Ireland champions.

'What happened in 1991 went beyond anyone's expectations,' says McGrath. 'Because Down football had been in the doldrums. In All-Ireland terms, it had been second rate, so for us to win the Ulster title and then to go on and win the All-Ireland …'

A good coach can plan and strategise to do everything possible to win, but one of the hardest things to legislate for is the effect that winning has on the players and the team as a whole. It happened with Kerry when a youthful, swaggering team won on their first outing in 1975; it took three years to regain the title, and for Down, the victory in 1991 was overwhelming.

'Given the euphoria and all that went with winning the All-Ireland,' says McGrath, 'for many, many Down people who thought they would never see what others had seen in the 1960s, and indeed for people who had experienced the 1960s and were now heading into middle age, suddenly they were able to savour it all again. The players were really feted and they were paraded all around the county, there was such excessive demands placed on them after that win.'

Success also brought its own consequences on the pitch, and the reaction from fellow Ulster counties was that if Down could do it, so could they. Unlike Down's previous success in the 1960s where they were dominant in Ulster, in the 1990s there was much tighter margins between the counties. This, plus a loss of focus, meant that the following two seasons were disappointing for Down and they didn't even reach the Ulster final. Donegal and Derry were dominant in 1992 and 1993, and leaving the field after a chastening eleven-point loss to Derry in 1993 meant the Down team were at a crossroads. McGrath asked his players coldly if they were to become known as one-season wonders or if they had anything else left to give. 1994 was to prove the ultimate litmus test for both the players' hunger and McGrath's managerial skills.

'In all my years of training teams and coaching teams,' he says, 'I never saw a team that was as driven as that panel of 1993 going into 1994. People like Greg Blaney, D.J. Kane, James McCartan and Ross Carr, they realised that all the glory and recognition that they got in 1991 might be severely tarnished if their careers ended without another All-Ireland success.'

McGrath could take them so far but ultimately the drive for more success, the honour and pride, had to come from within; it was up to McGrath to shine a light on what it was the players wanted from their careers.

> *To a certain extent, the motivation and hunger is something that is inside a player. What a player wants to achieve, the type of player that person is, comes down to themselves. But we also had very established leaders within the team who wanted to achieve again and they were getting others by the scruff of the necks and pulling them along with them.*
>
> *Four new players came into the team in 1994 – Brian Burns at full-back, Gregory McCartan in midfield, Michael McGill at right-back and Aidan Farrell at full-forward – which had a freshening-up effect. As well as that, Pat Burr,*

*who has since passed away, joined me on the management
team and had a galvanising affect as well.*

The first round of the 1994 season pitted Down against reigning
champions Derry, who had handed out the eleven-point thrashing
just twelve months previously. Just how far Down had come in that
year would be put to the test in the championship opener.

'We all knew this was going to be a high-noon situation,'
McGrath remembers, 'and so we started training the previous
October – this was the one game we were training for.'

The match served up in Celtic Park at the end of May has been
described as one of the game's greatest. On a bright summer's day,
the two teams tore off at a blistering pace that never let up for the
full seventy minutes. It was a masterclass from both sides, one
of those days where both are at their peak in terms of skill and
commitment. No quarter was asked or given as the lead changed
hands a number of times. With just six minutes to go, substitute
Ciarán McCabe scored what proved to be the winning goal and
Down won by 1–14 to 1–12. The Down players had answered the
questions that McGrath had put to them in the best of fashions.

'When we came away from Celtic Park that day,' McGrath
recalled afterwards, 'we knew we were going to win the All-
Ireland. We didn't say it, but the players knew there was nothing
out there to beat us.'

They reclaimed Ulster, beating Tyrone by six points, before
dispatching Cork to face Dublin for their second All-Ireland final
in four years and seemed destined to capture Sam Maguire. With
eight minutes to go, Dublin were awarded a penalty. Behind by just
three, a goal would have put Dublin back in the driving seat and on
course for their first All-Ireland since 1983.

The penalty hoodoo for Dublin's Charlie Redmond was to
continue, however. Having missed penalties in the 1988 Leinster

final and 1992 All-Ireland, his shot this time was saved and he sent the rebound wide. Dublin had lost another All-Ireland to the Ulster champions and Down had won their fifth title, a second under Pete McGrath.

'The fact that we were able to beat Dublin in Croke Park and with all those circumstances I think was most definitely a final vindication of this group of players,' he says.

He had put it up to them in the wake of the humiliation of 1993, forced them to look at themselves and question what they wanted to be remembered for. However, in his usual humble manner, McGrath refused to take the credit for what he had achieved with this group of players and how he had shaped them.

'The players weren't conditioned by me,' he said afterwards. 'They were conditioned by what they were told when they were younger, by their parents or their uncles or people who knew. It's a process of conditioning that takes place over a long period of time.'

Such was the competitiveness in Ulster, Down were unable to retain their Ulster title, but they were to reach another final in 1996 against Tyrone – 'the last shot for the 1990s team' as McGrath described it.

Tyrone beat us 1–9 to 0–9 on a really wretched day and it was a game that we certainly could have won. The team broke up after that and the last couple of years were difficult because you were really swimming against the tide in terms of trying to get a team on the field and trying to motivate players and the material really just wasn't there. My last game in charge was against Longford in a qualifier match down in Pearse Park. I remember when that game ended Longford had beaten us by five or six points and I just turned to John Murphy, the selector who had been with me from the very start, and I said, 'John, is this the end?' He said,

'Yes, I think it is.' So in the changing room I just announced,
no fuss no ceremony, that I was stepping down. It was very
painful and it was a long journey home that night.

Having given his life to coaching Down teams, and despite having
been in charge of the seniors for thirteen years, it was inevitable
that, at some point, Pete McGrath would be involved again with
underage sides. He managed the under-21s to the 2009 All-Ireland
final, losing narrowly to Cork by a point, before coming full circle
and taking over the minors a year later. Coaching young players
is something he finds energising and he is in a great position to
compare the teenagers of the twenty-first century to those of thirty
years previously.

'Dealing with the seventeen- and eighteen-year-olds, they are
more streetwise and more mature than young fellas were in the
1980s,' he says. 'But essentially they are still young footballers
who love the game, who are enthusiastic playing the game; they
want to improve, want to be the best they can be and all have a
vision of moving on and playing for the seniors and that's exactly
what they had in the 1980s.'

Pete McGrath had started out by imparting a simple coaching
philosophy of doing the basics well, and it has stood the test of
time, as his managerial career took him from colleges to minor all
the way to the heady heights of All-Ireland success.

'I suppose when you look back on your life and football
generally, there were all kinds of heartaches and great days,' he
says. 'There were disappointing days and traumatic days and days
that will live with you forever while other days you will never
remember again.'

More importantly perhaps was the fact that in guiding Down
to All-Ireland victory in 1991, he helped point the way for other
competing Ulster counties to achieve similar success. The glass

ceiling had been broken, and the influence of Ulster's coaches was now to hold sway over the development of the game for the next quarter of a century, which was the real legacy of Down's and Pete McGrath's achievements in the 1990s.

'Donegal people would say to this day,' says McGrath, 'that when Down won the All-Ireland, they sat back and said, "Damn it, we know we're every bit as good as that lot and they have done it and shown us how to get there." Then came Derry in 1993 and I'm sure people in those counties would say that in all probability they would have won their All-Irelands – only it was Down who lit the fuse.'

Chapter 12

'Wise men learn from fools and fools learn from wise men'

Like Pete McGrath, Donegal's Brian McEniff was born to manage. Whether it was in sport, life or business, McEniff has been an organiser his entire life. His introduction to management happened in Toronto, Canada, of all places, where he had moved in his twenties to gain more experience in the hotel business in which his family was involved. Playing soccer with Toronto Roma, he found himself gravitating towards being captain, secretary and manager, and began to take a real interest in the coaching side of things.

'I was always a curious chap,' he explains. 'I would want to know about things, and I suppose that, if I had a success, it's that I was always looking to learn. Every day you get up you learn, and there's an old saying that goes, "Wise men learn from fools and fools learn from wise men", so you can apply that.'

Coming back home to help out in the family business, his involvement with sport and the GAA in particular took off. It began with playing and managing the local club side before being asked to help out with the county minor side. He was also playing for the county seniors and, remarkably, was able to juggle work life with playing and coaching. Multitasking was a skillset he needed because he then became player-manager of the Donegal team in 1969 aged just twenty-seven. It also helped that he had spent most of his youth outside of the county and so hadn't got caught up in the club politics of the time. He was delightfully ignorant of Donegal football, which was probably the best way to be at that time, struggling as they were most years to field teams.

'When I came out of boarding school in Monaghan, I went to college in Dublin,' he says. 'And then from there, I went to Canada. I never saw a Donegal senior final until I played in it myself and didn't know a pile about the county scene.'

Nevertheless, even when he was managing the minors, he was conscious of the political divisions that were going on in the county at the time.

> *When I took over the minor team, the one thing that I did want to knock out of the Donegal people was this fragmentation of divisions. The northwest had been a very strong division in Donegal and the south were the poor relations when I was a boy growing up, and the boys would tog out in little groups of their own. The first thing was I wanted the lads to mingle, those from Gweedore or Ballyshannon or Letterkenny, and I would just get them to talk to each other and become more Donegal people.*

Having come back from Canada earlier than expected because of his father's ill-health, McEniff was thrust into managing the Holyrood Hotel in Bundoran, which his father had bought fifteen years previously. Still only in his mid-twenties, leadership and management were necessary in the world he was thrown into, and he found they came naturally to him. When Donegal came asking three years later, he was a young man with old shoulders, and it didn't daunt him.

While Tony Hanahoe achieved remarkable success as a player-manager with Dublin, winning the All-Ireland in 1977, what McEniff achieved as player-manager with Donegal over a short few years was even more impressive. The county had only ever appeared in two Ulster finals – in 1963 and 1966 – losing on both occasions, and yet within three years of McEniff taking over the team, they won their first provincial crown and captured a second two years later. It was a remarkable turnaround in fortunes for the county and one spearheaded by McEniff's management skills.

Upon taking over, however, McEniff had a mammoth task ahead of him.

We had played Leitrim in the last match of the league before Christmas. And Leitrim hadn't won a match for some eighteen months; they were our neighbours and they didn't just beat us, they played us off the park. I remember coming home and I was to go to a party that night in my brother's house on the road out to Leitrim. But on the way, I said to my friend to let me off beside the church. I just jumped over the wall and into the darkness of the parish and didn't appear until the evening of the following day. I was too ashamed to show my face.

The players had a meeting in the aftermath of the Leitrim defeat, to sort out just what the hell was going on. Had things really got that bad?

Some of the lads were talking about travelling expenses for the year, another guy said he was at a party the night before and he wasn't feeling well, plus there was indiscipline there.

> *It was tough because I was also captain and I was playing*
> *good football, playing with Ulster too, played my heart out,*
> *but in vain. We decided amongst ourselves that we would*
> *go out and source a manager for the team and as I had*
> *played under the great Mick Higgins of Cavan with the*
> *Ulster Railway Cup teams, I asked him if he would do it.*
> *His answer was no, but then he said, 'Why don't you do it*
> *yourself and I'll give you a hand if you need one?'*

Mick Higgins was a legendary figure in Gaelic football. A former captain of the great Cavan team of the 1940s and 1950s, he won seven Ulster titles and three All-Irelands including the famous 1947 Polo Grounds final. His success continued as he turned his attention to coaching his native Cavan to three more Ulster titles – and their last All-Ireland final appearance, when the minors lost to Dublin in 1959. He then achieved incredible success with Longford in the 1960s, managing them to their first and only National League title in 1966 and their only Leinster crown two years later. His stature in the game was remembered when he was awarded an All Star All-Time Award in recognition of his achievements and success as a player and manager.

For Higgins to suggest that McEniff try his hand at managing the team, despite his tender years, meant he saw the potential in the young Bundoran man. Plus, having someone of Higgins' experience to call upon when needed was to prove an invaluable mentoring aid – something that McEniff was to provide himself to a young up-and-coming manager in the form of Jim McGuinness some forty years later.

Playing on Railway Cup and All Star teams was opening McEniff up to other footballing spheres and talents, playing alongside some of the game's leading players, such as Mick O'Dwyer, and playing under Kerry's Jackie Lyne and wanting only to talk about football and management with them. He was learning from some of the game's leading minds from the outset.

Just as Maurice Hayes had done in breaking down the divisions within Kerry and as Heffernan was to do in scouring Dublin for players, so too Brian McEniff began reorganising and looking far and wide for players.

'I used to run tryouts to see what was available,' he says. 'And sometimes they were able to call up some players for you, but not all the time. You would be constantly sussing out players all over the place to see who could play where. I had nothing to lose, but we always had good footballers in the county, I firmly believed that. Within a year, we came back to play Leitrim and we beat them 5–16 to 0–1.'

Things were turning around for Donegal and in the back of his mind McEniff's target was set on an Ulster title. He hadn't expressed it to the players just yet, but he knew that it could be achieved. Having played on All Star teams made up of Kerry greats, he looked around the Donegal dressing room and thought to himself, *Our players are just as good, we can compete.* Even looking to the great Down team of the 1960s, he believes that what really drove them, apart from their talented players, was the organisation and unity behind the team.

Instilling that self-belief and organisation into the team, Donegal reached the Ulster final in 1972, only the county's third appearance in the provincial decider, and this time they won, beating Tyrone by five points. The county was ablaze with bonfires celebrating their first Ulster title, led by a man still only thirty years of age.

Another Ulster title followed two years later, but McEniff's biggest regret was that they never pushed on for an All-Ireland which he believed was within their grasp. McEniff was always studying the opposition and tweaking his own side, looking to create player match-ups that would disrupt the other team and play to their own advantage, a tactic that gave Donegal the edge most of the time. Every player on the team was delegated a specific job to do under McEniff's watch. Much as he had to do with his burgeoning hotel business.

'It's all about man-management,' he says. 'The real successful managers are those who can man-manage well. I was also working in the hotel industry where you would meet a huge cross-section of people and you had to get on with them. I would go around the tables in the hotels, saying hello, just checking how things are. You meet some very interesting people, and people want to talk to you and you might want to talk to them because they might be bringing in some sort of qualification or expertise, something that is new to you and being the curious boy that I am, I would have to find out for myself what they were at and what it was.'

But Donegal was also to toughen up, which helped in their success in Ulster particularly, and he credits Heffernan with raising the levels of coaching and fitness at that time.

'Our football, to put it simply, was too pure in Donegal,' he says. 'I remember when we went down to play Wexford, looking good for promotion, and Wexford arrived like a junior team can, in bits and pieces; my boys were all prepared, but for want of a better word, in Wexford Park that day, they physically just horsed us out of it. It wasn't dirty but it was damned tough. After that, we got into the gym and we started to build the lads up, to develop the upper body strength, because they had to.'

Although McEniff's association with Donegal football was to last over a quarter of a century, the nature of county GAA politics meant that it was an on-off relationship that saw him step away only to come back and revitalise the county at key periods in their development over the next three decades.

His first departure came off the back of the county's second

Ulster title in three years and he wasn't short of offers to manage, and, for the 1975 season, he got involved with Sligo's championship campaign which saw the minnows beat Mayo after a replay to win only their second Connacht title – their first since 1928.

McEniff came back for another stint with Donegal in 1983, and with the under-21s winning an All-Ireland in 1982, hopes were high that the county would push on at senior level. They had never built upon the success achieved under McEniff in 1972 and 1974, and he seemed to be working more magic for Donegal again as they won an Ulster title in 1983, beating Cavan by three points, but again losing out in an All-Ireland semi.

Surprisingly, they lost to Armagh by a point in the next year's championship and, in 1985, Monaghan, the reigning league champions, sent them on their away. The team had never built on their earlier promise and McEniff says it was time for Tom Conaghan, the manager of the under-21 All-Ireland-winning team, to take over and have a go.

'But I didn't go, I was pushed. I deserved it,' he admits frankly. 'I hadn't done as well with the team as maybe I should.'

Despite his sackings, McEniff remained on good terms with the county board, also spending time on the County Board Executive Committee. There wasn't a man in Donegal GAA whom he didn't know, from either the playing or administration side.

Now into his forties, with his hotel interests expanding and having been on the road with Donegal for the best part of twenty years, McEniff could have been forgiven for wanting to take a step back. He had achieved great success with Donegal, but there was still one item of unfinished business gnawing away at him.

'I want to win an All-Ireland before I am fifty.' That's the exact statement I told the county board when I went looking for reappointment once more in 1990. I said we would

win one within three years. I was going to be fifty in two
years' time so I had time to make up. But I knew the talent
was there. I had been sacked, and now I was back. I was
confident then in myself more than ever before, and I knew
the players. I had been managing Ulster teams for years
and knew them well. I knew there was a mindset amongst
those players, a winning mindset. But the age was creeping
up. It was now or never.

Once more McEniff's impact was immediate. The team had been there or thereabouts in Ulster, reaching the provincial final the year before, but McEniff's tactical nous and attention to detail saw them win Ulster in his first year back in charge. It was a remarkable record. It was the county's fifth Ulster title and McEniff had managed the team across three decades to each one. It wasn't that he toiled for years with them but, once in charge, he led them in the right direction·and they were invariably provincial winners shortly thereafter. For a county that had never won Ulster titles before his arrival, the McEniff factor was obvious.

Like any good manager, he also brought along top-class men for his backroom team, people he trusted implicitly, who were expert in certain areas. McEniff was at the head of the pyramid, leading and co-ordinating, but he was also helped greatly by those he pulled in to help out.

Michael Lafferty was a former Donegal player on whom McEniff could rely for his insights and knowledge of the game.

'He was a great reader of the game and was very quick to spot a difficulty on the field and point it out,' McEniff said. 'He was very forthright too and was never afraid to speak his mind, but always commanded the respect of the players and the rest of the management team.'

Seamus Bonner was another with a glittering Donegal career

who was now based in Dublin where he was the link man to those Donegal players also in the capital.

Naul McCole was involved with the Donegal County Board and county executive for most of his adult life, acting as chairman at the height of McEniff's success. He was an important link to the county board and administrators, a key relationship to keep in place as the county team pushed on in pursuit of success.

Anthony Harkin, a player with the county in the late 1970s, was to be a vital cog in the setup as the team trainer just as sports science and weight training was starting to become more important. He had studied and played at Thomond College in Limerick, winning an All-Ireland club title alongside the likes of Brian Mullins and Pat Spillane, and went on to become one of the game's leading authorities on training and coaching.

His input into the team's physical development was vital, says McEniff.

> He was a brilliant trainer and a real driving force behind the success. He had the players in great shape and he was a good football man too. Anthony knew his football and was not afraid to give his opinion and advice on how well a player was going in training. He was well ahead of his time as a coach and was one of the top coaches in the country at the time.

Brian McEniff was also one of the first to utilise 'eyes and ears in the stand', someone to give a different perspective and a bird's eye view of what was happening in a game. Pauric McShea was that man in the 1990s.

'Pauric was, and still is, a good football man and had a good football brain and was a good reader of a game,' explained McEniff.

Finally, and always looking for that edge over his opponents,

McEniff had Sean Ferriter, a former team-mate of McEniff's who was based in Dublin, attend their training sessions and take meticulous notes on what they were up to and who was going well and who was not.

Donegal reached their third Ulster final in a row in 1991 where they were dominating the province and seemingly on course for another tilt at an All-Ireland final. But Donegal weren't the only ones on the up playing an improving game with a solid foundation of technical fitness programmes behind them. Down beat them to the punch that day and went on to be the county that led the way for Ulster's rise in the 1990s.

The loss that year still sticks in the throat for McEniff, and one can easily believe that he feels Donegal should have been rhe torch-bearers for the province in the years to follow.

> *The All-Ireland we should we have won was 1991. We had hammered Down in the McKenna Cup and the league – and I mean hammered them. But that final day in Clones ... they turned on a show ...*
>
> *We gave away a bad first goal, then we got back into the game [with a goal] and I can remember it so well. That goal would have put us ahead but they went back up and got a point. Now, fair play to Down, we had a leaky defence that they exploited but we had a very good forward line and I felt that based on what I knew of the team, that we should have won the All-Ireland that year.*

Despite the success the following year, it's always the ones that get away that hurt the hardest and even defeat in 1993 to Derry remains a source of consternation, losing as they did on a monsoon of a day and a pitch that was so waterlogged it was a safety concern.

'That was a good Derry team that year but we should have

won in 1993 as well,' McEniff believes. 'I nearly wasn't coming out of the dressing room that day in Clones and I gather Tommy McDermott, the referee, didn't want to proceed with the game either but he got direction from the Ulster Council to proceed. It was dangerous, it was very dangerous on the hill, there was just a massive waterfall. It was savage.'

Speaking to McEniff twenty years after that period, you'd hardly think that sandwiched in between those losses in 1991 and 1993 was an All-Ireland success, the county's first. It was an incredible success. In many ways the last throw for that generation that had promised so much by winning the under-21 All-Ireland ten years previously and which had never truly delivered on their potential until McEniff stepped in to take over in 1990.

Our team was an amalgamation of the under-21 side and the good work that had been done at underage level. And then the introduction of two very good players, Noel Hegarty and Tony Boyle, who galvanised the side. There was a togetherness on that team but they were tough men and they weren't easily managed, I can tell you.

I had earned respect from my previous successes and most of the players you could get through to but there was always some difficulty. One interesting fact is that phones became a lot more important and there was more contact. When I was there in the 1970s, the players didn't have phones, their fathers and mothers didn't have phones, so it wasn't easy to contact players. But everyone had them by the 1990s, and it kept me in closer contact with the players and I would have known not only the player but his girlfriend, his wife, his parents. I remember I phoned every one of the players on Christmas Day wishing them a Happy Christmas – you could keep that closeness there over the phone.

Again, his man-management skills were to the fore. Making sure he knew every one of his players, what was going on in their lives, what was making them tick, what was holding them back and what they needed to be driven on further.

'It's like me walking into any hotel and talking to the girl in the dining room and saying, "Hello, Mary", and finding out how she is,' explains McEniff. 'What it comes down to is it's all about people.'

With the team challenging for honours, a lid was maintained on any internal problems and the players were all rowing in behind McEniff and his management team. The campaign of 1992 will forever be remembered as Donegal's All-Ireland breakthrough year. After losing Ulster the previous year, the team came storming back to recapture the provincial title, beating Derry by two points, and then overcoming Mayo in the semi-final to reach the All-Ireland final, where Dublin awaited.

McEniff was always a man with an attention to detail and their preparations for the final were not going to be left to chance. He even had the team sit down in Letterkenny to watch the hurling final two weeks beforehand just to get a sense of the day.

In the end, despite Dublin being hot favourites, it was Donegal who won through 0–18 to 0–14, and over twenty years since he first took up the reins of Donegal football, McEniff and his county had reached the promised land. Donegal were All-Ireland champions for the very first time.

Winning, though, was to bring unforeseen problems.

I never legislated for what was going to take place afterwards. I remember reading a quote from Joe Mercer, the successful Manchester City manager, who described what happened to City when they started to win things. Winning and success he thought was brilliant – all the

*hope, joy and satisfaction – but he also said there was a
lot of internal bickering and jealousy and stuff like that. At
the time, I didn't really understand what he meant but after
our success in 1992, I started to understand how things had
changed.*

*There were huge internal rivalries there – not bitterness
– but between them they were knocking against each other
in league and championship and other tournaments. There
was a great head-to-head with them and it could be a bit
ratty, so it was about trying to keep things afloat in a good
way by sitting on top of it.*

The writing was on the wall for the team and the 1993 season
was to see them lose their Ulster title to up-and-coming Derry in
that infamous waterlogged game in Clones. The champions were
out and McEniff didn't have anything left in the tank to give. It
had been a crazy year since the previous September, between
functions, celebrations and being on the go 24/7. While there was
regret about what might have been achieved in 1993, things were
slowly starting to unravel from that point on and McEniff walked
away from the job, this time an All-Ireland winner, his name etched
forever in Donegal history.

McEniff was to look on as Derry and then Down continued the
remarkable Ulster success with further All-Irelands for the province
in 1993 and 1994 and he witnessed the rise of Armagh and then
Tyrone onto the national stage at the start of the 2000s. By then,
it had been ten years and he was starting to itch for the game, the
competition and the challenge of managing Donegal once again.

*I had been watching football for ten years as a spectator,
enjoying it, going to games, reading my programme and
watching the matches. I had been helping out a bit with*

*the training to get them ready for the league when all of
a sudden, it's 1 January 2003, and I find myself becoming
team manager again. We were playing Galway in the league
in January and here I am beside John O'Mahony, who's
there with his stopwatch and he is up and down the sideline,
he's working the referee, and I'm thinking, F–, what am I
doing here?*

*It was ten years later, and the change in the game was
incredible ... next up was the All-Ireland champions,
Armagh, and holy Jesus these young boys were bursting
out of their jerseys, they had these skin-tight jerseys and
they were throwing us around like rag dolls, they just blew
us away. I thought, it was more akin to rugby league.*

It was a rude awakening for McEniff, and he realised there was so
much work to do to prepare the team for the championship. In the
new world of Gaelic football, to compete with the Armaghs, the
first thing was that the players had to be bigger, stronger and fitter.
Patsy McGonigle was brought in, as McEniff says, 'To knock
sparks out of them, but that's all we could do at the time to sort
them out the physically.'

They were so far behind other teams in terms of physique and
fitness that the league itself was a lost cause and, by the fifth defeat,
Donegal were relegated.

Anthony Harkin was brought back into the setup by McEniff
and within the group a few home truths were aired. Did this group
really want to achieve and win things or were they content to let
everyone else overtake them? The team wasn't that far behind –
they had reached the Ulster final in 2002 only to lose to Armagh,
who eventually won the All-Ireland – but were in danger of never
catching up. Despite an early loss to Fermanagh, the introduction
of the qualifiers meant that if Donegal could get a run of games

under their belt, they could build up a bit of momentum and turn their season around.

They were drawn against Longford in round one of the 2003 qualifiers. McEniff knew he needed to change things around and decided to drop a number of the big names, including Jim McGuinness.

'I did a revamp just to get things going,' says McEniff. 'And I remember Jim being very upset about it, but it worked. It was a nice sunny Saturday evening in Ballybofey and I remember after winning the match going over to the crowd and applauding them for coming because they didn't have to, we had no reason to have support at all.'

Sligo, Tipperary, Down and then Galway were all dispatched in due course and, suddenly, Donegal found themselves in an All-Ireland semi-final, meeting Armagh, the team that had thrown them around like rag dolls just months previously.

We had to do huge work and preparation for Armagh. I got it into their heads that it was going to be a physical game and that we could not engage with them because we hadn't got the upper body strength at that stage. What we had to do was to keep the ball moving. Then I also put Damien Diver in front of the full-back line to counter the diagonal balls Armagh were playing. Everything was going swimmingly, we got a goal before half-time, goal of the year it was. Steven McDermott went through the middle like a f–ing rocket, passed the ball to Toye who then hammered the ball into the net.

But Armagh were a tough team. Heffo's Dublin team of the 1970s was a tough team. Armagh didn't introduce that side of the game, they just brought it on to another level. It's not the way I would like to coach teams. I would

always want to play an extrovert game, not always the most
successful but always expressive.

I remember Colm O'Rourke saying back in the 1990s
that Donegal were never anything, they were too nice,
and nice guys don't succeed. And then I remember him
apologising in the Sunday paper after we had won the All-
Ireland. 'Apologies,' he said, 'nice guys do succeed.'

McEniff looks back on 2003 as another potential All-Ireland that slipped through his hands. Leading Armagh into the second half, they were dealt a body blow with the sending off of Raymond Sweeney. The system of containment, utilising a sweeper in front of the full-back line, was now lost as the team went a man down. Still, though, they kept on battling and it was only in injury-time that Armagh grabbed the winning score to put them into their second successive All-Ireland final.

Despite the defeat, Brian McEniff takes pleasure in looking back at that game and how his team had so nearly managed to find a way to overcome the Armagh tactics of swarming and blanket defence that were starting to come into vogue at that time and would develop further over the years with the success of Tyrone and Donegal under Jim McGuinness.

'There is a way around it,' believes McEniff. 'But it is up to each manager to see the way around it.'

Armagh were to be McEniff's nemesis once again in 2004 when they beat Donegal in the Ulster final by thirteen points, the heaviest defeat of his managerial career. The scoreline had shown just how far the game was developing and how far ahead Tyrone and Armagh were of the other counties in the province – in the previous year's Ulster final, Tyrone had beaten Down in a replay by fifteen points.

Surprisingly, Donegal lost to Fermanagh in the qualifiers, and in the following year's defeat to Armagh in Ulster, despite taking them to a replay, McEniff's team ended up losing by seven points before suffering a one-point loss at the hands of Cavan in the qualifiers. For the first time in McEniff's success-laden career, Donegal had not managed to win an Ulster title. As he says himself, football had changed so much in the ten years he had been away from the game, and despite attempts to take on Armagh's rise to dominance, the closet they had come to fulfilling their own potential was that agonising All-Ireland semi-final defeat in 2003.

Finally, after three decades of involvement, it was time to step away for the third and last time.

Football was changing and it needed new ideas, new thinking, and a younger manager to take Donegal on to the next level, not only to compete with the Armaghs and Tyrones but to beat them in a new and different style of play. For twelve years, from 1999 to 2010, Armagh and Tyrone shared the spoils in Ulster with nobody else getting a look in. After McEniff stepped down, Donegal spent five years in the wilderness, never getting beyond the All-Ireland quarter-finals.

But as McEniff stepped away from Donegal football, in the background down at the club scene, one man was quietly making waves. Jim McGuinness, who had been a member of Donegal's All-Ireland winning squad in 1992, had retired as a player in 2003 and had recently taken over the management of Naomh Conaill's. In his first season in charge, they won their first Donegal senior county championship. Unknown to Donegal GAA and the Gaelic football world, the makings of the county's next great manager had begun.

Chapter 13

'Forget about the rain and just go for it'

Ulster's domination of Gaelic football has continued since the 1990s. The thinking, the studying, the excellence in coaching have been led, in the main, by Ulster men. John Morrison, the outside-the-box thinker and hugely influential coach, puts it down to a number of factors, including identity and the Troubles, but also the fact that more money was being pumped into the universities and sporting sectors in Britain as a whole. Northern Ireland was a beneficiary of such largesse over the years and it has encouraged the furthering of coaching and skills development, so much so that it is the likes of Morrison who is in demand all over the country to give coaching clinics to clubs and county setups.

Jim McGuinness has been another beneficiary of Morrison's ideas and techniques, learning and soaking up much when Morrison was a selector with Mickey Moran, who managed Donegal from 2001–2002. McGuinness was coming to the end of his playing career at that stage but what he learned from the Moran–Morrison double act formed much of the basis for his future thinking on training and coaching.

Mickey Moran, who has been described as one of Gaelic football's most influential coaches, has had All-Ireland success with Derry and has spread the gospel with Sligo, Donegal, Mayo and Leitrim. For much of that career, he has also been assisted by Morrison, and it is their far-sighted and revolutionary approach to coaching and training that has seen their expertise so much in demand.

In many ways, Moran was of the same mould as Down's Pete McGrath, a former player who found himself, much to his surprise, thrust into management at a young age. After achieving a rare two-in-a-row in Ulster in 1975 and 1976, as well as a National League final appearance, Derry football went into decline. Moran had been an inter-county player on the team and as he had completed a coaching course in Manchester and had some experience training the club team, he was asked to step into the breach to train the seniors – though it was to be only a temporary measure until someone else was found.

Such was the state of football in the county, however, that nobody could be found.

'I kept waiting and waiting,' Moran remembers. 'And then as a manager didn't appear and I had been taking the training, I ended up player-manager at twenty-eight years of age.'

Similar to Brian McEniff's situation, Moran found himself, suddenly and without looking for it, manager of an inter-county team while still playing and still only in his late twenties. It was a strange scenario to find himself in but a lot of his team-mates were now deciding to move on anyway.

'The players in the team were pretty close,' he explains. 'So they understood the situation and, at that stage, the team was in transition and a lot of the lads I had played with were retiring and there was a lot of new players coming in.'

He spent four years in charge but, unlike McEniff, without any spectacular success. Derry failed to reach an Ulster final, which in the early 1980s was changing hands between Armagh, Down, Donegal and Tyrone. Ulster football at that stage was at a low point overall, with only Armagh in 1977 and Tyrone in 1986 actually making the All-Ireland final – and the margin of defeat was fifteen and eight points respectively.

Continuing to teach PE at St Mary's High School in Limavady, Moran was soaking up new ideas all the time to further his own coaching education, citing Kevin Heffernan's arrival and his ideas on the game as the real revolutionary change to hit Gaelic football.

> *He started the revolution, you know. Dublin were way ahead and while Kerry had the tradition and the silverware and the fitness, Kevin Heffernan brought that new dimension of working with the ball and so it slowly filtered into other counties. At that stage, I would have been always thinking about that – how to train with a ball and how to make it relevant.*

It was to become a hallmark of Moran's career. While other counties ran their players into the ground just because that was how it was always done, for Moran the reasoning behind it didn't make sense. If players were going to get fit, it had to have a connection to the game, to drills, to getting the ball in hand and having an end result in mind.

> *I remember Frankie Kearney, the manager of Derry at the time, he had been down in Gormanston at one of Joe Lennon's coaching courses, and he came back with all of these new ideas and I was stunned, there was just so much more to it that I hadn't realised or thought about. Up to then, basically when county training came along, you did your warm-up, you might play a bit of a game but just basic*

skill and not a whole lot really – in fact, the majority of the session was physical fitness, laps and stuff like that. But with Heffernan and Lennon's courses, it all changed then and that's when the seeds were sown and it made me start to think about things too. Football became drill-oriented but we had to move on from that to make the drills game specific and bring in a shot at the end of the drill or a tackle.

You listen to everybody you can, the managers who I trained under and played for in Derry and Ulster. Down's Sean O'Neill who coached Ulster Railway Cup teams, he was a man ahead of his time too. You just listened and learned; basically a good coach, or somebody who was aspiring to be a good coach, is somebody who formulates their own theories and ideas – you have to work out things yourself. A lot of coaches starting off might just want handouts of drills but that's not the way it works, that defeats the purpose, you have got to have a thinking approach, you have got to find out for yourself.

As a PE teacher in school, I was involved with youngsters for over thirty-one years and you're able to try things and develop things. You get a good broad spectrum from coaching at underage right up to inter-county level – every sort of different age group. Everything should be allied to the development of the child, right up to adult level.

Moran's exposure to the new ways of thinking about the game meant the seeds of change had been sown, and while it wasn't to have an immediate impact with Ulster counties at the time, the development of their coaching philosophies and improvement in their techniques was happening apace. While Cork and Meath were dominating in the 1980s real change was taking place in the North, and was set to break through onto the national consciousness, just as Down had done in 1960. As Pete McGrath noted, their success in 1991 lit the fuse and the others in the province were thinking they could do the same and follow them up the Croke Park steps to collect Sam Maguire. Donegal had done it in 1992, and the standard of play in Ulster was such that, while Donegal were strong, Down and Derry also had their own notions of being kingpins.

Eamonn Coleman took charge of Derry in 1990, the same year that Brian McEniff was in control across the border in Donegal, and while McEniff's team made an immediate impression capturing Ulster that year, and Down showed the way by winning the All-Ireland the following year, Derry were also making their own strides, quickly gaining successive promotions and then capturing the National League in 1992 – the first for the county since the 1946–1947 season. One of Coleman's first acts as manager was to bring Mickey Moran on board as the team trainer and it was their managerial combination that was to prove so successful.

Like Moran, Coleman was of hallowed Derry pedigree, having won Ulster and All-Ireland minor and under-21 medals with the county, before progressing to the senior team. As a manager, he mirrored his own career, leading Derry minors to Ulster and All-Ireland success in 1983, with four from the panel going on to win at senior level ten years later. While Coleman was the manager, Mickey Moran's insights and thinking on the game meant he was more than just a number two and his influence on the setup was far-reaching. Eamonn Coleman was the man-manager while Moran was the trainer.

'He would have known what made people tick,' remembered Coleman's son, Gary, in an interview with the *Sunday Independent* in 2007, a year after his father had passed away. 'He told Joe Brolly he was the best forward in Ireland and he had told Enda Gormley the same thing.'

'He was such a vivid presence for us,' remembered Brolly, now a pundit on RTÉ who was also an All Star forward on that Derry team.

'The leader of that group. He was a totally inspirational person. He spoke a version of the English language which you wouldn't find in a textbook, but he had a terrific turn of phrase. He told us we would win an All-Ireland. He used to say to me, "You're the best corner-forward in Ireland. I just can't believe how good you are." I only realised in hindsight that it was a lie, but I believed it at the time.'

Playing Donegal in 1993 on that waterlogged pitch in Clones showed the grit and determination the players had to succeed. No excuses – monsoon weather, rain-soaked pitch or not, they won their first Ulster title in six years and were reigning league and Ulster champions.

But heading into 1993, it looked as if the wheels were about to come off. Playing Donegal in a league quarter-final, Derry led by six points at half-time and yet allowed their neighbours to come back and beat them in the second half, scoring only a single point in the process. Had the team peaked and become satisfied with all they had achieved thus far?

'That was the result when it all changed,' remembers Moran. 'We had training the next night and I was there early to set the whole thing up and the next thing they called me in for a meeting. Eamonn had called in a sports psychologist by the name of Craig Mahony, he was originally from Tasmania but he was working at the university and that night he earned his crust. The meeting lasted four hours and we just sat there and slashed it all out.'

'The boy Craig Mahony stood up and said, "I have some questions,"' recalled Gary Coleman. '"Dermot McNicholl! You came over to the sideline for water after fifteen minutes – why? Enda Gormley! You missed five frees – why? Anthony Tohill! You started drop-kicking the ball and giving it away – why?"'

'The meeting was very personal,' says Moran. 'Mahony just got up and cut everybody off and to one player he said, "Don't speak again", other players got really irate, and he said, "No, no I'm not telling you not to speak but, if you speak, instead of saying, 'This

is wrong, this is wrong, this is wrong', put forward your account."'
And that just checked everybody then. He had pinpointed things
they had done in matches, he asked one player, "What did you do in
the thirty-seventh minute?" And he says "Why, I don't know what I
did." He said, "You came across to the dugout for a sip of water and
the ball was still in play." Wee simple things like that, you know.

'We had a wild rivalry within the clubs then but, at that stage,
players just stood up and said, "Right, f– it, lads, we're going to
get together and we are going to work in groups." The Lavey and
Bellaghy boys sat down to work together – and those two hated
each other – and all the other lads came together as well, so we
bonded that night. That was a turning point for me. Everything
lifted, they were doing extra work on their own, they gave up the
drink and that got us over the line, everybody pulled together. Even
the county board rolled in and we got a free run for a year.'

The backbone of the team was built on the success of the Lavey
club team that had won the All-Ireland club championship in 1991
– only the second Derry side to win the title.

'We had great players,' says Joe Brolly, a member of that Derry
team. 'We had the Lavey boys, we had Henry Downey and Johnny
McGurk on the half-back line who had been the guys who had
pioneered Lavey's All-Ireland club title, and then you had Seamus
Downey in full-forward, these guys were serious, serious Gaelic
footballers. Then to complement that, you had boys like big
Anthony Tohill, six foot five inches, brilliant athlete, kicking off
both feet, scoring a goal every other game. Our half-backs were
really good attackers, we had terrific defenders like Tony Scullion,
once in a lifetime players. We had a very simple tactic, which was
the attacking side of the pitch on the right side was mine. So if
Dermot Heaney was playing in front of me, he vacated and that
whole side was mine and then the ball was kicked long into that
area. But, ultimately, we really enjoyed it. You could express
yourself, which was important, you weren't yoked to the plough.'

And seeing the success of Down and Donegal in preceding years spurred them on.

'Down's winning spirit spurred Donegal and ourselves on and maybe others at that stage had taken their eye off the ball,' says Moran. 'Maybe it was these three counties that put in that wee bit extra work at the time. I'm sure we were all saying, "Look if they can do it, we can do it too, you know", and that was really it. Then we had the emergence of Lavey who had won an All-Ireland, which actually really helped the setup and Lavey coming back to us as All-Ireland champions and knowing that they were winners, knowing that it can be done was a big help.'

Such was the nature of football in Ulster that one slip-up in the championship meant you were gone. Thankfully, for Derry's sake, their slip-up came in the league quarter-final against Donegal, but they regrouped and went on to beat the same opposition in that waterlogged Ulster final later in the year.

Summing up the campaign and Derry's achievements thus far, Mickey Moran said at the time:

We were very single-minded and our concentration was excellent in the first game against Down. We finished well against Monaghan and even though we didn't score very much, we played lovely football against Donegal in the second half. We got up off our knees in the Dublin game and put in a great second-half performance. I'm not totally happy with our performances but I will be if it all comes together on September 19th.

Cork were their opponents for only their second All-Ireland final appearance and yet it was Derry who were to continue the incredible Ulster record, making it three All-Irelands in a row for the province. Moran pinpointed Cork's hand-passing game as one that Derry had to break down on the day.

'They play a lovely brand of football and can get in for goals but hopefully we can cut them out. A good team's defence starts up front and off the ball the whole team must defend,' he highlighted in the build-up to the game.

The tactics worked despite Cork starting well but a Seamus Downey goal in the first half was to prove crucial and Derry finished the stronger, turning around a one-point deficit to run out 1–14 to 2–08 winners. Remarkably, for the second year in a row, it was a breakthrough All-Ireland success.

It was the ultimate accolade for Eamonn Coleman and Mickey Moran and what they had sought to achieve with this group of players. Anything Down or Donegal could do, Derry could match. It was proof that, allied with talented players, the winning mentality was key and, according to Moran, that team were the most committed bunch of players he had ever worked with.

Speaking in terms of commitment shown, it outreaches anything I've ever known. All the players and management staff deserve a lot of credit. They've put in hours upon hours of dedication and it's been a magnificent team effort.

Presciently, at the time he also raised the spectre of what would befall an All-Ireland-winning team. 'If we win the All-Ireland, a lot will depend on whether or not it goes to their heads,' he said. 'But they have a good attitude. They celebrate well but when you call a stop to it, can they get back to business?'

The problem wasn't to arise with the players, but with the county board controversially removing Eamonn Coleman from his job less than a year later after defeat to Down in the Ulster championship. Such was Ulster football in the 1990s that none of the All-Ireland champions went on to retain their provincial title, and for Derry in 1994 it was no different as they lost to Down.

Mickey Moran stepped into the breach, with the team going on to collect a third league title and retaining it the following year, beating Donegal on both occasions in the final. However, with first Coleman gone, and despite league success, losses in the aftermath of the Ulster Championship meant the bitterness of Coleman's departure was not to heal easily and Mickey Moran also left in 1996.

Derry's greatest hour had come and gone and with it went the two men most responsible for it. It was Down who responded when Pete McGrath asked his players if they wanted their legacy defined by 'just' one All-Ireland success, and they were the only county to go on to achieve glory the second time around. McGrath was also the only one still in charge of his county more than two years after winning the All-Ireland title; McEniff and then Coleman and Moran were all gone shortly afterwards.

Eamonn Coleman and Mickey Moran never rekindled their partnership, both going on to have varied fortunes with different county teams. Coleman had a second spell with Derry from 1999–2002 when he captured another league title as well as reaching the 2001 All-Ireland semi-final, only to lose to eventual champions Galway. He then took over Cavan but had to step down from that position, fighting as he was non-Hodgkin lymphoma, but it was to be a losing battle for him and he died in 2007, aged just fifty-nine but he left a legacy and memories of his achievements with Derry in that historic 1990s period.

Mickey Moran moved on from Derry to Sligo, where he reached the Connacht final in 1997. After four seasons there, he moved on to Donegal. His stint with Donegal was a short one – just two years – but while the team didn't win in Ulster, under his leadership, the techniques and ideas he imparted to the players resonated with one man in particular, Jim McGuinness, who was coming to the end of his playing career and looking ahead to future managerial days. For Moran, there were to be further short-lived spells with Derry, Mayo and Leitrim, including an All-Ireland semi-final appearance with Derry in 2004 and a Connacht title and All-Ireland final appearance in 2006 with Mayo.

While rightly regarded as one of the game's leading coaches, Moran's influence on the game has spread farther afield. The work that himself and John Morrison passed on, in terms of modern training techniques and ideas, bears a direct lineage to Joe Lennon's work done in previous decades. By training different counties in different provinces in the subsequent years, their thinking and approach to the game has disseminated to a wider audience, influencing the next generation in turn.

However, the rise of Armagh and Tyrone in the 2000s brought an increased emphasis on physicality and blanket defences and, suddenly, all other counties, including Kerry, were struggling to overcome the modern way of playing and trying to mimic what they were going up against. It's an approach that Moran is opposed to. Every coach needs to think for himself, he believes. The only thing is, this takes time, and it's not something that modern coaches are being given much of these days.

> *Teams are trying to stop the ones that have set or have raised the bar. They're not concentrating on going for their own style or trying to develop their own game plan. The thing is, the coaching of game plans, ways of beating another team and getting scores, is the most difficult thing to coach. You can do your strength and conditioning, you can do your skill work and small-sided teams, but in terms of being able to unlock defences, that takes a lot of time and effort, it's not just a matter of walking it through in a matter of days.*

But ultimately, it comes down to the players and what they want to achieve. A bridge was crossed that night in Derry in 1993 after their hammering at the hands of Donegal in the league. Changes were needed and it was the players who stood up to be counted, and that, ultimately, was the difference.

'You have to motivate them and to get them to buy into what you're about,' says Moran. 'Because at the end of the day, that's what coaching is about. You can only set the parameters, you can only set the guidelines, but if the players don't buy into it and don't take it on board and don't push things, then you're going nowhere. It's okay when things are going well, but when things are not going well, can you think on your feet and change things or can you turn it around? That's what real coaching is about.

'Part of man-management is actually unannounced to the players, you have to look inside his own head because despite all the tactics of the day sometimes it's just a matter of facing the moment. You need players who can face the moment and say, "Right, I've got to roll up the sleeves here, just have to absolutely forget about the rain and just go for this. You just have to put your body on the line and mentally just say, to hell with it, and just go for it."'

Ulster football's glorious years in the 1990s lasted just one more season, when Down won their second All-Ireland in three years, and it was to be another eight years before the Ulster counties would return to dominate. Then it would be under different managers and with different counties, but the message for the future of Gaelic football was becoming clear: Ulster was producing the minds that were thinking and influencing the future development of the game and soon the other provinces would be playing catch-up.

For now, though, Ulster's rising was to be confined to the early 1990s while traditional powers such as Kerry, Dublin and Galway sought to leave their imprint on the All-Ireland series with titles in the remainder of the decade. None of it would be lasting, however. Success would only be fleeting as the last of the old-style football was being played out and Ulster would soon return to dominate.

Chapter 14

'If you change the way you think, you'll change the way you act'

As Mayo's painful experience in All-Ireland finals continued, with successive defeats in 1996 and 1997, a Mayo man was ready to oversee the next All-Ireland success for a Connacht county, except it was to be in the colours of Galway as they captured their first title since the great three-in-a-row side of 1964–1966.

John O'Mahony had made his name as a manager of some experience and clout with his native Mayo back in the 1980s when he took charge of their under-21 team and guided them to All-Ireland success in their first year and reaching the final again the following year only to lose to Cork. Four years later, when the Mayo senior job came up, O'Mahony was called upon to see if he could end the county's barren years and follow through on the team's promise and potential of previous seasons.

As a teacher and communicator, O'Mahony was at the top of the game. He had a plan, which he set out, but then, most importantly, he sought to empower the individuals and the group to buy into it and implement it from within. He is a people person first and foremost, as described by his ex-players, while also being autocratic and the boss – ultimately it's up to the players to follow through on his messages.

He's a natural leader, someone who has the self-confidence and belief to stand up in front of a group of people and say, 'Follow me, I know the way', and it's no coincidence that he ended up in politics, becoming a TD for Fine Gael, representing Mayo in the 2007 general election. Out of the frying pan of inter-county management and into the fire of politics, some would say. 'In sport they might knife you in the back,' he jokes, 'and in politics they'll knife you in the front.'

He took Galway to three All-Ireland finals in four years. Some would say that team was full of such talent that it took very little to lead them to Sam Maguire success, but for the game's great managers such as O'Mahony, success comes no matter what the era, the age group or standard. From Mayo to Leitrim to Galway to St Nathy's, his CV is one of success. For such managers, it is more than about being in the right place at the right time, there's an x-factor in their DNA that sees them take on a group of players in almost any setting and turn them into champions.

O'Mahony was your typical GAA man, Gaelic football was his only hobby and as a kid, and as a boarder at St Nathy's, he was always kicking a ball around. His inter-county career saw him win minor and under-21 All-Irelands with Mayo before graduating to the seniors, playing in losing Connacht finals in 1973 and 1975. With the success of the under-21s, eleven of the team were thrown into the seniors for the 1975 season and it was, he says, too much too soon for many of them to be expected to win at senior level. O'Mahony's own playing career faded away and it soon became apparent to him that he needed another means to continue his involvement in the game.

He was St Nathy's club secretary, trained the team and did some refereeing, but it was as a manager that he was to get the buzz that made him realise that this was what he was going to pursue. He quietly learned his trade in the club scene with Ballaghaderreen and at St Nathy's, flying under the radar, trying things out, learning about management and communication skills along the way.

'I got a huge buzz out of getting fellas to improve themselves collectively and as individuals,' he says. 'I remember the first club success I had was with a minor Ballaghaderreen side – it was a divisional round robin competition in 1976 and nearly forty years later, I'm still remembering it. We played Charlestown in the first round and they hammered us, but then, later on, we beat them in the final. Knowing we'd come so far and improved so much, seeing the progress the lads made having applied themselves, that gave me the greatest pleasure.'

Just a few years later and he was asked to manage the Mayo under-21s, a big step up from club level.

> I knew if I got the opportunity, the next thing I wanted to do was manage at county level. I managed at club level, got to county finals and then got the Mayo under-21 job. Liam O'Neill, who had been the manager, had stepped up to the seniors and must have seen me in the club scene, he asked me would I put my name forward. I did and in our first year, we won the All-Ireland in 1983 – that springboarded me into the limelight, so to speak.

The success O'Mahony achieved in just two years showed that he wasn't out of his depth, and despite stepping down after the final defeat to Cork four years later, he returned to the one position he coveted the most when the Mayo senior job became available. Having won the All-Ireland in 1983 as under-21s, this was a group of players whom O'Mahony knew well but they had never fulfilled their potential, the closest being an All-Ireland semi-final defeat to Dublin in 1985. Time was ticking and, by 1988, they needed to win quickly if they were to win anything. But having had the Midas touch for so long, things didn't begin well as the team were relegated from Division One.

'I remember the heads were down and it was a huge challenge for me and the team,' O'Mahony recalls. 'The final games were against Kerry in Ennis and they beat us and then we also lost to Armagh. But I remember saying to the guys, "We can still win a Connacht championship", and we did, beating Roscommon. We then played Meath, the All-Ireland champions, in the semi-final.'

Meath were reigning champions and hardened and experienced pros, and after only forty-five minutes, they had Mayo beaten into the ground, ten points to the good.

'Only when the game was gone did we start playing and we got to within five points,' says O'Mahony. 'They had relaxed and started to play but, up to that point, everything that could go wrong did go wrong. I remember afterwards asking, "Why did it happen like that? Why did we allow ourselves to be humiliated for those first forty-five minutes?" Then I realised it was all about belief and confidence, it was the head not the body. We were as fit as them but effectively we didn't believe.'

The power of self-belief is a recurring theme for O'Mahony's teams and their successes. If the players bought in to what he was saying to them, if they really believed within themselves, then there was no saying how far they could go. However, it wasn't something that he alone could give them and so he decided to introduce a radical new approach by bringing in a sports psychologist to deal with the demons inside the players' heads.

We had to bring it in secretly even then. If word got out that Mayo was using a team psychologist, you'd have been

committed yourself. Bill Cogan was our psychologist, he
was in HR in Digital in Galway and had an interest in the
mind and motivation and that sort of thing. He was from
Scotland and didn't have a clue about football, but I met
him in the winter of 1988 and told him what I wanted. He
was there for the 1989 season and made a huge difference
in turning around how players viewed themselves. We had
to swear the guys to secrecy on it, it was a radical advance,
but no Connacht team had won an All-Ireland since Galway
in the 1960s and for Mayo since the 1950s, so something
radical was needed. Different rumours did get out, but we
just denied it all.

We needed to maximise each individual's potential and to
gel it collectively and we worked on that constantly from the
spring onwards, using techniques like visualisation, one-to-
one sessions and team meetings. We also used motivational
speakers, and brought in Ireland's triple-crown-winning
manager, Mick Doyle, to talk about winning and what it
took to win. He spoke off the top of his head and he was
brilliant and was able to talk about how Irish rugby had
succeeded. The guys could relate to what he was telling
them and that too made a huge difference.

The effect was immediate, with O'Mahony's Mayo team
successfully defending their Connacht title, the first time the county
had done that since 1951. Was it an omen for what was to come?
Just as that 1950s team had succeeded at All-Ireland level, so too
would they – O'Mahony set Sam Maguire as the target.

'As a manager of Mayo, if you won Connacht your job was
safe, All-Irelands weren't on the horizon,' says O'Mahony. 'But I
felt we had to look at pushing the bar higher and, in 1989, when
we won Connacht again, the big barrier became the semi-final

against Tyrone. But I was confident that year, we had corrected our mistakes, addressed the belief and psychological thing and so I was confident. After all, if you change the way you think, you'll change the way you act. Tyrone walked into the trap, they were super-confident – and there were even T-shirts printed in advance looking ahead to the final. But we beat them.'

Reaching their first final in thirty-eight years was a major milestone for Mayo, they had banished memories of 1985 and they were facing a Cork team that were now into their third successive All-Ireland final. Having lost the previous two to Meath, the favourites tag rested with Cork now that the Leinster men were gone.

'We missed an open goal and didn't take a few good chances that came our way,' remembers O'Mahony, but the three-point defeat still rankles as one that got away. 'We didn't win it, it's as simple as that. I've digested it and looked back on it only in recent years and ultimately we lost by three points. But if Mayo had won that day, we would have gone on to more titles and the barrier would have been broken through for the county.'

As it stands, the anguish for Mayo football has continued since that final in 1989. There have been five more All-Ireland final losses – in 1996, 1997, 2004, 2006 and 2012 – each one more painful than the last. *Will this be the year we rid ourselves of the hoodoo?* they have wondered each time, but by the end of the seventy minutes they are staring another failure in the face. But as O'Mahony recalls, talk and expectations of All-Irelands within Mayo at that time were non-existent – Connacht was the sum of the ambitions – but their double provincial success in 1988 and 1989 changed that. O'Mahony had raised expectations and, with them, the spectre of 1951 has haunted them ever since.

If there's a blot for O'Mahony, it must be 1989. Up until then, he had been cruising in terms of managerial accomplishments with under-21 All-Ireland success, then senior Connacht titles, and having addressed the mental-belief issues in the team over the winter and spring, it seemed inevitable that the Sam Maguire would be next on his list of achievements. It wasn't to be. For Mayo the what-ifs continued for another twenty-plus years. 1989 was O'Mahony's best chance of an All-Ireland with that particular team and they knew it. Shortly afterwards, the team broke up with some retiring and new players coming in, and the rebuilding process had to start all over again.

Mayo's time had come and gone and a resurgent Roscommon in Connacht, who had lost the two previous finals, went on to capture their own two-in-a-row, defeating Mayo in a replay in O'Mahony's last year in charge. He stepped down after four years, a tenure which had begun so brightly and promised so much, but which ultimately faded out after the 1989 All-Ireland final defeat.

For O'Mahony to end up in Leitrim just two years later in 1993 seemed the unlikeliest of destinations and yet the success he was to achieve with the Connacht minnows was to seal his reputation forever in the game as someone whose managerial talents really could transcend the traditional big counties and be put into practice with lesser lights.

I would never have thought about managing an outside team. And I was surprised to be asked by Leitrim if I would be interested in managing them. I met the officials and some of the players, wanting to be convinced that they were ready to buy in to what I wanted to do and what they needed to do. They wanted a Connacht title and I wanted to be convinced of it, but I also knew that in 1990 and 1991, they had run Roscommon very close; they had won an All-Ireland B championship and the standard of football in the county had been lifted. The danger is sometimes you come in with

a track record of success and people think it's a given when
you arrive that it will also follow.

   But I met the Leitrim officials and players and felt they
were very passionate. In the first year, I had to deal with
a lot of ingrained doubt, this thing of it being acceptable
that you got a moral victory by running Galway to a few
points. I wanted to get that out of their system but it took a
while. One of the things I did was put together newspaper
headlines about Leitrim's Connacht championship over the
years and it didn't make for impressive reading. I was trying
to get over to the players, asking them, 'What script do you
want to write here?' I was trying to empower them, saying,
'You can change the script here if you want', but it was
ingrained for sixty-seven years so they were slow to come
around to change.

O'Mahony's methods were working, however. They beat Galway
in Tuam for the first time in forty-four years and it was then that the
players and management realised it could be done, the big powers
could be beaten, and in their own backyard. Leitrim's success
wasn't just a Connacht storyline, even the national newspapers were
latching on to it, running with images of that successful day on the
front pages the following Monday. The fairytale hit a roadblock,
however, in the next game against Roscommon, described as a
'setback' by O'Mahony, 'but importantly, the project was up and
running'.

'The key to success with Leitrim was in the mind,' explains
O'Mahony. All these years later and it's hard to fathom just what
impact Leitrim's achievements in 1994 had on the county but also
on the wider footballing landscape. The 1990s were a historic period
in Gaelic Games with previously unheralded minnows in both
hurling and football coming out of the woodwork and disrupting

the natural order. John Maughan achieved miracles when Clare won only their second Munster football championship two years previously, beating Kerry in an historic final. In hurling, Clare won their first Munster crown in over sixty years and then followed it up with All-Ireland successes in 1995 and 1997, while Offaly and Wexford were also to win the Liam McCarthy Cup, keeping the traditional Cork-Tipperary-Kilkenny powers in the shade. It showed just what could be achieved with good organisation, fitness and belief, and even with a limited talent pool, if they believed in themselves, anything was possible. For Leitrim, it was O'Mahony who made that possible.

'You were dealing with players who wouldn't have been on Galway or Mayo panels. 'In the stronger counties, players have a shorter time to prove themselves and adapt. But in counties like Leitrim you sit down with the players and say to them, "You need to improve and adapt better because you are going to be on our squad either way." It wasn't as if, after the defeat in 1993 that I could drop five or six players.'

Identity to the county was also key.

I always tried to tap into the culture of the county, tap into the history and what resonated with them. I got videos made of landmarks and scenic places in Leitrim, and I was saying to them, 'You have a chance of rewriting the history of the county here.'

Then there was the self-empowerment.

In my first couple of years, we had as many meetings as training sessions to get inside their heads. They would have set targets for themselves, such as how many points they could score in the next match or how much they could restrict

*their opposition. You build on that, and then come back to
them if they didn't achieve the targets, asking why not?*

*Importantly, it was the players who set the targets in terms
of what they could achieve as a group and as individuals.
After we beat Galway in 1993, I got the headlines from the
national papers and local ones. I enlarged the headlines
and there was one particular one that said: 'Miracle Men,
how the old traditions are being thrown away. First Clare,
then Donegal, now enter Leitrim.' I put it in front of them
and said, 'Look at that, ye built that, ye wrote that script, ye
made that happen.'*

The icing on the cake came in 1994 when Leitrim captured their
first Connacht title in sixty-seven years beating O'Mahony's
native Mayo by two points. Along the way, they had also beaten
Roscommon and Galway, all three big guns of Connacht dispatched
by the minnows of Leitrim, making their success all the sweeter.

For O'Mahony, dealing with a limited talent pool showed the
power of the mind if players could believe. If he could achieve that
in Leitrim, the sky would be the limit with one of the country's
traditional powerhouses.

Three years later, O'Mahony was in Tuam to see Mayo beat
Galway in the Connacht championship. Galway had never won
an All-Ireland since the heyday of the three-in-a-row 1960s team
but as he watched Mayo's archrival lose out, he knew that there
was an extremely talented bunch of players coming through. If he
could harness that potential and ally it with the mental belief that
Leitrim showed, then surely he could fulfil a lifetime's ambition of
capturing an All-Ireland.

'I remember when the Galway job became available later in the
year,' recalls O'Mahony. 'And thinking if I could get it, I'll win an
All-Ireland with them.'

What his native county would have given to have tasted the success that O'Mahony was about to bring to Galway. At the interview for the job, there was still suspicion of hiring an outsider, especially one from Mayo – despite O'Mahony's record of success. 'Why should we appoint a Mayo man to this job?' they asked him suspiciously.

'I presume it's because you want to win an All-Ireland?' was O'Mahony's jaunty reply.

They did want to win one, so much so that the officials managed to overcome their reticence and appoint Galway's first outsider as manager. It was a decision they would not regret.

'I never thought they would hire an outsider,' admits O'Mahony. 'But when I was given the job, I felt that a quick impression was needed to be made, the team needed to get winning and get confidence up and the league was the vehicle for that. I met the players, told them of my plans, and took it from there.'

'When Johno came in, he brought with him phenomenal experience – he had the kudos,' says Ray Silke, who was team captain in O'Mahony's first season with Galway. 'When he joined, everyone got on board, even the county board were eating out of his hand – they had put all their eggs in that basket and they were going to make sure it worked.

'We needed somebody to put the different pieces together and that's what Johno did. He came in and he facilitated, he put a structure in place to enable us to achieve. Planning, organisation, leadership, motivation, he brought all that with him. And he didn't suffer fools gladly either. My first training session, I had to tell him I was going away with my fiancée to Texas for two weeks. It had been booked and paid for nine months previously and on Tuesday I had to tell him I was leaving on the Friday for two weeks. He said to me, "That's very disappointing, you'll have to do your own training out there, won't you?" So straightaway he was laying down the line. There was a certain amount of ruthlessness, he was the boss.'

But the team were hungry for success, they knew they had the players, they just needed somebody to pull it all together for them.

'I remember something that Bosco McDermott, who had managed Galway previously, used to always preach to the players which was "the daily bread", as he used to call it,' remembers Silke. 'He tried to drum into us that playing inter-county was not about Tuesday, Thursday, Saturday. It was a daily thing of diet, lifestyle, going to bed early, of living your life the right way to ensure that you could make the most out of your Gaelic football career. I remember in 1994 in the gym and we had to pull our own body-weight up the ropes and I couldn't do it, just couldn't physically do it. Then I started going to the gym three or four times a week, built myself up and the following February, I pulled myself up the ropes and Bosco saw me do it and then he knew I had bought into it. And I think managers need to know that you are buying into it and to see the proof of that also. It's a lifestyle choice and ethos to life overall for the good of your game. I remember Seán Óg de Paor taking it to extremes, taking the coleslaw out of his BLT sandwich. That's how much people can buy into it.'

'What I did was recognise what the players needed to do and motivated them and outlined to them what they had to do,' says O'Mahony. 'Galway up to 1998 had won only one Connacht title and that was a disgrace for Galway. You had fellas like Ja Fallon, Seán Óg de Paor, Tomás Mannion hitting their peak and being beaten by Leitrim. They were saying to me they wanted an end to the bad old days. The year before I went to see Galway versus Mayo, it was Michael Donnellan's first championship game, and then there was Pádraic Joyce, Derek Savage who were all in their twenties; they weren't on that team in Tuam but I would have known them from schools football and I was thinking if I could get these guys and gel the two elements between the younger and older lads, then we'd be onto something.'

With the talent and hunger already there, O'Mahony set about not radically overhauling things, but tweaking and perfecting. With such a talented forward line at their disposal, it was about getting fast, direct ball into Joyce, Savage and Fallon.

'It was partly to do with pushing the mental bar higher to get the little things absolutely right,' explains O'Mahony. 'There was an acceptance amongst the players of the very fine line for success. For instance, when Mayo beat Galway in Tuam in 1997, the Galway team had a tactic whereby the goalkeeper Martin McNamara would kick the kickouts very close to the sideline but the ball would go out over the sideline a good few times during that game. Then the following year, I asked Martin about the tactic and he said he wouldn't do that anymore as it contributed to losing the game. But I said, "What about if we try to do it properly?" It was practised and practised and in the second half of the All-Ireland against Kildare, we won five kickouts to perfection of what they had done wrong the previous year. It was just about fine-tuning it.'

While being regarded as autocratic by some, O'Mahony also wanted to empower the players, show them that he trusted their instincts and talent.

'Michael Donnellan's thing of coming back to get the ball in the full-back line wasn't my idea,' he says. 'But I tried to empower the players on the field of play. Even with our long-ball play. Donnellan was getting frustrated that the ball was going in over his head, but to achieve a certain tactic, there's still an awful lot of other play around that and I remember Ja Fallon telling him it wasn't going to be an issue. It gets to the stage where players would suggest trying things, and you'd say, "Have a go at it." My philosophy of management is if you get players to buy into a system where it is coming from them at times, they will implement it far better than if you come in with a dictatorial approach saying if you don't do it this way you're off.'

For Pat Comer, who had been with Galway teams since 1983, O'Mahony's arrival signalled a new and novel approach, and the new manager succeeded in convincing his players of its usefulness.

'When John O'Mahony was first signed up, I would have been totally against it myself personally as a Galway player,' admits Comer. 'It was the first time that they went out of the camp to get an outsider and secondly the manager before that, Val Daly, was a close friend of mine. But part of O'Mahony's success was in the detail of the small things. The training format was new to us in that we would train very hard and then nothing the week before a game, we had one training session on the Wednesday and then we would get together on the Saturday.

'When we would get together, he would literally, once or twice, walk us through moves with the starting fifteen lined out on the pitch and to be honest, it was all a bit silly to us. But it was novel and this mental mapping on the field, mapping out if you get the ball, what is the first thing you are going to try to do, kick it in or send it up, was a bit of creative thinking and a fresh approach. He had a folder under his arm and he kept records, plotting people's form, and he would have made calculated decisions rather than just impulsive ones. I think he was no smarter than anybody else, but just the attention to detail was what stood out. There is no one way to success. It's like the old Buddha saying, "There is no way to happiness, happiness is a way." It's about the journey; this life is all about the journey and about doing your best every time and working hard.'

'All that matters at that stage is just the god-damn thing,' says Silke. 'I didn't get on that well with Johno but you don't give a shit, you'll work so damn hard for it, you don't want to step off the plate because you've put so much into it. I remember an argument with him once where he said that Leitrim could have won the All-Ireland in 1994 and I said, "Come on, John, that's crazy talk", but he really absolutely believed it with such conviction and that's what you need, someone of such conviction who believes so strongly that you're going to succeed.'

Their first championship outing in 1998 was against Mayo in the Connacht quarter-finals and there would be no better game to see how far Galway had come since O'Mahony took over. This time it was the Tribesmen who came through, winning by three points, and an important marker had been laid down. Leitrim were dispatched by fourteen points, before it took a replay to overcome Roscommon in the final with three players – Donnellan, Savage and Joyce, who had only been on the fringes the year before – scoring 1–11 of the 1–17 total. Derry were comfortably beaten by five points in the All-Ireland semi-final, leaving Galway to face a Mick O'Dwyer-inspired Kildare in the final.

The story of the season was O'Dwyer leading the resurgence of Kildare, managing them to their first Leinster title in fifty-six years and first All-Ireland appearance since 1935. O'Dwyer was working his magic again and the story would be complete if Glenn Ryan were to lift the Sam Maguire. It was a magnificent footballing occasion with only twenty-seven frees in total and the scoring feats of Pádraic Joyce and Ja Fallon outstanding on the day. Galway won out by four points – 1–14 to 1–10 – and despite Kildare's All-Ireland romance coming to an end, Galway were applauded widely for their style and approach to the game.

'Galway's All-Ireland victory will convince many that transferring the ball quickly and accurately by foot should be the principal method of moving the ball,' wrote Colm O'Rourke. Eugene McGee went even further, saying, 'The GAA should get down on its knees and give thanks for John O'Mahony and his gallant Galway players ... And if Galway's example is followed by others then maybe Gaelic football will regain its former greatness.'

McGee's comments and the outpouring of goodwill towards Galway's success was a riposte to the way the game had developed over a number of years, first with the robust physicality of Meath and Cork's rivalry and then with the success of the Ulster counties' short hand-passing style.

Even though Galway would go on to reach two further All-Irelands, winning their second title under O'Mahony in 2001 as the first beneficiaries of the back-door qualifier system that had been introduced that same year, those who believed that Galway's success would represent a new development and breakthrough for the game with a focus on the catching-and-kicking game were to be disappointed. Ulster football hadn't gone away and, in Armagh, Crossmaglen were making waves under their new manager, Joe Kernan, while in Tyrone Mickey Harte was having great success with the county's underage teams.

But that was for the future. In 1998, the goodwill surrounding Kildare and Galway's rise meant there was a yearning for a return to a more expansive, kicking style of play. It has been a constant point of discussion throughout the history and development of Gaelic football, with certain styles more successful when espoused by certain counties in different eras. The glamour and rivalry of the Dublin–Kerry years represented a high point for the game (though not necessarily from a coaching perspective) and in the aftermath of the Meath–Cork–Ulster years, Galway's success was seen, hopefully, in some quarters, as a beacon of hope for a return to the 'good old days'.

Another unique element of Galway's victory that year was the remarkable capturing on film of their journey to All-Ireland success. Pat Comer was a documentary maker by trade and was in a unique position to record their story from within the dressing-room walls.

A Year 'Til Sunday is probably the greatest Irish sports documentary made. For the first time ever, fans could get an insider's glimpse of just what it meant and what it took to go all the way to lift the Sam Maguire. Incredibly, it was never even formally sanctioned by O'Mahony; Pat Comer had an idea for this story and just started showing up at training sessions with his camera, leaving it under a towel on the pitch or in a bag in the dressing room.

'There was no discussion with anybody, we were just doing it,' Comer explains. 'I used to bring it onto the pitch under a towel, not trying to hide it, but just letting the lads know that I wasn't being brazen about it. I felt a little uncomfortable myself doing it because I wanted to concentrate on my own training. I would be in goals, there would be a game on and I would start shooting with the camera; as soon as the ball went past the forty-five, I would have to drop the camera and resume playing.'

Incredibly, the year of the project was also the year that Galway went all the way and lift Sam Maguire, so what started out as a side project ended up becoming the first fly-on-the-wall documentary of an All-Ireland-winning team.

'There was a bit of serendipity to everything, there was no grand scheme,' Comer admits. 'When we got to the final we just cut a short piece together that we showed to RTÉ and asked if it would have the potential for a story. There was a very quick turnaround in terms of the documentary, the only time that it really kicked in was the week of the final; even on the day of the final, we had six crews going. When I say crews, some of them were just mates with cameras over in London or New York, but those things helped build up the scene and then we had the two camera crews in Galway and one in the Curragh and then two in Dublin and then me, hammering around the dressing room and stands after the warm up.'

The remarkable thing about the footage that Comer shot was how unaware the players were of the camera being there. He was part of the squad himself and slipped into the scenery just as any of the other players did.

'The first game against Mayo, O'Mahony is giving a speech before we go out and the camera is on the bench and there is a body right in front it, that's me trying to hide the camera from O'Mahony! I wasn't being deceitful, I just honestly believed in the story and I was taking a chance, taking a punt, and I was the oldest guy by a country mile on the team and I think that he kind of respected that this is what Pat does, sort of thing. I was doing a documentary with the D'Unbelievables at the time and I had to tell him, "Look, John, I am recording these guys and it could be two o'clock in the morning and it could end up being a bit of a session, I might have a pint with these guys and I know that it is not kosher, and I just want to tell you that." I wasn't going to enjoy a rock'n'roll lifestyle and then try and be a county footballer, it would have been on my conscience, I wanted to get my excuse in before I was charged.

'Fair play to him, he said to me, "I think it's going to be an interesting nine months, Pat, and I think you should stick around." I thought he would say, "Pat, fair enough, I appreciate you saying it to me and we will find someone else", but he didn't. So I don't know what he saw in me, maybe because I was a voice, spoke with a bit of experience, and he just needed someone like that. I wasn't a rebel, I wasn't against him. I would have been on board. Whilst I had reservations of him coming in, once he was the manager, I was committed to him, like any player.

'He respected players' integrity and he gave them a mature way of dealing with it, saying look this is your opportunity, you have to bring something to the table here and we will give you every chance to do that, it wasn't like do it my way or the highway. At the time Kevin Walsh was missing a few training sessions because he couldn't get off work as a garda. O'Mahony said to him, "Well sure, look, what time do you finish?" and he said, "I'm not finished till twelve", to which O'Mahony said, "That's no problem, I'll wait. We'll be finished at nine, but I'll hang on here for you." O'Mahony's approach was there was no way out of it but instead of bollocking the guy out of it or letting him off, that was a fantastic way of dealing with it.'

While Pat Comer never asked for formal permission for his documentary, O'Mahony was aware of it and allowed it as it was one of their own doing the filming. He trusted Comer, he knew that was what he did and he never once asked for editorial say or control.

'We did give him a viewing of it before we went to print,' says Comer. 'That was out of respect. And he did have concerns with the language because he was a school teacher, but it was just the natural language of the dressing room. I remember at the time we were in a bit of a dilemma because if we took out all the curse words we would lose the impact sometimes. The editor was great when it came to cutting them out, and instead he would put in a little cough, or maybe the sound of a stud mark on the ground and we trailed the f-word.

'There was one scene where O'Mahony was reading the paper and someone had written an article about Galway after they drew at Roscommon, saying Galway were "fancy dans". O'Mahony lifted the paper and declared, "There's only one f–ing answer for that." I heard the most fantastic stories about people buying the documentary at Christmas time and to this day people come up to me and say, "It's my favourite film", which is a wonderful thing to hear.'

After the high of 1998, the following season ended in disappointment when it was Mayo who got the upper hand on them in the Connacht final, beating them by four points.

In 2000, they came back to regain the provincial title, beating Leitrim and then met Kildare in the semi-final, beating them once more. This time they faced Kerry in the All-Ireland final and despite being seven points down at one stage, Galway clawed their way back into it to force a replay, only to lose that by four points. Although of little consolation to the Tribesmen, the standout moment from that game was one of the best goals seen in an All-Ireland final when Galway worked an eight-man move from their own goal line to end with Declan Meehan scoring to the back of the net.

Just as Pete McGrath put it up to his Down players in the 1990s, asking them did they want their legacy tainted by only having a single All-Ireland to their names, O'Mahony and his panel felt they hadn't fully done themselves justice by collecting just the one Sam Maguire, but time was running out.

'With John, his first few years were his best years,' says Ray Silke. 'It gets harder as time goes on as the players are hearing the same voice. *Ní bhíonn in aon rud ach seal* – there's only a while in everything, as the Irish saying goes. Life moves on.'

And only for the introduction of the back door system, the legacy for Galway and O'Mahony might have remained at only the one All-Ireland. For in the 2001 Connacht championship, they were to lose to Roscommon at the semi-final stage but for the first time were given a reprieve, playing Wicklow in the second round of the qualifiers. From there, they built up a momentum, beating Armagh, Cork, Roscommon (gaining some revenge in the process) and then Derry in the semi-final, to leave them facing Meath in their third All-Ireland final.

Unlike Galway, Meath had won their provincial crown, and there were unhappy rumblings in the game about the appearance of Galway in the All-Ireland final, as they had already lost in Connacht. But this was the new system, designed to appeal to

GAA fans and give teams that had spent so long in training for the championship a second chance.

Galway didn't need to be asked twice after they were given the opportunity and overwhelmed Seán Boylan's Meath after Nigel Nestor was sent off for the Royal County, with Pádraic Joyce giving another masterclass in scoring, notching up eight points in a row. This superb Galway team were no longer one-hit wonders and proved that their legacy in the record books would go down as double All-Ireland winners.

The All-Ireland victory of the Galway under-21s in 2002 proved that there was more talent coming through the county and O'Mahony must have relished the thought of building another side capable of going all the way. However, as the class of 1998 moved on, the same success wasn't to be replicated and despite going on to win two Connacht titles in a row (the first time Galway had done this since 1986–1987), the qualifier system meant that it was becoming harder to win All-Irelands. Plus, the football being played was starting to change radically with the rise of Armagh and Tyrone.

In 2001, O'Mahony's team had beaten Armagh by a point on their way to All-Ireland success and yet within a year Crossmaglen's Joe Kernan had taken charge and turned the Ulster county into a ferociously ruthless, tightly organised team that captured its first ever All-Ireland in 2002. The effect and impression they made was immediate.

'The biggest change to come into the game tactically was with Armagh in 2002,' says O'Mahony. 'And from there now it's gone to a whole different level. There's good and bad in that. Donegal in 2012 epitomised the good by taking on board the criticisms and fine-tuning it by being more offensive and more up-front. However, the danger is everyone thinks this is the only way to win and play. But you must never forget the talent at your disposal and that it is still a simple game.

'As a manager and coach you're instilling into players, "Don't lose possession", and how is that done? By short passing, but the problem is much of it is across the pitch. I always encouraged players to keep possession but not by playing five-yard hand-passes. You can go down the wrong road if you take certain principles to the limits and, as a manager, you also have to create a system to allow the talents built in the team to express itself.'

There were no greater expressive talents than those of Fallon, Joyce and Donnellan and, on their day, Galway were a joy to behold. But would they have won playing the same way in 2002 or 2003 when the different style of Armagh and Tyrone was dominating?

'I often wondered would Galway have won with the same team and tactics in 2002–2003,' admits O'Mahony. 'I think it would have been more difficult to win it, to be honest. We would have been challenged by it and dealt with it in our own way. But would we have won? I don't know ...'

After stepping down in 2003 after six seasons in charge, Mayo were the coming force in Connacht and would reach two All-Irelands in the next three years. But the *House of Pain*, as sports writer Keith Duggan memorably described Mayo's All-Ireland pathos, continued and in 2007 they sought out O'Mahony to provide that final answer. This time it couldn't be done, though he points out that the team were in transition and he was trying to build a new one, a process that was going to take time. Time isn't what Mayo football wanted to be waiting on and O'Mahony's new career into politics, after the 2007 general election, meant that time wasn't on his side either, nor was everyone in the county pulling in the one direction.

'There were certain members of the county board who didn't want you to succeed,' O'Mahony believes. 'You didn't have that unity of purpose that I would have found in Galway or in Leitrim. That was the difficulty and when you are in politics, people start imagining things about who should be given games or trials or whatever. I would never have allowed politics inside the door when I was in Mayo, I wouldn't allow that to happen, but reality and perception are two totally different things.'

After four seasons in charge and with one Connacht title won, expectations for O'Mahony to succeed went beyond provincial titles. Critics asked why he wasn't winning All-Irelands with Mayo when he'd done it with Galway. He stepped down after a shock defeat to Longford in the qualifiers in 2010, to concentrate on his political career full-time.

He sees similarities between his career as a manager and now his involvement in politics, the power of the group buy-in being particularly relevant.

In sport it's unbelievable the power a group of people have if they buy into something. On the Galway team that I managed, we had some ordinary players but because everyone bought into the collective, you can actually get a whole group carried across the line. I've never seen the same amount of buy-in and belief together than in my experience of successful sport.

What happens in sport is applicable in business, in life, in politics. It's the same characteristics that are needed to win: leadership, teamwork, individual excellence, trust. They're all there in the winning teams. Sport is a public examination of what you do behind closed doors for the rest of the year. You're in front of 85,000 people and every plan that's been hatched in those long winter nights is exposed, everything is there to be examined. In business, you can carry a loss from one year to another, but you can't do that in sport because the loss means you're out.

I always used to confront players with what winners do and what losers do. If you let in a goal in the first minute, which Leitrim did in the 1994 Connacht final, you have two choices – you can stay calm and try and put it right, or you can panic about it. If some of your team-mates make a mistake, you f– him out of it or you can encourage him. You have a choice when things happen in a match – you can either react this way or that way. And that's where the mind and psychology comes in, if you get fellas thinking in a certain way, the controllables are themselves and not the opposition. On the one side there's calm, encouragement, belief, team-play and on the other there's panic, blame and doubt. Winners do one; losers do the other. The question I ask is: which team do you want to play for?

Part V

Amateur Games, Professional Players

'Do not let what you cannot do interfere with what you can do.'

*John Wooden, record-winning UCLA basketball coach, revered
as one of the greatest coaches of all time*

Chapter 15

'Good teams don't have an escape route'

When you're losing year in, year out, when what you've always
tried isn't working, sometimes you're forced to confront tradition
head on. What's the point in sticking to tradition if it means always
being on the losing end come the final whistle?

Joe Kernan remembers the bad times. His commitment to
Armagh and Crossmaglen football was never in doubt, flying
home from London at weekends for games as a young player in
the 1970s when the team was unable at times to gather enough
players to fulfil their fixtures. From that low, the county began to
pick itself up, winning three Ulster titles in ten years and reaching
an All-Ireland final in 1977 only to be hammered by Dublin. Ulster
counties were so far behind Leinster and Munster that getting to
an All-Ireland semi-final was the height of their ambitions. After
Armagh in 1977, there was to be only one other Ulster county in an
All-Ireland final – Tyrone in 1986 – before the breakthrough years
of 1991–1994.

Joe Kernan had given seventeen years as a player to Armagh
football and, when he finally hung up his boots in 1987, he thought

he was leaving Armagh football behind him. But within a year, he was to be sucked back in when Paddy Moriarty, who was in charge, asked Kernan to give him a hand – and changed the rest of his GAA career forever.

'I didn't know I was going to go into management when I quit playing, that thought never entered my head,' Kernan says. 'But then I was doing nothing, so I said yeah to Paddy, it seemed a good idea. Sometimes, until somebody says something to you and opens your mind to it, you don't consider it. I thought to myself, *I'd like to get back into it. I can't play any more and hopefully what I've learned in seventeen years playing might be of benefit.* The three years with Paddy, I probably learned more in some cases than the next five years because coming in and seeing it from the other side was eye-opening.'

Although other counties were dominating – Donegal, Down and Derry especially – and despite Armagh's lack of success, Kernan's appetite had been whetted. The idea of managing, shaping and driving a bunch of players on, while studying the game, dissecting why some teams are better than others, became a source of fascination to him. So much for walking away from the game in retirement.

Crossmaglen dominated his life. It was (and is) the exemplar of where the GAA's club-community ideal was perfectly in harmony. The club was the community and the community was wrapped up in everything that the club did. The presence of the British army base on their grounds during the Troubles merely brought the people closer together; in dignity, they carried on their GAA commitments, not letting it stop them no matter what harassment or difficulties were encountered.

On the pitch, the Cross tradition was that of attractive football, a culture rooted in playing a kicking game, but one which was never tough enough to stand up to the rigours of more 'street football' from neighbours in the county or province.

'Everybody used to tell me that they would be supporting Cross, but Jesus it was tiring,' says Kernan. 'It used to be a great club, they were saying, and it was tiring not winning, everybody was feeling sorry for us.'

Crossmaglen had always been one of Armagh's leading lights, but success had become sporadic and when Joe Kernan took over management of the club side, it had been seven years since their last county championship. *Why was the club focusing only on one approach all the time?* Kernan pondered. Players were getting caught out and a new tactic and style was needed, with more emphasis on keeping possession and quick recycling of the ball.

'I was sick of losing and didn't have one problem going against the Cross tradition,' he says determinedly. 'I looked at the great teams, such as the Kerrys, the Meaths, the three Ulster teams that won in the 1990s, and you try and pick out what is good and will suit your team. We were going through traditional catch-and-kick and I had to change the boys' mindsets into thinking that you don't have to kick it all the time. To get out of trouble, it might take two short passes instead, it's all about move the ball, move the ball. When I was involved with Cross, it was seven days a week. Twenty-four hours a day, my mind was thinking about football.'

However, in the beginning, even those closest to him were questioning his tactics.

We were winning matches but not playing well because we didn't all click into the system. Thomas Cassidy, a good friend and colleague, said one night in the dressing room, 'Joe, Plan A isn't working. What's Plan B?' It stunned me coming from him, because I thought I had his full support, which I had, but he was getting frustrated too because not everybody believed. Some of the boys were coming to him and saying, 'We've got to go back to the old way of catching and kicks.' Later on, I met Thomas and I said, 'Listen to me now, this is the way this works: if Plan B doesn't work, do we go to Plan C? Do we go to Plan D? Because everybody looks for an escape route when our backs are to the wall. The good teams don't have an escape route, they join forces and their mental strength and their ability gets them through.'

Such was Kernan's belief in what he was doing, there was no Plan B. Plan A was going to work no matter what. It had to work, otherwise they would always be looking for excuses. They had thrown their hats over the wall and now they had no choice but to climb over to get them.

The one thing about Cross was that I got a team that was young. I had eleven or twelve young lads along with a few old heads who trusted me. I'll never forget the one night that was pivotal to everything that followed was when we had to face Mullaghbawn, our fiercest rivals; we had lost to them the previous year and the knives were out at Cross, everybody was questioning what I was doing. In the previous round, we had won 0-9, 0-8 and were very poor, it was a desperate game. I remember one of the parents saying to me afterwards, 'Joe, that's desperate, you can't win.' But I said, 'Did we lose today? No, we won - if we lose, then come to me and tell me about it.'

Next up was the showdown with Mullaghbawn. This was going to be their fiercest test yet but training on the Tuesday was not going well. Were they willing to stand up to the plate, answer the questions that were being asked of them?

*That Tuesday night, the training was dead. I pulled the
boys to one side and said, 'Boys I've a problem here. We
are now in a situation we wanted to be in. We were beaten
by Mullaghbawn last year and we wanted to prove them
wrong. I get the feeling you are all afraid of Mullaghbawn,
that you feel you can't beat them. If that's the way you feel,
we leave here right now because I'm not going to waste my
time.' Then one lad said, 'I'm f–ing not afraid of them.' And
I said, 'F–ing act like it then.' From that night on we turned
it around.*

*We played them and it was a battle – there was blood
spilled. But I tell you what, that night got them to think the
way I wanted them to think. Instead of crying twelve months
over, 'Why didn't we play well the last time? Why didn't
we beat them?' They went on, won this time around then
won in Ulster – something we had never done. Fair play to
Mullaghbawn, I was jealous of their success, but it turned
our boys around into saying, 'We're not afraid of them, we
can go for them.'*

Self-belief and never giving up are the central tenets of Kernan's
philosophy in life and football. He cites the example of Munster
rugby who for so long were so close to winning in Europe before
finally cracking it, then came Leinster's turn and now Ulster are
knocking on the door again. 'We got beaten for three years before
we won the three All-Ireland club titles. Was there much in it? No.'

Overcoming Mullaghbawn, who were reigning Ulster
champions, was like breaking through the mental barrier for
Kernan's team. They had shown to themselves that they could
win and overcome their own doubts and those on the outside. The
shackles had finally been loosened and what was to pour out has
been nothing short of historic and revolutionary and the benchmark
for every other club in Ireland since then.

In 1996, Crossmaglen went on to capture their first Armagh title in ten years, and followed it up with their first ever Ulster title, before, incredibly, going all the way and lifting the All-Ireland. It was an amazing season and turnaround in fortunes for the long-suffering Cross. Joe Kernan had got them playing to a new style, and though it may have had its detractors from the traditionalists, it was actually winning matches. And not only winning local battles, but becoming champions of the entire country, a feat never before achieved by an Armagh club.

However, nobody could have foreseen what Crossmaglen were set to achieve in the coming years. Having broken through in 1996, they went on to win a historic thirteen Armagh titles in a row, not losing a game in the Armagh club championship for fourteen years. When their run came to an end in 2009, their dominance didn't stall, and instead the club came back to regain the title in 2010.

After winning the first All-Ireland and then winning the second, reporters used to come to me and say, 'Joe, we know, everybody knows what Cross is going to do.' I said, 'That's good, but can they better it?'

And my challenge to my players was: 'Have we played to our full potential yet? Can we be better at what we do? We're ahead of everybody else playing this way but can we be better?

After we won the three All-Irelands, myself and my selectors, Ollie McEntee and Donal McKenna, sat down and Donal said we could win ten county titles and now we've actually won sixteen out of seventeen, six All-Irelands and ten Ulsters so far. But an awful lot of credit has to go to the players and the managers in each of those categories that came after me. We started it, but to continue it, to me that's the greatest legacy of all.

The Crossmaglen success was also having an effect on the county team and they captured the first Ulster title in seventeen years in 1999 and retained it for the first time in their history the following year. However, on both occasions Armagh fell in the All-Ireland semi-finals to the eventual winners – Meath in 1999 and then Kerry after a replay in 2000. They lost their Ulster title to Tyrone in 2001 at the quarter-final stage and were to lose again to the eventual champions, Galway, by just a point in the third round of the first year of the qualifiers. They were close but needed someone who could drive them on that extra mile if they were to fulfil their potential.

Brian McAlinden and Brian Canavan stepped down from the Armagh job and in November 2001 when the new manager was announced, there was only one name that people expected to hear. The question was now: could Joe Kernan bring the success of Crossmaglen to the county setup? This time, there was to be no questioning of his tactics or system. It had worked with Crossmaglen and didn't need three years of bedding down with the Armagh team. But could they overcome traditional club rivalries and unite together to win an All-Ireland title? It was to be the ultimate test for Kernan's philosophy and tactics.

Always looking to tweak and improve things where possible, Kernan had the idea of bringing the team away for sun training before the championship started. Bad weather had been playing havoc with training schedules, and with Kernan's first championship game against Tyrone, the reigning Ulster and league champions, looming, he needed to get the team together.

Winter training in the sun is nothing new nowadays, a week's training in the sun is seen as worth three or four weeks back at home and is a great opportunity for team bonding. From group sessions in the hospitals of Killarney and Ballinasloe in the 1930s to weeks in La Manga and Dubai in the 2000s, collective training has come a long way. However, Kernan's Armagh were sticking their necks out – they were one of the first teams to go abroad and so were inviting derision at the time. The sunshine boys and all that would be slung at them if 2002 didn't work out but it was just another of those edges that Kernan was looking for to get his team that extra inch.

One evening in Spain as the team was reviewing video of Tyrone, Kernan also knew that any worries about the team overcoming club rivalries for the cause of Armagh were well and truly buried.

Cross and Mullaghbawn hated each other, there was an awful rivalry, there was blood spilled. That night we were talking about unity and the bond that should be there when John McEntee stands up and says, 'I tell you what, whenever I'm wearing the Cross jersey and you're from Mullaghbawn, when we meet it'll be head to head, but when we are wearing an Armagh jersey, I'll never let you down.' And there was a silence in the room. It seemed like ten minutes but it was only about ten seconds. You could hear a pin drop, the hair stuck up on the back of everybody's head and I said, 'Right, boys, that's enough for tonight.' As soon as they went out the door, I said to Paul and John, 'We have these boys, now, they're there.' It was one of those moments where you know that, right now, they're all thinking the one way and they won't let each other down.

A few weeks later, Armagh beat Tyrone by three points in a replay having scored an equalising goal in injury time in the first game, and then went on to recapture the Ulster title. They beat Sligo in the All-Ireland quarters before facing Dublin in the semi-final. The last time Armagh had been in Croke Park was the 1977 annihilation by

Dublin, a defeat that spurred Joe Kernan into the winning mindset with his own teams years later. This time, it was a much tighter affair, with the resilience and mental strength of Armagh seeing them over the line – albeit with Dublin's Ray Cosgrove shooting an injury-time free that hit off the bar.

Winning games in the last five minutes was becoming a hallmark of Kernan's team – they never gave up the fight and knew they could win a game in the last moments if needed.

We won more matches in the last five minutes and you know why? Some teams are in front to play safe. It was the same with the good Meath team in the 1980s, you played to the final whistle; teams would know that and they would retreat back and we pushed forward. Francie Bellew used to push up to the middle of the field, give a pass, draw somebody to give a pass to and that was opening up space. We got them to believe that you can play bad for sixty-five minutes and still win it in the last five.

The All-Ireland final against Kerry was one fraught with nerves for the players – there were decades of disappointment and hope resting on their shoulders. 'Everything about that day heightens the worst emotions possible … It's more than a test of footballing skill,' wrote Oisín McConville afterwards. But Armagh had to dig the game out of the bag – after losing the inspirational John McEntee they were trailing by four points with Oisín McConville missing a penalty. 'I thought of Bill McCorry who missed a penalty in the 1953 All-Ireland,' recalled McConville.

This time it was different. This was a team built off the back of Crossmaglen's All-Ireland successes, a team that had been winning Ulster titles and had been steeled and prepared mentally to deal with situations going against them. In the dressing room at half-time, they weren't allowed to feel sorry for themselves as Joe Kernan pulled out his runner-up medal from 1977 telling them he was ashamed of it, throwing it against the wall. Kerry waited out on the pitch while Kernan roused his players. 'Do you want a runner-up medal? Do you want to be losers like I was?'

Remembering 1953 and 1977, Armagh threw everything at Kerry. The teams exchanged points for the first twenty minutes and Kerry were still four ahead. Then it all changed with fifteen to go. McConville, determined not to be remembered for having cost Armagh the 2002 final, played a one-two with Paul McGrane before burying the ball into the back of the net. They were only a point down. Kerry were to remain scoreless for the rest of the game as Armagh squeezed the game from their grasp with Ronan Clarke and Steve McDonnell scoring the vital points that gave them a one-point victory and the county's first All-Ireland title.

Redemption at last, thought Kernan, going back over thirty years of defeat and humiliation. He had changed the mindset of his club and now his county. He had made them believe; he made them tougher; he steeled them to become winners. Most importantly, he had ditched tradition and found a new way to play, a way that meant winning. And it had all paid off in just his first year in charge.

'There were a number of things that Joe improved in 2002,' explains Enda McNulty, the defender and All Star winner that year with Armagh. 'We improved tactically, there is no question about that. Our tactical understanding and execution significantly improved in 2002. From a defensive point of view we got tighter; from an offensive point of view, we became more structured in our approach. So we knew if we were going with a free-kick from a centre half-back for example, we knew what to do if we had a sideline ball on the right-hand side – we knew the process to go through in order to create a goal-scoring opportunity. Our ambition wasn't to play the most stylish football in the country. Our ambition wasn't to be the most glamorous or sexy footballers going forward or in defending. The ambition and the mission was to win the All-Ireland. Not to please journalists, not to please supporters, not to please our opposition. But to win the All-Ireland.

'Joe helped with the belief of the team because he had been in Croke Park with Cross and had won an All-Ireland which was a major feather in his cap in terms of when he walked into that Armagh changing room.'

Armagh's 110 per cent dedication and focus to the game at hand, their intensive preparation, the monastic approach espoused by the likes of Kieran McGeeney, Enda McNulty and John Toal, raised the bar tactically and fitness-wise and came as a wake-up call for the other counties.

'A lot of those players were all or nothing,' says McNulty. 'There was just one thought in their heads when they woke up in the morning and one thought when they went to bed at night. And that was football. If you look at the personalities and the psychological profiles of a lot of those leaders on the team, they were all similarly predisposed. They were all hugely committed, had a huge work ethos, one focus and were very, very intense. Now of course if you look at it, there is not too many of those guys that says let's go out at night and have a training session and enjoy it and have a bit of fun. It's let's go out guys and get absolutely stuck into each other and make sure we are working maximally and making sure we don't make any mistakes – that will not be acceptable.

'Before they even got near that Armagh panel, those players all displayed a serious intent on being successful in sport. A lot of those guys won with St Colman's or in the Abbey; some went on to win the Hogan Cup and then in college we all won Sigerson medals with either Queen's or with Jordanstown. A lot of the players did. Then on through under-21, a lot of the players won All-Irelands or Ulster medals and even at minor level a lot of us had won with

Armagh in Ulster and got to an All-Ireland final. Crossmaglen had
won the All-Ireland and Mullaghbawn had won an Ulster in 1995,
so the players had a lifetime of being successful even before they
moved into the Armagh team.'

No stone was left unturned as Armagh sought the Holy Grail.
Enda McNulty, who was to become a sports psychologist and
motivator himself, setting up his own company, Motiv8, introduced
leading sports psychologists Hugh Campbell and Des Channing to
Joe Kernan, who in turn brought them into the backroom team
helping to develop the team's mental toughness.

'The group became very ambitious in embracing anything that
would help the team improve,' says McNulty. 'Whether it was
speed development, whether it was hydration, nutrition – I even
remember getting a hygienist so the team's teeth would be sorted.
If your teeth are dirty or have a lot of plaque on them you are much
more likely to get sick or to get infections, whereas if they're clean
and glistening there's less chance of it happening.'

Such was the level of detail in their preparation, nothing was
left to chance.

The 2000s saw the footballing landscape shift radically. Armagh
and Tyrone, physically and tactically, were to take the game to new
levels and Kerry were determined to match them. For the next
eight years Armagh, Tyrone or Kerry were to win the All-Ireland,
with Ulster titles being divided up between Armagh and Tyrone
from 1999 to 2010.

The next few years were dominated by the fierce rivalry between
Armagh and Tyrone at the highest levels, with the sides meeting in
an All-Ireland final, Ulster final and All-Ireland semi-final in three
consecutive years from 2003 to 2005. Despite winning four Ulster
titles to Tyrone's two during Kernan's years in charge of Armagh,
it was Mickey Harte's Tyrone who were to go on and capture three
All-Irelands to Armagh's single success in 2002. It's the biggest

regret that remarkable group of players and management still harbour to this day.

'There's a massive regret that we didn't win more,' admits McNulty. 'Eighty per cent of that team invested ten years of their lives playing for Armagh. And I'm not talking about ten years of your life giving two nights of the week to it, I'm talking about the full-on commitment for ten years.'

In a strange way, because it meant so much to them, they were nearly over-committed to it, to last at the top for any length of time they needed more balance to what they were doing.

'I remember showing Shane Horgan [the former Leinster and Ireland rugby player] my training diary,' says McNulty. 'There were weight sessions, speed sessions, skill sessions, there was a collective team session, and so on, all marked down in it and Shane just looked at it with amazement and said, "Enda where is your recovery? Where are your down days? Where is your time-off?" In hindsight, we were massively committed and, on reflection, I would have to say we didn't rest well enough. I would have to say that we probably left a hell of a lot on the training pitch.

'I am not blaming coaches or Joe for that, I am blaming us as individuals sometimes for going over the top. I remember in 2003, the week before the All-Ireland final, we had a brainwave – we would go and do a four-day training camp in Belfast, and we trained like dogs for four days and I personally went into the All-Ireland final with the flu.'

In 2002, after their general had led them up to the mountain top, from the steps of Croke Park they lifted Sam Maguire above a sea of orange who acclaimed their heroes. They had reached the promised land, but staying there was to prove even more difficult.

Winning back-to-back All-Irelands would have been the icing on the cake for Kernan's Armagh, an opportunity to cement a legacy in the record books that said more than just first-time winners –

historic and momentous as that was in itself. But as with Meath, Cork or Down, winning it the second time was a chance to really go down in history.

'We know we should have won more than the one All-Ireland and that's a regret that I have and the players have,' says Kernan. 'After being beaten by Kerry in 2006, and looking back on it now in the cool light of day, I could have said, "Right, it's time to weed out and refresh the whole thing down", but it was going to take another two to three years and at that time between work and everything else, I just said I need a break, something has to give. I was after giving nine years with Cross before that, so I was after giving fifteen to sixteen years at it. In 2002, as we drove through the gates of Citywest to head home, I looked around and asked myself, "Will we be able to monitor the monster we're after creating?" I felt it straight away and, to be honest, we weren't able to do it.'

The warning signs were there when the reigning champions were dumped out of Ulster in the preliminary round by Monaghan by seven points and Tyrone went on to win the provincial crown in Mickey Harte's first year in charge, hammering Derry by fifteen points.

Luckily, Armagh had the qualifiers to fall back on and went on a run to rediscover their form and hunger to reach their second consecutive All-Ireland final.

They faced Tyrone, who had been defeating teams in Ulster by a minimum of eight points before trouncing Fermanagh by nineteen points in the All-Ireland quarter-final. Kerry had been a stiffer prospect in the semi-final but Mickey Harte's team held the Kingdom to just six points, beating them by a seven-point margin. It was to be Páidí Ó Sé's last game in charge as Kerry realised they had to change their ways.

Indeed, such was Ulster's second coming in the 2000s that three Northern teams competed in the semi-finals that year (Donegal were the third). With Armagh and Tyrone to face each other for the 2003 final, it was the first time that it was an all-provincial clash and it was no surprise that it was to be an all-Ulster final such was the rising strength of the province once more.

It was in the aftermath of Kerry's semi-final defeat to Tyrone, when their game was strangled up by the swarming packs of Tyrone players, that Pat Spillane described the spectacle on TV as 'puke football'. Kerry's Colm Cooper compared it to a train ramming into them. 'It was like we didn't have air to breathe,' he said afterwards.

Revealing much of the same philosophy and mindset to winning as Joe Kernan, Tyrone manager Mickey Harte countered, 'There's no use in us playing flamboyantly and losing.'

Armagh and Tyrone had shown that physical, in-your-face, tackling pressure when brought to a constant high-tempo could cause teams to crack. As Kernan explains:

You can run all you want, but if you don't know how to hold the ball, you're in trouble. The first thing you have to do is stop the player – if I stop you, where can you go? You have to go back or sideways. We always had a man coming in on the far side and so had Tyrone, so he has to get rid of it. But when three or four men swarm round you then that's when the thing got a bit messy and the referees and people didn't like it. But the thing about a tackle is I can't let you past me, so I've to try and stop you without fouling. I can't pull you from behind so we used to say 'boys get in front', if you're the man in front, you're on your toes and your feet are well balanced so that if he gives you a dummy you're able to go with him.

But the thing is to get the hands up and push him back. We used to do it and then that would stun them – it's not a foul – but it would stop you and if you don't go past me

*you have to go somewhere else because the referee is going
to blow you off, so you turn back and the next thing you
meet the same thing again, then you're in trouble. John
McCluskey had the players working on it in training and
the thing is, in the game situation, it's always the best way
to do it. So we would stop games and say, 'How did he get
past you?' We'd look at videos and say, 'He can pass you
and it left an extra man, if you had stopped him there that
problem wouldn't have occurred.' So our idea was always
stop the man without fouling, but stop him, that's where the
weights and the strength and conditioning came in.*

The 2003 All-Ireland final was a tight and scrappy encounter
between two teams that knew each other well. Joe Kernan believes
the sending off of Diarmuid Marsden was the turning point between
the sides.

*I still reckon we would have won it if he had been playing –
there was only a few points in that game. Some days you get
it and some days you don't. There was only a kick of a ball
any day between us.*

It was to be a sore, three-point defeat for Armagh and was to
represent the last All-Ireland final appearance for them under Joe
Kernan, while Tyrone were to build on their legacy with two more
All-Irelands in the wake of their breakthrough success. There were
similarities and memories of the 1990s when Down, Donegal and
Derry won their All-Irelands, but the manner and style of Armagh
and Tyrone's All-Irelands meant that Gaelic football was on a clear
tactical evolution that others would have to embrace if they hoped
to be on a par in future years.

For Armagh, however, despite further Ulster success, a second

All-Ireland was to prove elusive and it's the one that got away
that remains the talking point. At their tenth anniversary dinner
remembering the 2002 title, the reflections and conversation turned
to asking out loud why there was only just the one. From Enda
McNulty's perspective it was a combination of the hunger not
being what it was and being overtaken tactically by others.

> *In retrospect – and some players would be very honest about
> it and say that maybe their hunger for winning another one
> wasn't as strong or as steely as it was in 2002. As Down's
> manager, Pete McGrath said after their 1994 success, your
> hunger can be taken away like a ghost in the night. Another
> thing that happened was that obviously our competitors
> realised what we were doing and in hindsight we were far
> too open in the secret ingredients of that success. We needed
> to advance our game plan when other teams realised what
> our game plan was.*

Joe Kernan's belief in Plan A and no other escape routes perhaps
contributed to this, and as the game evolved quickly in light of
Armagh's success, so further adaptations were needed. Likewise,
as Kernan himself admits, a new crop of players should probably
have been brought in. But by that stage, he had been on the road
as a manager with Crossmaglen and Armagh for over fifteen years
and the eight-point defeat to Kerry in the 2006 All-Ireland quarter-
final was to mark time up for his remarkable tenure.

The game had come full circle by then, Kerry were learning to
catch up with the Armagh and Tyrone style of play, and Kernan
stepped down knowing that the winning culture and mindset, so
often discarded and not believed in, had been bedded down deeply
within the psyche of his club and county. They had won four of the
last five Ulster titles, had won their county's first All-Ireland and

meanwhile Crossmaglen were to win the first of three-in-a-row in Ulster as well as further All-Ireland club titles.

'Self belief, work ethic, a commitment and unity – that's what's needed in any walk of life,' says Kernan. 'You might have a bad day but you have to say to yourself, "That's it gone, move on." We've had plenty of hassle in our life, we've had bankruptcy and different things, but you get on in life, there's no sense in sitting back and worrying about it. After a bad defeat, it will annoy me worse for a while, it will take me longer to get over it with the team and then you'd say, "Right, we've been here before, hundreds of teams have been here before and there's only one way you want to go and that's back up."

'When I go to places to talk I get two people to stand in front of me and see if they can separate my hands joined together. I've done it with international rugby players, club players and county players and nobody has separated those two hands. Now which team do you want to play in? The team that isn't joined together and unified or the team that can't be separated? That's the team that wins.'

The motif for Kernan's Armagh team was a circle inside a triangle which was sewn onto the county jerseys. Every time they looked down at the symbol it was a reminder of what the team represented, the character and soul of them standing together and it's the philosophy that has carried Crossmaglen and Armagh on to further success over the years.

'When the All-Ireland final is over every other team is looking and wondering, *Could we be the team up there? Could we be the one?*' says Kernan. 'I dreamed about it and woke up thinking about it. I would tell the players this could be our year.'

Chapter 16

'Success is not a lucky break, success is a choice'

The 1970s was about new levels of fitness in Gaelic football and the 1980s focused on man-management, while the 1990s saw an increased level of organisational skills – but it wasn't until the 2000s that the expansion of the backroom team began in earnest, with increased levels of specialisation and the dedicated application of sports science in areas such as psychology, strength and conditioning. The other major leap forward was in tactical developments, seeing the game in a whole new light with emphasis on systems of total football with interchangeable positions and increased tactical awareness needed from players who were expected to stick to game plans under pressure.

Tactics have always been part and parcel of the game since its codification – Erin's Hope student teachers introduced new skills and formations in the 1890s, hand-passing as a means of retaining possession and moving forward was perfected by Kildare and Dublin in the 1920s. Each decade saw an evolution of sorts, but, in general, any tactical considerations focused on the forwards with the question being how to create space to open it up to scores. Tony Hanahoe's role under Heffernan being the main example of this.

The 2000s, however, saw a radical development with the rise of Armagh and Tyrone. Joe Kernan's Armagh showed the way in terms of the importance of size and strength in stopping players – raising a question once more about the definition and place of the tackle in the game which has still not been addressed – and a willingness and confidence to keep possession in defensive situations. Mickey Harte and Tyrone were to take things even further. Harte ridicules the notion of there being a 'Tyrone style of play' or a 'Kerry style of play' or any style of play for that matter that is particular to a county, believing instead that any team coached well plays to its own strengths at that time. Nonetheless, each coach's thinking is still a reflection of his particular time and place. The winning mindset and culture is a universal one, but the product of a person's thinking and reading of the game is set at that place in the game's evolution and development.

At the end of 2002, Tyrone were reigning league champions but it was Armagh who were All-Ireland winners. After nearly twenty-five years' involvement with Tyrone as manager at different times, Art McRory, along with Eugene McKenna, stepped down and Mickey Harte, the promising coach who had managed Tyrone to All-Irelands at minor and under-21 level, was appointed senior county manager. The aim and the target was simple: to replicate his underage success and bring a first senior All-Ireland to Tyrone football.

Tyrone's first Ulster titles arrived in the 1950s, a decade of breakthroughs for a number of Ulster counties that finally broke Cavan's long-held stranglehold on the province. Armagh led the way, resulting in an All-Ireland final appearance in 1953, and then Tyrone captured their first Ulster titles in 1956 and 1957, followed by Derry and Down.

'At that stage the prerequisite for a Gaelic footballer was strength,' says Art McRory. 'You had to be physically strong and direct, they were the requisites for a Gaelic footballer. But that Tyrone team in 1956 had something different – there was Iggy Jones and Frankie Donnelly, neither of whom would fall into that mould, but both of whom were top-class footballers who used their speed and work rate around the pitch.'

Also key was the fact that Tyrone had won minor titles in 1946 and 1947 and were able to build on that ten years later. Success at underage level has always been a good marker for future success – but only if it can be built upon, something that Mickey Harte was to be so successful at fifty years later.

'You go nowhere unless you have the players and you will go nowhere unless you get success,' says McRory. 'We did not build on that success in the 1950s and that was our biggest problem.'

With Art McRory and Eugene McKenna stepping down after the 2002 season, the time was ripe for Mickey Harte to step in. There has been speculation that McRory and McKenna were pushed to make way for Harte but this is something that McRory firmly denies.

There would have been a school of thought that said that I did not pull out, that I was chased – that is complete and utter nonsense – at the September meeting of the county board, which is the meeting of all the clubs, every club in the county, the management team was unanimously returned. Now when I say unanimously, I mean unanimously.

But by end of October I had to step down, some of my reasons were medical, some were not, but I had to get out. I simply had to quit and I was very disappointed, for I knew that we had the team. And the other thing was, if I stayed would I have been a drag on the whole thing if I wasn't fit to give it what was required? Would they have realised

their potential? That's what I had to consider and it would
have been very selfish of me to stay on, and so I personally
recommended Mickey Harte for the job. I had Mickey Harte
as a minor player, I also had him as a senior player and I
also watched him managing the minors and under-21s. I
knew what he was capable of.

Growing up in Tyrone, Mickey Harte was obsessed with Gaelic
football, looking to play it day and night, be it around the house or
with the local club Ballygawley. His older brother Peter had played
with Tyrone in the 1960s and another, Martin, was on the under-
21s, so it was no surprise that he was soon following in his brothers'
footsteps, making it onto the Tyrone minors in 1972 and winning a
second successive Ulster title before losing the All-Ireland final to
Cork. Soon afterwards, Harte made his debut with the seniors and
added an Ulster under-21 medal to his growing collection.

By the mid 1970s, Tyrone had won Ulster minor titles in 1971,
1972, 1973 and 1975 and had Ulster under-21 success in 1972 and
1973; however, that underage success wasn't translated into senior
success. 'We hoped we might win,' Harte wrote in his autobiography.
'We didn't think about how success in one year could feed into the
next. There was no sense of process or improvement.'

What also stood out for him was the lack of togetherness on
those panels, team ethos and building connections within the group
was unheard of, it was the best players who won matches, not the
best teams. Watching the Dublin team of the 1970s gel together and
seeing Tony Hanahoe moving unselfishly out of position to create
space for his team-mates opened him up to a different football
world. In Dublin, Kerry and other places, the hunger and attitude
to win was dominant, and he knew that this mindset had yet to be
instilled in his own county.

Importantly, though, his years training as a teacher in St Joseph's

College and playing in the college team brought him under the influence of Derry's Jim McKeever, a man whose methodical, detailed approach to the game was to influence generations of inter-county coaches in Ulster.

Graduating as a teacher, Harte's natural affinity for the game saw him gravitating towards coaching the school teams and, like so many others who succeeded at the highest level of football management (John O'Mahony, Billy Morgan, Pete McGrath, Art McRory, Mickey Ned O'Sullivan, Jack O'Connor), the school teams were to be the testing ground for his own development in team training, communication and management.

Working with Robbie Hasson at St Ciaran's opened up Harte to the practical application of attention to detail and in doing things right – there was no shouting and bawling on the field, no talking back to referees and no bad language in the dressing room. Training, limited to the twenty-five minutes at lunch-time, was refined and focused, with everything revolving around ball work. Even with Peter Canavan starring at that age, the emphasis was on teamwork and soon the school was winning Ulster Vocational Schools titles at every age grade.

Along with coaching his club, Errigal Ciaran, Harte's growing reputation led to him being appointed Tyrone minor manager in 1991. There was only one goal in his mind: to avenge the 1972 loss and prove to himself and Tyrone's footballing community that they were better than they believed, to prove that in Croke Park they deserved their place alongside the Kerrys and Dublins of the Gaelic football world.

The same principles that worked for them at St Ciaran's continued: ball work and ball skills lay at the heart of the team training.

'I wanted to fit them into a system of play that didn't define them,' said Harte, 'but offered them a solid baseline from which to work

– one with the flexibility to accommodate flair, to accommodate uniqueness.'

While Harte was bringing on the young players' development, instilling in them an ethos of respect beyond the pitch, he was also looking to develop and improve his own skills in terms of management. Two winless years with the Tyrone minors meant that he wasn't sitting on his laurels but looking around him all the time for techniques and methods that would help him improve his input.

George Zalucki was a guru of network marketing whose simple message was that if you give a little of yourself to help others, it will come back two-fold, and when Harte came across Zalucki's motivational videos, it opened up a whole new world to him. One that said that no obstacle was too big to be overcome, defeat and rejection only gave you an opportunity to try harder until you do succeed, and it was a philosophy that he preached to his teams from that point on.

In Harte's third season in charge, Tyrone won their first Ulster minor title, but were beaten by Meath in the All-Ireland semi-final. There was still much more work to do if they were to be better than the sides outside Ulster. However, having won in Ulster, it was to be another four years before they were to repeat the same feat, winning another provincial title, and finally, twenty-five years after suffering heartache as a player, his team were in an All-Ireland final.

But finals aren't won because of neat endings and sometimes, even no matter how hard you work and train for something, it's just the better team on the day that wins. And so it was as Laois, already reigning champions, beat Harte's Tyrone team by three points in 1997, and in the process brought seven years of work for Harte to an abrupt end. The team had endured tragedy and heartbreak when their team-mate Paul McGirr had died from an accidental clash in a game against Armagh earlier in the year. It had brought them together like nothing else, Paul McGirr always in their minds, but maybe the script wasn't meant to be, maybe Harte just had to accept that. He announced his resignation that night, but the players pleaded with his family not to let him quit. One more year, they said, we can do it.

Our best-laid plans have more twists and turns than we can imagine. Harte believed it was written in the stars that Tyrone would win the All-Ireland in 1997 – but what if they had? He believes that his ultimate goal would have been satiated and he would have retired from football management, happy at last that the wound of 1972 was healed.

'Success is not a lucky break. It is not a divine right. It is not an accident of birth. Success is a choice,' wrote Rick Pitino, the American basketball coach, lines that Harte came across years later. In 1997, it was being put up to him by the teenagers on his team. The dream hadn't come true, but they weren't giving up. That night, his daughter, Michaela, wrote out on a napkin the targets for the coming years:

- Winning the All-Ireland final in 1998 (minors)
- Winning the All-Ireland final in 2000 (under-21)
- Winning the All-Ireland final in 2003 (seniors)

It would seem that some things after all were written in the stars.

Starting over the following year, Harte decided to go back to fundamentals and find ways to not only improve the players but to ensure that the players were looking to improve themselves as well, starting with the principle that defending would begin from the front. 'Once we lost the ball, every player became a defender. When we broke out from defence, everyone became an attacker,' wrote Harte, in what was to become the bedrock of the tactical evolution of the senior game in the twenty-first century.

A possession-and-support game was being nurtured and developed by Harte. It was about controlling the percentages, giving players options and support, based around intelligent running of angles. 'Players never ran in isolation,' said Harte. 'Other players chased them in support. Players upfield moved to make themselves available.'

It was a philosophy espoused by Phil Jackson, legendary Chicago Bulls and LA Lakers basketball coach – the ultimate in team effort and collectiveness, each and every individual submitting to the group system – it revolutionised the development of the game. It was not without its critics either and the swarming pressure of play is one that still engenders plenty of debate about style and aesthetics versus practicalities and the group collective.

Tackling and holding on to the ball were key to Harte's tactics. Getting the ball back quickly and effectively meant that, in possession, they were in charge of the controllables and then had multiple options with the support play and running that had been drilled into the players. In those training sessions, and on the rudimentary diagrams hanging up on the back of the dressing-room door, was a glimpse into the future of the game, and here it was being pioneered on the fields of the Tyrone minors.

The system worked. A twelve-point win over Armagh, five over Derry and six over Antrim to regain the Ulster championship followed, but that was never enough for this team that was overpowering all before them. They hammered Leitrim by eleven points in the All-Ireland semi-final and faced Laois once more in the final. This time it was different: the team was a shadow of that from 1997, it wasn't about the cups anymore but the players, and Tyrone won out by six points, 2–11 to 0–11. The All-Ireland final dream had finally been achieved and as Harte looked back in future years with multiple All-Irelands to his name, the 1998 minor success was still the one that ranked as the best.

The ongoing success of Harte and Tyrone can be traced to those years – from defeat in 1997 to turning things around in 1998 and developing the system and principles of teamwork and support on the pitch. He had also developed a unique team bond with this particular group of players, over half of whom went on to win All-Irelands at senior level.

The natural progression for Harte was the step up to the under-21s the following year and eight of the minor panel from the previous season were brought up as well. Success, as Harte noted, wasn't just an expectation, it was an obligation and they collected two All-Ireland titles in a row in 2000 and 2001. By 2000, nine of the under-21 panel had been drafted onto the seniors, reflecting the standard that these players had achieved at such a young age, although it wasn't something that Harte agreed with, believing the players needed to be phased into the senior setup, 'not flung in too early and burned out'.

Mick O'Dwyer was to claim in later years that with such a talented bunch of players, five All-Irelands could have been won and, to him, seeing the likes of Stephen O'Neill, Owen Mulligan, Brian McGuigan, Ryan Mellon and Kevin Hughes must have reminded him of the great All-Ireland-winning under-21 Kerry side in the 1970s.

When Art McRory stepped down in 2002, Mickey Harte seemed the obvious choice to succeed him, but he still had to go through an interview process, competing with the other incumbent, Eugene McKenna, as well as other applicants, Brian McIver and Peter Doherty. Having achieved so much in the game already with the core group of players who were now on the senior panel, forcing Harte to go through an interview justifying and outlining his plans might seem disrespectful, but sitting in front of the county board officials, there was only one target he and they were interested in: an All-Ireland for one of the most talented group of footballers to have come through Tyrone's ranks.

Harte continued to develop his concept of total football, working on the collective, the culture and ethos within the team circle, and to succeed he realised that a coherent and all-encompassing defensive system was needed.

Philip Jordan, a wing-back under Harte since the minor days and who went on to All-Ireland and All Star success at senior level, says they needed to strengthen up defensively.

When we played under Mickey, we had good individual footballers but when you get into the senior game, having individual players just isn't enough. You need a system to try and nullify the attacking teams, you would go through the Kerry forward line and every one of them was someone who was probably capable of being a Player of the Year. If you went out to play one-on-one against those players, there wasn't any defence in the country that was going to be fit to stand up to them.

He developed a system over time that, in the early years, our centre half-back was the sweeper and our midfielder dropped back into centre half-back – it was as basic as that. We were lucky enough to have someone like Brian Dooher playing wing-forward who was fit enough to get up and down the pitch and people probably said that Brian's role was a defensive role, but Brian always played that role. The one benefit we got was the opposition didn't always have the players to get back up the field and take a couple of points, which Brian always did. As long as you are able to get back up and support your forwards, you want your half-forwards getting back and defending and getting up and down the pitch all day. That's really what the modern game is about.

Emphasising the tracking and support play was crucial to Harte's teams, each player had to increase their work rate; everything done on the training field was done to match speed, with high-intensity sessions lasting no more than the duration of a game and with ball work central to it all. Video analysis and stats became more important, communication, two-way between management and players, was encouraged. It was all about the individual's self-improvement – for the good of the team.

For Mickey Harte's first championship season in charge, the script couldn't have been written any better. Derry were beaten by nine points in the opening game in Ulster, followed by an eight-point win in the semi over Antrim. Down took them to a replay after Tyrone conceded four goals in the Ulster final, but in the replay a fifteen-point trouncing – 0–23 to 1–5 – meant they collected the Ulster title, the county's tenth, with the biggest margin of victory in an Ulster decider since Down's 2–16 to 0–7 mauling of Cavan in 1959. Were Tyrone set for similar greatness?

They blitzed Fermanagh in the All-Ireland quarter-final by nineteen points – 1–21 to 0–5 – a warning shot sent out across the footballing landscape that Croke Park held no fears for them any longer. But facing Kerry in the semi-final would be a different proposition altogether and Harte studied their shape and approach, tailoring Tyrone's tactics to suit by stationing Gavin Devlin around the D to snuff out the main attacking threats from 'Gooch' Cooper and Mike Frank Russell. Despite the free-flowing football of previous wins, the Tyrone team needed to tighten up and snuff out the oxygen of space that Kerry used to build on.

That day, Tyrone hounded and pressurised Kerry players in every corner of the pitch, not giving them a second on the ball anywhere. At one stage, Darragh Ó Sé, Kerry's totemic midfielder, was surrounded by a pack of hunting Tyrone players and could only hack the ball away in desperation. Tyrone led 0–9 to 0–2 at half-time and continued to smother Kerry into the second half, winning in the end by 0–13 to 0–6. Tyrone were into their first All-Ireland final in eight years in what would be an all-Ulster encounter against Armagh, but it was the storm of controversy in the aftermath of the Kerry win that was to generate most coverage and talking points and for which Tyrone and Mickey Harte's tactics were to come under the microscope.

Spillane's 'puke football' comment became the stick to beat them with, while Sean Walsh, the Kerry County Board chairman, was talking about the mark and other rule changes to counter-attack the new style of football that was taking over. But to Harte, single-minded in both his philosophy and convictions, it meant nothing – after all, blanket defence and swarming were the ultimate in the teamwork ethic that he so espoused and cultivated in his players.

'I saw the first half as one of the best thirty-five minutes of football we ever played,' he wrote. 'It contained everything you could ever wish for from your team. I'm not interested in foul counts. I'm into sheer energy, work rate and determination. That was all there. If the foul count is high the referees are there to deal with it.'

'We wanted to pick up big scores ourselves and to limit the scores that the opposition was getting,' explains Jordan. 'When we got to the All-Ireland semi-final, in the first half of that game we played as good a football as we played all year, but in the second half we didn't expect to be 0–9, 0–2 up against Kerry. It wasn't something we had prepared for and I suppose the Tyrone team in 1986 in the final were in the same position and they didn't expect it but they ended up getting beaten in the game.

'There was a natural fear in the team, they didn't go out and play the same way in the second half, we didn't set out to defend the lead, it wasn't orders from the management. I remember Chris Lawn, one of our trainers, saying after the match that it's going to be hard to keep the hype down on us because our thoughts were we had played so well in the first half and that's what people would be talking about, but obviously after the game it was a lot different. I remember a conversation with Chris saying that we're going to be built up to be this great team, but it wasn't the case. So, thankfully, we didn't have to worry about that.'

The criticism stung, how could it not have? Turning in your finest performance but to hear it reduced to 'puke football' – two words that would remain in the lexicon for the rest of the decade – hurt, but it also steeled their resolve. Unwittingly, it was a tag that became associated with the rise of Armagh and Tyrone in the 2000s and once more the notional battle for the heart and soul of Gaelic football was deemed to come down to another fight by Kerry to be pure to the traditions of the game in the face of Northern tactics. It was just another rerun of the same conversations that had been ongoing in Gaelic football for the past one hundred years.

The 2003 all-Ulster All-Ireland final of Armagh versus Tyrone threw up a scary vista to the traditionalists who saw themselves being hounded out of games, losing the battle of strength, tactics, wits and will, overpowered by the Ulster hordes who were coming through in droves from the qualifiers. Where would it end? When would non-Ulster teams ever appear in an All-Ireland again?

The doom merchants wanted to paint an apocalyptic vista but for Mickey Harte and his team, the season up to that point was being too easily dismissed and forgotten about. Seventeen points against Derry, twenty against Antrim, twenty-three and twenty-four against Down were proof that Harte's system was working and that he and his players had raised the bar even higher that year. Now only reigning champions Armagh stood between them and glory.

The hype and the build-up to the final centred on the storm of criticism after the defeat of Kerry, to which the Tyrone camp responded by giving the players media training with local reporters schooling them in PR responses.

'The players learned to just say that we take on board whatever criticism is levelled at us and we want to play good football and that's how we responded to it,' says Philip Jordan. 'I suppose it's a bit of a game as well, we had been coached in what we were going to say at that stage.'

Harte saw Armagh as a more one-dimensional team, built on a rigidity and singular strength in contrast to his more flexible unit. They both happened to be from Ulster but that was where the common traits ended. Nothing was left to chance in preparation and, just as Brian McEniff had done with his troops for 1992, on the day of the hurling final, Tyrone headed to Donegal to watch the game, soak up the noise, the schedule, the build-up to the game. Then the week before the football final, he brought the players down to Dublin to do a dress rehearsal, timing everything to coincide with what would happen exactly on the weekend of the final, stopping off in Monaghan for food, arriving at their hotel in Killiney, checking into the rooms. Everything had been meticulously planned in advance.

Even on the morning of the game as the team gathered one last time, Harte wanted to leave them with one more nugget of motivation. Keen to counter the hype around Armagh's size and strength, he had done the calculations of both teams and found that Armagh were just seven ounces heavier and three-quarters of an inch taller. Seven ounces of coffee granules and a three-quarter-inch folded piece of paper were produced and held up before their eyes. Was this what they were afraid of?

The game itself was a tight affair with Tyrone leading 0–8 to 0–4 at half-time. 'Keep knocking on that door, boys,' urged Peter Canavan as he came off to rest his ankle. 'Inside will be heaven.'

'We'll not be f–ing knocking it,' replied Brian Dooher. 'Start kicking it down, boys!'

The second half was, in Harte's own words, a pitched battle, with fouls aplenty and no space anywhere. Diarmuid Marsden of Armagh was sent off and, with six minutes left, Peter Canavan, Tyrone's greatest player, was sent back on to see them over the line.

A three-point lead against Armagh, who usually saw teams off in the final few minutes, meant nothing and, sure enough, in the dying moments a breaking ball fell to Armagh's master marksman Steven McDonnell, who shot for goal but then out of nowhere came a diving Conor Gormley to get a hand on the ball to deflect it away. The victory was Tyrone's and with it their first All-Ireland. Michaela Harte's predictions, written on the back of a napkin six years earlier, had come true. The trilogy was finished. Within five years, Mickey Harte had brought All-Ireland titles to the minors, under-21s and seniors. The journey was complete.

Mick O'Dwyer had experienced it; Brian McEniff had felt it; Pete McGrath saw it; John O'Mahony knew about it; and just twelve months previously Joe Kernan had wondered about it. Once success comes, how do you control it? McEniff and Kernan would rue it, wondering about what-might-have-beens, McGrath put it up to his players three years later to deliver on their legacy, O'Mahony was saved by the introduction of the back door, and Mick O'Dwyer brought in the Bomber to change their formation.

In the coming years, it was Mickey Harte's Tyrone that outmatched all of them bar O'Dwyer's Kerry, winning three All-Ireland's in six years, competing with Kerry for top honours in the decade. But what was most remarkable was the setbacks they had to overcome to achieve and cement their place in Gaelic football history.

Coming off the high of 2003, with Peter Canavan injured and the twenty-four-year-old inspiration Cormac McAnallen now captain of the team, Tyrone came out of the blocks in 2004 to win the early season McKenna Cup. McAnallen had already lifted All-Ireland minor and under-21 cups and was determined to complete the trinity come September.

'I've got an All-Ireland medal at twenty-three,' he told the team upon his appointment as captain. 'I don't want to look back, saying, "Did I only get one?"'

But tragedy was to fall upon Tyrone football once more when Cormac McAnallen died tragically of Sudden Adult Death Syndrome at his home the night of 2 March 2004. It was a shock to all of Gaelic football and to the entire country that such a fit, respected and inspirational person could be struck down so suddenly without any prior warning.

It was, as Harte wrote of the days that followed: 'Unlike any other tragedy we had encountered as a group … Paul's death had brought us together as friends. This transformed us into a family.'

As the team grouped together in the weeks afterwards, Harte himself wondered if they could survive such a death. Was this the end of the line for something so special? In the end, the choice was as it ever was and ever will be in life: give up or go on.

As the 2004 season kicked in, that old monster, 'success', was rearing its ugly head. The 'Disease of Me' as Harte described it (borrowed from NBA coach Pat Riley) was becoming noticeable: players feeling underappreciated, resentment against others, personal efforts at the expense of the team, the team ethos that had been so steadfastly developed and built upon over all those years was in danger.

Despite starting the championship strongly, beating Derry by eleven points and then overcoming Fermanagh, Donegal caught them in the Ulster semi-final. They even got to the All-Ireland quarter-finals having overcome Down, Galway and Laois en route, but that year's finalists, Mayo, were to have the beating of them and they went out of the championship. After the year they had gone through with Cormac McAnallen's death, injuries, retirements and departures, 2004 was a year they were glad to put to bed.

The next year was a key season for Harte's management and the team's future as a whole; how they bounced back would determine how they would be remembered. Peter Canavan and Brian Dooher were fit again and Brian McGuigan had returned from Australia; the pieces it seemed were starting to fall into place again.

They reached the Ulster final to face old rivals Armagh, and such was the interest in these two counties, the provincial decider was moved to Croke Park for the first time in its history. Harte's Tyrone team had come back that year with renewed vigour and determination, the resolve coming from within each of the players in the dressing room; it was a team of energy and pace against one of power and strength. Despite Tyrone being four points up, Armagh pulled out their customary last-minute surge to bring the game to a replay and once again Tyrone were four points up into the second half when Peter Canavan and then Stephen O'Neill were sent off. Tyrone were stunned, and Armagh marched on with six unanswered points to win by two.

It was only a stumbling block to Tyrone however as they had bigger goals in mind, and blowing Dublin away in the All-Ireland quarter-final with a sublime Owen Mulligan goal struck the tone for what lay ahead for the rest of the summer. They faced Armagh in the All-Ireland semi, a chance for revenge in Ulster, and it was seventy minutes of hits and no quarter given. Croke Park was becoming accustomed to these thunderous clashes. A point down with less than ten minutes to go and Tyrone's future was about to be decided. Defeat would probably mean the end of the road for this team, come through with a victory and they would be another step closer to a footballing legacy.

For once, it wasn't Armagh that sealed the deal in the closing stages, this time it was Tyrone who had the mental resolve, and an equalising point from the corner-back, Shane McSweeney, followed by the winning score kicked from the hand of Peter Canavan (who else?) saw them through to their second All-Ireland final in three years. Their opponents were Kerry, the team they had squeezed the life out of two years previously, the reigning champions who had regained Sam Maguire in 2004 and who wanted revenge. They wanted to prove that Kerry's way could match and beat Tyrone's style, that the tables hadn't turned irreversibly, that they were ready to play for their footballing tradition and future.

Kerry came at them in waves from the outset but Tyrone hung in there and went ahead, leading by three at half-time. In the second half, Peter Canavan was sprung late once more, this time for his final encore, and he helped see them through the last fifteen minutes. With points from Canavan, Dooher and Jordan, Tyrone were champions once more. The second one was about fulfilment and so much more.

'We had left our past as a footballing county behind us forever,' Harte wrote. 'Two All-Irelands meant that we could aspire to great things every year. So could the generations who came after us. We had laid the foundations for a new era in our history.'

Three years later, in 2008, it was the same All-Ireland final pairing. Kerry had addressed their weaknesses and adapted to the new style of football in light of the defeats to Armagh and Tyrone. When Jack O'Connor had taken over from Páidí Ó Sé, they had won All-Irelands in 2004 and 2006, and Pat O'Shea continued the winning streak in 2007. Each of those victories however came against Mayo (twice) and then Cork and many in Kerry were itching to prove a point, that the Kingdom still held sway over whatever the best of Ulster could throw at them. The semi-final and final defeats at the hands of Tyrone in 2003 and 2005 still rankled and they had never had a chance to avenge those losses in the meantime. They were going for three-in-a-row, and what better way to finish it off than with victory over their past tormentors.

For Tyrone as well, this was a final to prove themselves once and for all against the Kerry insults over the past few years. It was about identity, the right for Tyrone football to stand on its own two feet and be recognised for what it had achieved and what it represented. 'We were going into a final striving to become a team to be remembered,' said Harte.

In the run-up to the final, Brian Cody, Kilkenny's most successful manager, spoke to Tyrone's players telling them that it was their example of teamwork, commitment and pursuit of excellence that served as the model for Kilkenny hurlers. It was a ringing endorsement of what Harte and his teams had become since taking over five years previously, and as they faced the game's most successful county, here was another great telling them they were now the benchmark.

In the end it was a tactical battle. Kerry switched between the 'Twin Towers' of Kieran Donaghy and Tommy Walsh and the sublime skills of Gooch Cooper up front; Mickey Harte called upon Justin McMahon at full-back to cope with the Kingdom's aerial physicality, and the emergence of Martin Penrose and the return of Stephen O'Neill up front gave them added artillery.

Kerry were a point ahead at half-time but just after the restart Brian McGuigan's scrambled shot gave Tyrone the goal to go two points up before Kerry came back again. Once again, it was the indomitable self-belief and courage that held sway on Harte's team and they closed out the game, scoring five unanswered points to win by four and collect a third All-Ireland in six years. Having been dumped out of the Ulster championship by Down at the quarter-final stage, it was the most remarkable turnaround for this Tyrone team and the one that sealed Harte's and Tyrone's place in the history books.

Further Ulster titles were added in 2009 and 2010 while, for Kerry, in typical Kingdom fashion, they bounced back to capture another All-Ireland the following year, this time defeating Cork. But Tyrone had proven to be the thorn in their side and in the battle between the two for team of the decade, it was Harte's men who had come out on top.

Mickey Harte has remained as Tyrone manager in the face of everything that has befallen him, including the death of his daughter Michaela. And while Jim McGuinness' Donegal have now risen up to become the top team in Ulster and the country, Harte is determined to plot another All-Ireland for Tyrone with a new group of players.

The minors followed in the class of 1998's footsteps with All-Irelands in 2004, 2008 and 2010 and the next challenge will be to see if he can likewise empower the next crop of Tyrone seniors to emulate their record-breaking predecessors.

For Harte, it's about the team, the circle and trusting the players. He will find ways to outsmart Donegal's system of play, but can the players find it within themselves to do it as well?

'If you have good natural footballers you are going to trust them to make the right decisions on the ball,' says Philip Jordan, who is now part of the backroom team with the under-21s. 'It takes a brave manager to go out and do it. Some day, they might go out and get hammered off the pitch, but ultimately, in the long term, what will benefit the team the most is if you trust your players to take the right option.'

For ten years from 1998 to 2008, Mickey Harte placed his trust in his players, himself and a higher power. Life, as he has said, is not about an ending but a continuing path. Life moves on, football too.

Chapter 17

'Burning the boats'

Defeat to Tyrone in the 2003 All-Ireland semi-final was the line in the sand. Football had changed, Armagh had beaten them in the 2002 final and now Tyrone had shown that the pressing, swarming game was not about to go away. Once more, Kerry had to learn to adapt or die.

When Jack O'Connor stepped in to the Kerry management position, he was the first manager since Dr Eamonn O'Sullivan not to have won an All-Ireland as a player (or even to have played for the county). But Kerry had finally accepted that they had to ditch the old traditions – relying on the past was not going to win them All-Irelands in the twenty-first century.

Mick O'Dwyer was a playing legend when he took over the greatest side to grace Croke Park, and various incumbents had tried and failed to build another dynasty in his wake – Mickey Ned O'Sullivan, Ogie Moran, Páidí Ó Sé – all from the class of 1975. Jack O'Connor was a step into the relative unknown as the modern game threatened to overtake them.

However, he was a complete outsider. Like Mickey Harte, he

was a teacher, and the Dromid man had made a name for himself in the Vocational Schools competitions with Scoil Ui Chonaill as well as training his own club team which was starting to do well in the South Kerry championship. Despite never having been good enough for inter-county level, O'Connor was a fanatical Gaelic football man, always playing and being involved in the local club wherever he was, be it New York or Kerry.

It was always his single-mindedness that made him stand out, and when it came to football in Dromid, he was the one that cared the most and was training teams even at the age of just nineteen. Coming back from the States in 1989 and setting up home again in south Kerry, he threw himself into the game and in the 1990s was coaching three teams – the school, the club and the Kerry techs.

'I wasn't the organising type,' he says. 'But I would have been the type that questioned stuff that I'd heard in dressing rooms when I was there myself. I wouldn't just have gone along with everything the manager said. If you've got any independent thinking, you can't be a sheep, you can't just go along with everything that is said to you. I wouldn't have been a shrinking violet.'

Such traits would be badly needed when he did take over as manager and oversee the county's own adoption of Ulster tactics.

O'Connor was brought in as a selector when Páidí Ó Sé took over the Kerry job in 1996 and served his apprenticeship over the next seven years, working his way up to the senior selector role as well as training Kerry's under-21 teams, including an All-Ireland in 1998 as well as All-Ireland Vocational Schools titles in 1997, 1999 and 2000. When Páidí stepped down in 2003, O'Connor knew he was ready for the next challenge.

I felt I was ready. Whatever obstacles were there, I was going to have to deal with those but I felt I was ready for the job and I was only thinking of the positives going into it. Obviously, Kerry football was at a low ebb, but all I could see was getting a really good Kerry team back and competitive again and I had a few ideas myself on how I would go about doing that.

However, I wouldn't have come from the background that you would normally associate with Kerry managers. I wouldn't be seen as a big one down here because I mean, when you look at the line of fellas who had managed the team before me, the two guys before me had sixteen All-Ireland medals between them, and obviously O'Dwyer's shadow is always going to be over Kerry managers because that is what you are going to be judged against.

The similarities between Harte in rising up the football management ranks with underage success are obvious, as was the ability to get the best out of youthful dressing rooms. Good man-management was an important trait to have, and O'Connor also liked to believe in empowering the players.

I would be a fellow who would try and treat them well, who would do the right thing for them. I would expect huge commitment back as well. The way I operate is I would give a player every chance but there would come a point when I would draw a line and say, 'That's it.' I wouldn't be the type of fella who would keep nagging at the player. I would encourage them and I would support them, but there would come a point where I would just draw a line and say, 'No more.'

A lot of it has to do with the mix in the dressing room, the characters. There are players who are leaders and there are players who are followers and if you have got your leaders onside and you have got strong enough characters and leaders, that makes your job very easy. Ideally, the leadership needs to come from the players.

Of course, the manager needs to set the tone but the players are the most important. It's critical that you have leaders. Leaders in the dressing room, leaders on the field, because when games are in the melting pot, it's the leaders that can pull you through. Go back to 2005 when Tyrone needed to score a free out on the left-hand side of the pitch against Armagh, it was Peter Canavan who came up and kicked it. It's the big players and the leaders that make the difference at the end of the day.

The contrast in approaches to the game between Ulster counties and Kerry is never more striking than in the personalities of Mickey Harte and Jack O'Connor – one is a pioneer, calm and almost scientific in his analysis of the game; the other a fiery man from the rugged Toorsaleen mountains in south Kerry who wears his emotions on his sleeve. Northern coaches are seen as almost cerebral in their thinking about the game. In Kerry, it's still seen as something instinctive, coming from within. But for both, as their counties were re-emerging in the 2000s, the core principle to succeed remained the same: teamwork and togetherness. How they got there might have differed greatly in approach and emotion, but ultimately the same result was in their mind driven on by a fierce determination to win.

'I wouldn't be into gimmicky stuff at all,' says O'Connor. 'The manager has to try and transmit a bit of his own personality across to the team. The team should be a reflection of the manager's personality and so rather than bringing gimmicky stuff and trying tricky stuff, it's better just to be honest and be passionate and try and transmit some of that passion across and then let the team try to be a mirror image of your vision and your passion.'

In a county such as Kerry, however, where the divisional structure of the place meant there was more politics involved in the club football, and where certain footballing families held a sort of royal dominion over things, getting a mirror image was always going to be a difficult thing.

'Kerry football was at a crossroads really,' O'Connor says. 'They were beaten in two consecutive years by Northern teams and it appeared that they couldn't handle the intensity and the tackling. So I suppose when I came in, it was a big challenge to take over Kerry, especially taking over from Páidí Ó Sé, an absolute legend and Páidí obviously wanted to stay on and wanted to try and redress the situation, so that was a difficult situation for me because his nephews were on the team and they were big players. I wasn't going to be welcomed with open arms.'

For O'Connor, taking over after Páidí Ó Sé also meant having to deal with the old guard from the O'Dwyer years.

'They almost work as a cartel, those boys,' O'Connor wrote in his autobiography. 'In Kerry, it's as if they'd invented football … but the game moved on.'

Weeshie Fogarty of Radio Kerry rates O'Connor as one of the top three Kerry managers in their history – placing him alongside Dr Eamonn O'Sullivan and Mick O'Dwyer – with his ability to bring Kerry football into the twenty-first century and not only keep up but beat the rising Ulster teams as important as any other achievements that had gone before.

'He came along at the time when everything was changing,' explains Fogarty. 'All the tactics in the game had changed completely and in particular the professional training and then the swarming on the pitch that the Ulster counties brought in. But Jack O'Connor was able to come along and he was able to adapt. He put an awful lot of time and an awful lot of effort into it and he was able to motivate the players and get them to accept the challenge. He came along at the right time, even though he thinks himself that people thought that he wouldn't be able to do it. But also, importantly, he surrounded himself with good people.'

O'Connor may not have had the All-Ireland medals in his back pocket but he made sure that those selectors on the sideline with him did, and two of Kerry's footballing legends, Johnny Culloty and Ger O'Keeffe, joined his backroom team. The introduction of Pat Flanagan as trainer was also key. Flanagan, a physiology lecturer and former national 100-metre champion, focused his work on fast, intensive training sessions, with an emphasis on speed work, even proper running technique, not on bulking up to counter the size of Armagh.

Flanagan saw the game as a series of short bursts within a seventy-minute context and so every session was no longer than the seventy minutes, with players training more like sprinters than the traditional slog of lap-running that would have been typical in Mick O'Dwyer's management days. 'Train like you play' became the mantra, with speed, agility and quickness the key principles. Likewise, in the North, Mickey Harte's Tyrone team had long been focusing on ball work and speed in their sessions. Kerry were playing catch-up, however.

Despite winning the All-Ireland in his first year in charge, the real questions that were asked of Jack O'Connor's management of Kerry came with defeat to Tyrone in the 2005 All-Ireland semi-final, when they scored just six points and found the space in Croke Park squeezed out of them that day.

The harsh reality was that for Kerry to survive and beat the Tyrones, they needed to learn how to tackle like them – despite O'Connor asserting that in Kerry tackling was akin to 'heckling a tenor during his solo'. O'Connor didn't want them playing like Tyrone but he knew defensively they needed to be on a par. It was about proper technique, tackling with your body, not your hands, stop the man then go for the ball. It was new stuff for the team to take on board but some of the principles harking back to Dr Eamonn O'Sullivan's time also remained true, as Johnny Culloty, who played under O'Sullivan, reminded O'Connor. 'Fear fatal fouling' and 'close continual coverage' were the mantras that

Kerry's legendary trainer drilled into his teams in Fitzgerald Stadium over the decades and remained as true in the 2000s.

Firstly, O'Connor had to learn everything that the Ulster teams knew and did and he researched and pored over articles and drills on tackling from the Ulster council website, phoning contacts across the province, asking for any information on what Armagh and Tyrone did. A lot of Kerry pride was swallowed in the process, but for Kerry to survive and prosper once more, it had to be done. An Ulster contact was met in Dublin where information and notes on drills, techniques and an insight into the world of the Ulster men was passed on. If Kerry could be trained in meeting them head on, then maybe they could begin to find the spaces again to win Kerry's way. As O'Conner explains:

> *I felt that Kerry needed a slightly different type of player. For example, a player like Paul Galvin would fit into that mould. There was an awful lot of action going on around the middle of the field in that period, there was a furious intensity in the middle third, so you needed a certain type of player to match that type of intensity and work rate that the Northern teams were bringing to it. Paul Galvin was that type of player; Aidan O'Mahony and William Kirby were those types of player.*
>
> *There has always been a philosophy in Kerry that you have to win playing attractive football, that you have to win with style. That's fine and well and good, but it's also about being pragmatic and practical. It doesn't matter how artistic your football is, if you can't get the ball into their hands, you are wasting your time. So we just needed to get the balance right, the balance of the artistry and the hard work.*
>
> *We had to look around and say, 'Can we match what those guys are doing whilst still remaining relatively true*

*to what Kerry always had done (which was play not overly
defensive football but attractive attacking football)? That
was the key for us – to get the balance right.*

Having taken on board the weaknesses from 2005, worked on them
and drilled just what was required into the players, defeat to Cork
in the Munster final replay in the 2006 championship appeared to
have taken the team a step back. But there was to be a silver lining
in the defeat.

Kieran Donaghy, who lined out at midfield in the first encounter,
missed the replay having been sent off for an altercation with
Anthony Lynch. In his absence, Tommy Griffin did well at midfield
and the following week at training, Donaghy was put in at full-
forward to see how he would get on under the high balls on the
edge of the square. It worked a treat, reminding Donaghy of his
basketball days when he could attack the ball, bring it down, and
then use his quick feet to trick opponents. Suddenly, Kerry had
a forward line that was starting to fall into place. With Donaghy
as the target man, the Gooch and Mike Frank Russell could feed
off him, and the confidence began flowing again. Facing the firing
squad after the loss to Cork had been the making of them.

The Donaghy threat was reaping dividends: they beat Longford
4–11 to 1–11 in the qualifiers with Donaghy having a hand in all
four goals. Next up was Armagh in the All-Ireland quarter-final
and a chance for revenge for 2002. Kerry ran out eight-point
winners and it was to be the furthest Armagh would reach in the
championship for the rest of the decade.

Cork awaited in the semi-final, and O'Connor stoked the flames
of anger from what had happened in the Munster final, feeding
off Cork manager Billy Morgan's spiky comments about Kerry's
cynical play. 'Controlled fury' was O'Connor's description for
it, they were going to leave it all on the pitch for those seventy
minutes. Declan O'Sullivan, who had been booed off the pitch in

the Munster final, had quit his job and was living off his savings to concentrate full-time on his training and preparation to get back into the side. Such was the level of determination and effort that was going into their season and, in the end, Kerry blew Cork away, beating them by six points to reach another All-Ireland final.

This time they faced Mayo, and with Donaghy dominating on the edge of the square, Kerry ran out thirteen-point winners, 4–15 to 3–5, with the Gooch, Donaghy and returning captain Declan O'Sullivan each notching up 1–2 apiece.

What pleased O'Connor most was that they had done it their way. They may have adapted their approach to the tackle and dispossessing opponents, but they hadn't ditched their heritage altogether and had won the All-Ireland with a kicking game. The team mightn't have had as many stars as O'Dwyer's 1970s side, but Donaghy's emergence as the star forward that season was reminiscent of Bomber Liston's famed first season with the Kingdom.

'Kerry have always been able to come up with good styles to counteract teams,' believes O'Connor. 'As far back as 1955, they beat a Dublin team that was considered invincible. For a long time, Kerry has managed to come up with ways and means of counteracting certain styles. I am sure Kerry will always come up with something because by and large we have produced a lot of natural footballers and if you have got the skill, you will always find a way around systems.

'And Kerry fans have no choice now, they have to accept that certain things are here to stay, and they have to change; you have to take the style you are playing against, you have to take that into account. I remember in 2003 watching Kerry playing Tyrone and I was saying to myself, "If I get my hands on this team, I am going to have to change the way they are playing here." If the boys are getting men back, standing in front of the full-back line, there is no point in you lamping the ball in at your full-forward line because it's going to come back out at you. You have to change and you have to take the opposition and the style of football that they are playing into account. So the Kerry public are going to have to change as well.'

End the Struggle and Dance with Life was the title of the book on O'Connor's bedside locker that summer. In it, Susan Jeffers extols the virtues of positivity, letting go and trusting the future. When Kerry football was at its lowest ebb in 2003 after successive defeats to Armagh and Tyrone, they turned to O'Connor to set them on the right course in a break from tradition; and when his Kerry team reached their lowest point after defeat to Cork in the Munster final replay in 2006, they had nothing left to lose and found a way to play once more with a confidence and self-belief that wouldn't let any opponents put them down.

O'Connor stepped down after they reached the summit of the 2006 victory – having reached three finals and won two All-Irelands during his three years in charge – and the side continued its remarkable run of All-Ireland final appearances under his successor, Pat O'Shea, winning in 2007 before succumbing once again to Tyrone in 2008 in the battle for supremacy.

O'Connor returned for a second stint with the Kingdom in 2009, when the team set a county record of six All-Ireland final appearances in a row, beating Cork for the second time in three years. Cork finally got their All-Ireland, beating Down the following year, before O'Connor brought Kerry back to another final, but this time resulting in a defeat to Dublin, thanks to a last-minute free kick from Dublin goalkeeper Stephen Cluxton.

O'Connor's last year in charge of Kerry in 2012 was to see them fall by two points at the quarter-final stage to the coming force, Donegal, and it was a salutary reminder that while Kerry had overcome the rising tide of Armagh and Tyrone at the start of the 2000s, football has been on an increasingly quicker evolutionary curve in recent times. Dublin and Donegal took the blanket defence system to new heights (or lows) in 2011 with a dour, defensive low-scoring semi-final with fourteen men behind the ball on each side. By 2012, Donegal had moved it on a step farther having established the blanket defence but were now playing with more expression and verve in the forward line. No county in the country could cope with the total football system played at breakneck speed by Donegal in 2012 and in the aftermath of the final defeat, Jack O'Connor stepped down.

In his *Irish Times* column after the loss, Darragh Ó Sé, who had already retired in 2010, compared the state of Kerry football to that in the wake of the 2003 defeat to Tyrone and predicted a gloomy future.

> *It has to be said that the immediate future doesn't look great for Kerry. It's hard to see where Kerry can get the bodies to turn this thing around. People are worried that there's nothing coming through and that's what has made it even more depressing.*

Weeshie Fogarty is similarly worried in the short-term, comparing Kerry's situation to that of the 1960s when Down changed the game and Kerry were going through transition to cope, but ultimately he believes that when there's All-Ireland-winning experience to call upon, then, long-term, the players will emerge and ultimately the county will come through.

'It's a natural progression,' he says. 'When Maurice Fitzgerald packed it in, they said there wouldn't be anyone like him again, then Colm Cooper comes along and you had Mick O'Connell before Fitzgerald, you had all the great players, there's always somebody coming along, and when these current older players go, Kerry will be in for a very lean time, there's no doubt in my mind. But the game will change and the game will evolve and football will always win out.'

Jack O'Connor also wonders what lies ahead for the Kingdom. He works with development squads in the county and sees at first hand the future talent.

They are not producing them in the numbers certainly that were there before. That is one of the things that I found in my last few years with Kerry, that the players weren't coming through in the quantities that you needed. I was involved with the under-21s in the 1990s and we won three All-Irelands in five years and you look at the players that came through in the that period, the Ó Sés, the Seamus Moynihans, the Mike McCarthys, we got a bunch through in the 1990s that really stood the test of time and they were the backbone of the Kerry senior team for ten years. But Kerry hasn't won a minor since 1994 and to me that's a massive indictment of what is happening, because that would be like Kilkenny not winning a hurling minor for twenty years and there would be a steward's inquiry and that is the big challenge in Kerry to try and get a minor success and build on it for the future.

He's also pessimistic about the future of the game, having seen and dealt with one Ulster revolution in the first part of his senior management career, and now Donegal have taken it another step farther.

Somebody said one time, and I think he had a point, that the way Gaelic footballers are being coached now, they are like battery chickens because they are all the same. Maybe there is a lot to be said in that and maybe that's what the next revolution is, people will have to go back to basics. With all the changes in the game it still comes down to fairly basic stuff, the quality of kicking under pressure is a big thing and is one thing that has been neglected in coaching. It's a lot of hand-passing, a lot of tackling, but if you can move the ball properly and accurately, by foot over long distances that still can be effective.

Football constantly evolves, after 2002–2003 people thought that Tyrone and the Armagh style would stay in vogue but the game changed again. At the moment certainly, it seems to have been taken to another level altogether. The one thing that I would have to say about Jim McGuinness is he had serious balls to do what he did, because if I had tried to do what he did in Kerry, I would have no fan but myself. People just wouldn't have accepted it. So for him to actually be able to do it and get his players to believe in it and carry it out to the letter of the law, you absolutely have to give him credit for that. I'm not sure that's a compliment now, but you have to give him serious credit for that because it takes serious balls to stand on the sideline in Croke Park and have everybody virtually booing the style of play and stick with it. And fair enough tweaking it a bit the following year but to stick with his guns, you have to give him credit there.

In my time, I was labelled as copying the Northern style and being defensive. I didn't think I was being overly defensive at all, it's just that I was getting the lads to toughen up a bit and work harder. But the point I am trying to make is that you would not get away with an overly defensive style in Kerry because the public don't want it. Teams that have never won too much will buy into any system that they think will win for them. But you know, managers have a duty to the game as well.

As each championship year approaches, the angst and the debate in Kerry goes on for another season. They had a side that reached six All-Ireland finals in a row but it still didn't seem to be enough. They had addressed the changes in the game when Armagh and Tyrone came along only to see an even faster, slicker version introduced by Donegal. Since 2002, it has been the Ulster counties, and the Ulster coaches, leading the way in terms of tactical evolution. Sometimes you get the feeling that in Kerry, they wish for simpler days when good catching and kicking won out and when they were kings at that, lording it over the rest of the country. But society moves on and develops, new minds and new ways of seeing and thinking about traditional methods are introduced and the game moves on with it.

Jack O'Connor stemmed the tide at the start of the century and changed the mindset of the county, accepting they had to change their ways – not ditching them but certainly altering them – and it proved successful for four of those six final appearances. However, once more Kerry is at a crossroads and this time for the new manager, Eamonn Fitzmaurice, the issue lies deeper than mere styles of play, it's about the emerging talent from the Kingdom, a county that was always able to produce its crop of some of the most skilful players in the country. They worry that it's drying up, that over-coaching, systems of play, drills and hand-passing have overtaken them at even club and underage level. Or perhaps that's just the reality of the modern game and any harking back to the old days is what will leave them mired in the past. The question now is: can All-Ireland success still be achieved with one foot in the present day and the other still in the past?

O'Connor retells a story about the level of commitment needed. When the Moors, only 7,000 in number, landed on a beach in Spain to take on the might of the Spanish army, their leader asked them, 'Are you committed?'

They cheered they were.

'Then burn the boats.'

It was all or nothing, no going back.

Part VI

The System

'You are the programmer.
Write the programme.
Now run the programme.'

Stephen Covey, author of
The Seven Habits of Highly Effective People

Chapter 18

Flattering to achieve

Jack O'Connor's last taste of an All-Ireland final was defeat to Dublin. 2011 was the year for turning back the clock and reminiscing about the glory years in the 1970s and early 1980s. It had been twenty-six years since the sides had last met in an All-Ireland final, and the game had changed beyond all recognition in that time. Kerry had won six All-Irelands (a veritable famine by their standards), while Dublin had only added the solitary one in 1995. What was it about the Dubs, who seemed, perennially, to flatter to achieve?

In 1974, Kevin Heffernan had dragged Dublin GAA from the wilderness, creating an aura and mythology about 'the Dubs' and 'the Hill'. It was the first experience of urban culture popularising Gaelic games and so, whenever Dublin threatened to go on to great things, the city's populace was ready to embrace it, always harking back to the Heffo days. There was no getting away from it, and just as Kerry struggled in the wake of Mick O'Dwyer's departure (there was an eleven-year wait before Kerry captured their first All-Ireland post-O'Dwyer), it was the same for Dublin. It was twelve years before they won the Sam Maguire in 1995, upsetting the Ulster years of domination in that decade in the process. Much as Kerry leaned on former greats to lead the county, so too Dublin looked to their past with a succession of ex-players taking over – Paddy Cullen, Mickey Whelan and Pat O'Neill all tried their hand and found that following in Heffernan's footsteps was at times too big to handle.

In the early 1990s, Dublin did threaten, and with talented and battle-hardened players such as Keith Barr, Charlie Redmond, John O'Leary, Brian Stynes and Dessie Farrell, they won two league titles as well as reaching three All-Irelands in four years from 1992–1995. They lost the first two – to Donegal and then Down – which only reinforced the reigning superiority of Ulster teams at that time. When Dublin finally did get their All-Ireland title, beating Tyrone in 1995, it was to be the high point of the decade for Dublin GAA as they failed to win even a Leinster title for another seven years.

Whereas Kerry were forced to confront their deficiencies in the face of the next wave of Ulster superiority, and did so with Jack O'Connor taking on the job, Dublin were still going through a succession of managers, most lasting three or four years before a new face was found. Yet even still, the resurgent Laois and Westmeath under Mick O'Dwyer and Páidí Ó Sé were proving difficult for Dublin to overcome in their own province, whereas the real battles at the top of the game were being fought at All-Ireland semi-final and final level with Armagh, Tyrone and Kerry battling it out.

Colin Moran played with Dublin for eleven years and witnessed the stuttering evolution of the county team while other counties were taking giant leaps forward. The beginnings of change and the start of the sports science influence came under Tommy Carr, a former player whose background was also in the Irish army. This military background saw the introduction of a regimented regime with a lot of focus on hill running and stamina training. However, it did start to change over time when scientific influences came to be better recognised in the field of Gaelic games. Liam Hennessy, an elite trainer who also worked with the IRFU, was brought on board and the county team were one of the first to be brought away to Spain for winter training, years before Armagh and La Manga became known for it, although Carr admits he actually overtrained the players there.

> *We were a month away from the championship and we said, 'Right, we have them for a week and we will train the shit out of them and they will be so fit when they come back.' But they actually became staler and more tired as time went on and it took them a good three weeks to recover from that one week.*
>
> *My knowledge of what should have been done should have been better – we were out three times a day when, in fact, it should have been nearly less than what we were doing back home because of the climate and the ground and all that. We went from being amateurs to being professionals for a week and you can't do that in the space of seven days. Of course, I know all that now and there's much more knowledge, much more technology telling you that the players are good for training or they're not good for training.*

'It was the start of change,' explains Colin Moran. 'It wasn't in any way as sophisticated as it would be nowadays but it was the first signs of it. Tommy started bringing circuit training into it and we were doing short blocks of sprints instead of the traditional laps and laps of running. That was the beginning of change coming into it.'

However, after four years in charge, Dublin had lost three

Leinster finals in a row. 2001 was the first year of the qualifiers, which meant they had a second chance through the back door, but they faced Kerry in the quarter-final, with the game going to a replay after a miracle sideline equaliser from Kerry's Maurice Fitzgerald. Dublin then lost the replay 2–12 to 1–12 and while Dublin might have been close, Tommy Carr was ousted in a contentious split vote in the county board.

'The players were all very disappointed about that,' says Moran. 'We had been hoping that he would have been kept on because we felt that he had been learning over the four years and moving us on to more sophisticated training methods. We felt we were close and then he got shafted. Tommy Lyons came in then and when he took over I remember we all felt it was a backward step because we were going back to the continuous laps and that kind of thing.'

In the early part of the decade, Dublin were losing ground and instead of moving forward seemed to be harking back to old ways and ignoring the way football had advanced. A Canadian sprint coach had been brought on board and was teaching them key elements of running (as Pat Flanagan was to do with Kerry) but it wasn't gelling with Lyons' management philosophy.

'Tommy was saying, "Okay, on Monday you can do your weights with her in UCD or wherever, but on Tuesday you are mine in Cathal Brugha Barracks and I am going to run the hair out of you on continuous laps,"' says Moran. 'And then the Canadian sprint coach was saying, "Look, everything I am doing on the Monday and a Wednesday, you are undoing that work on a Tuesday and Thursday because it's counter-productive." She was building muscles for explosive strength and he was building middle-distance runners.'

2002 was Lyons' first year in charge and he brought with him an energised tempo and knew how to play the media and generate massive interest in the county. They won a first Leinster title in seven years and hammered Donegal by ten points to reach an All-Ireland semi-final. Only Armagh and seventy minutes stood between them and an All-Ireland final with Kerry. The good times were back, the hype machine cranked into overdrive. Yet one swallow does not a summer make, and Armagh were ready and waiting for them.

'The thing about Armagh was their physical strength, their real commitment to the gym programmes and their more structured approach to the game,' says Moran. 'In Dublin we were always pretty positive, but Armagh were very structured and didn't take chances. When Tyrone came in the following year, they took cynical tackling and defensive tactics up a notch. The bar had been raised and Dublin were a bit stagnant.'

Dublin weren't the only team to be caught out, of course – Armagh and Tyrone both overcame Kerry in the course of their All-Irelands in 2002 and 2003 – but by 2004 the Lyons bandwagon had come to a stuttering halt. The initial promise of 2002 had faltered and Laois and Westmeath were enjoying their title successes in Leinster. Dublin on the other hand were getting no further than the qualifiers. Change was needed once more and when 'Pillar' Caffrey, one of Lyons' right-hand men, was chosen, eyebrows and doubts were raised among the players. But to their surprise, he was willing to change things around and take on board what needed to be done now that the game was developing so quickly.

'I'll never forget the first night that Pillar took over,' remembers Moran. 'And I would say, being honest, there were guys in the squad who were disappointed that he had been made manager, worried it would just be a continuation of the same old thing, but that wasn't the case at all. I can picture him standing up in front of the room and it was just obvious that even though this guy had been working for three years under Tommy Lyons, he had completely different ideas on training and on the game, so that was a breath of fresh air.

'He didn't introduce that much new talent, the subs changed a fair bit, but it was still the core team. He was just a very good man-manager and he certainly put a resilience into the squad and a sense of pride in the jersey again. In Tommy Lyons' last match, we got an absolute hammering against Kerry and confidence was at a low and he just built us back up again, changed the training techniques and was much more professional about the whole thing.

'The weights became a much bigger part of it, there was a big focus on statistics, key performance indicators, video analysis, that kind of stuff. He brought in a big backroom team to handle all of this. Whereas Tommy Lyons would have been hands-on in a lot of the training, Pillar would just stand back. He had specific coaches for defensive stuff, stuff for the forwards, for fitness and conditioning, so he brought in stuff we hadn't seen before.'

Dragging Dublin into the modern had an immediate impact and, in Caffrey's four years in charge, the county won the Leinster title every year from 2005 to 2008 – the last time Dublin had won four-in-a-row in Leinster culminated in them winning the All-Ireland in 1995. Yet, while their dominance in their own backyard was supreme, outside the province Dublin were coming up against teams that were years ahead of them in terms of strength and conditioning.

Bookending the Caffrey years were defeats to Tyrone in the All-Ireland quarter-finals. The first time they lost by seven points but, by 2008, Tyrone hammered them by twelve and Caffrey's time was up. There were also semi-final defeats to Mayo and Kerry in 2006 and 2007 which probably represented Dublin's best chance of an All-Ireland in that period, but they were never able to get over that line despite knocking on the door. However, it was their weakness in the face of Tyrone that was to prove how they were still falling short against the game's yardstick, no matter how much Caffrey tried.

'He would have had quite an interest in the Ulster teams and what they were doing,' says Moran. 'And what he had brought in from them was that we had to move the ball a lot quicker than we had been doing. This was really to combat the blanket defences that you would be just getting sucked into by over-carrying the ball and going nowhere. Defensively, we were trying to be a little bit cuter and even a little bit more cynical as well; Dublin were always the kind of team that I think other teams might like to play against because we were pretty open and positive and that kind of thing. There was also an emphasis on the physical conditioning and the mental preparation to games, which we hadn't really spent much time on before but which were big changes that he developed and introduced.

'We felt that we weren't far away, you know. We had really got a stranglehold on Leinster which we were trying to use as a platform to go on in the All-Ireland series, but when you look back at the Tyrone and Kerry teams and the players they had at that time, a lot of them were in their peak condition and just they were two quite exceptional teams that just had that bit more than us.'

The twelve-point defeat to Tyrone was the end of the road for Caffrey, but he had established the foundation. They had their confidence back, they were dominant in Leinster, the physical conditioning programmes, mental preparation and coaching specialists had all been introduced. Now the county needed someone who could take them one step farther and with St Vincent's capturing the All-Ireland club championship earlier in the year, it seemed obvious that their manager, Pat Gilroy, was the man to do it.

Gilroy came with the necessary CV: a former Dublin player, a St Vincent's man, close to Heffernan, successful businessman, a thinker of the game and, importantly, someone who had All-Ireland-winning experience. Here, then, was somebody with all the knowledge and motivation who could finally lead Dublin to senior All-Ireland glory.

Colin Moran, who had retired earlier in the season, was asked to stay on as a selector by Gilroy and he witnessed the team and games as they unfolded. Leinster was retained – the last time five successive provincial titles was achieved was in the heyday of the 1970s – and Kerry were next up in the All-Ireland quarter-final. Dublin were ready for yet another tilt at Sam Maguire and this time it would be different.

'The squad was very competitive, had been knocking on the door, but was just short of Kerry and Tyrone,' says Moran. 'And I think he felt he could make a few tweaks and get them over the line by giving them a few per cent more and that would be enough to do it.'

The wake-up call that finally shattered the Dubs' myth about themselves and their place in relation to the modern game came on 3 August 2009. Dominance in Leinster had been an illusory garland, but while no All-Ireland finals had been reached, the county believed they weren't really that far behind the Kerrys and Tyrones of the Gaelic footballing world.

That day in August, Dublin ran out full of confidence and self-belief against Kerry and ran into a side that had been hurting after their 2008 defeat to Tyrone, ready to prove their doubters wrong and make their mark once more. This was a Kerry team that had been groomed since 2004 for taking on Ulster teams' strengths and proven itself capable of winning All-Irelands on its own terms, albeit with better tackling and defensive strategies. Kerry had five years of consecutive All-Ireland final appearances under their belts; Dublin, without a single final to their name, were in the ha'penny place in comparison.

Kerry won that day by seventeen points – 1–24 to 1–07. It was their joint-biggest win over Dublin, equalling the 1978 All-Ireland final pummelling and shattering any myths about just how strong the Dubs purported to be. No amount of tweaking could paper over the realities and for Gilroy, it was a sobering first season in charge.

'I will never forget him after that Kerry match,' remembers Moran. 'He was just furious. The night after the Kerry game, he tore it all apart and started over with a blank page. If it was a one-point defeat, there might have been the temptation to make a few more tweaks, which is what Dublin had been doing for years. But the nature of that defeat triggered a radical restructuring of everything.'

Dublin normally wouldn't have been thankful to Kerry for handing them down a seventeen-point drubbing, but finally the county was forced to face up to reality. An overhaul was needed. Everything had to go, everything had to change.

Pat Gilroy had seen how tight modern defences had become. They were about giving no space away, getting men back behind the ball when not in possession and then relying on a two-man forward line to work its magic when it received quick ball on the break. While Dublin didn't have the same number of talented scorers as Kerry or Tyrone, they did have two gems in the Brogan brothers, Alan and Bernard, who were All Star talents.

Nor would he put up with players not wanting it enough, not putting in the hours or not working for the team. Any pursuit of individual glory or pandering to the ego mindset was gone. It had to be a team in total togetherness singing off the one hymn sheet. The days of Dublin being open and positive were about to go out the window. Seventeen-point humiliations do that to traditions and principles. Just as Kernan was willing to go it another way with Crossmaglen and Armagh, and just as Mickey Harte was prepared to introduce total tactics and total teamwork across the pitch in pursuit of victory, so too Pat Gilroy was to embrace a radically new approach to Dublin's football.

There would be many cast aside along the way, and there would be grumblings and dissent within the county, but if the price was ultimately an All-Ireland, would anyone care in the end? Gilroy was betting they wouldn't. Dublin were sick of being the also-rans. It was time to turn them into actual winners. No matter what it took.

'He would have felt there were some individuals in the team who were interested in their own performance more than the team performance and he absolutely tore that up,' says Moran. 'There were some high-profile casualties, but he set his stall out that if you don't work, and you're not tackling, it doesn't matter how talented you are. Dublin had been conceding a lot of scores in the big games in the later summer, the ones that they were eventually knocked out in, and he just felt that the players weren't working hard enough without the fear. The official line was: no matter how talented you are, if you don't work, you aren't going to play.'

Playing catch-up, and to test the players' resolve, 6 a.m. sunrise sessions were introduced in the early part of the season, forty years after Eugene McGee had used them with UCD Sigerson teams.

'It's a very short burst of them just to make up for the time of the down season – it's a lifestyle thing that works for us,' Gilroy said at a press conference. 'There is a big benefit for us because of the traffic and distances being travelled. It sounds very exotic, but it's actually a very practical thing. We only do it around exam time, and they really like to be up, particularly the students, to get their study in for the day. If we were doing five evenings a week, they'd lose the evening and would get no work done, whereas in the early mornings they're in college by 8 a.m. and they're able to study. So there's a lifestyle thing that works for us.'

There were further evening sessions as well, seeing the players doing two rounds of training in a day, but for Gilroy the workload was required as he revamped the playing style, introducing the blanket defence, twelve men behind the ball when the opposition crossed the fifty and an emphasis on closing down space, with dispossessing and tackling beginning with the full-forward line. Mickey Harte's defensive system with Tyrone was now becoming the template for others to follow.

Defend first, men behind the ball, squeeze the space. Even a top-class forward like Bernard Brogan was being put into the wing-back position at training to improve his tackling and dispossessing skills. Athletes were required first and foremost, players over six foot who could run all day were quickly becoming the prototype of the modern Gaelic footballer, and Gilroy was looking to perfect the model with the Dublin players at his disposal.

His day job was as the managing director of a French energy services company, and he was used to early starts, long hours, commitment, attention to detail and ensuring things ran smoothly. With Dublin it was to be no different. The business model of Tyrone was a successful one and could be adapted to Dublin's needs. After the SWOT (strengths, weaknesses, opportunitiess and threats) analysis came the training and the implementation, and if there was any questioning of where they were going or why they were doing it, the MD in Gilroy ensured there was no deviation from the script. Total commitment. Here's the road map, he was saying to the players, I can guide you and give you the tools necessary but only you can decide if you're prepared to work at it.

'He brought structure, he brought tackling counts, his big thing was work rate,' explains Val Andrews, a leading coach in Dublin who also managed Cavan and Tralee IT. 'Any time Dublin out-tackled their opposition, they won. So he defined the tackle first and worked with the players on their technique. To stop the opposition forward momentum, you had to get him to turn, or take the ball off him, or make contact with the ball, that was their defining of it.'

Gilroy's new plan for Dublin wasn't without its initial problems. The first game of the 2010 Leinster championship saw them ship an embarrassing five goals against Meath and lose by eleven points

– 5–9 to 0–13 – the old bad habits of conceding big scores hadn't gone away, it seemed. But Gilroy regrouped his troops and the qualifiers gave them an opportunity to prove their mettle, prove that Gilroy's way was working, they just had to bed it down and stick with it.

'The instructions on day one of the 2010 season were, "No matter what happens this year, we are not going to concede loads of goals and big scores,"' explains Moran. 'There wasn't even talk about winning All-Irelands or anything like that in January, it was just, "We are going to be really, really hard to break down." I suppose for the players that humiliating defeat to Kerry probably hammered home to them as well that they couldn't go on the way they were.'

Tipperary in the second round of the qualifiers gave them a chance to dust off the cobwebs of the Meath defeat and they beat them by eight points before meeting Armagh. The game was, as expected, a tough, tight encounter, and in the second half, down by a point, Armagh closed in on the Dublin goal. A three-point score at that stage and Armagh would have been through and Gilroy's Dublin record would have read: two years in charge – Year 1, a seventeen-point defeat to Kerry; Year 2, a five-goal hammering at the hands of Meath and beaten in the qualifiers by Armagh.

Managers and players always talk about inches, the little things that can make the difference, especially when you're at your lowest. As Armagh's forwards looked to hammer the goal home, Philip McMahon got back to clear the ball off the line. Dublin's season had been retrieved and they went on to win by three points.

'If they had been beaten in an innocuous game by a poor Armagh team,' says Moran, 'that could have been the end of the line for Pat Gilroy. If Phillie McMahon hadn't cleared that ball off the line …'

Louth were dispatched in the next round, as were Tyrone in the quarters and suddenly Dublin were into an All-Ireland semi-final without playing or winning convincingly, but their doggedness, the ability to come through tight contests, had shown that defensively they had tightened up, the system was working and the players were starting to gel under it.

They faced Cork, the previous year's beaten finalists, in the semi-final and played their best football of the year, leading by four at half-time and continuing to hold on to that lead as they moved into the final stages. However, while physically and tactically they might have been looking good, they were still lacking the mental toughness to close out a game. A sloppy penalty was given away, which Cork's Donncha O'Connor duly converted, and when Ross McConnell was sent off minutes later, the writing was on the wall. Having dominated for so long, conceding 1–03 in the final minutes was a hammer blow to their ambitions and they lost by just a point, 1–15 to 1–14.

It was all the more galling when Cork went on and finished the job by capturing their first All-Ireland in twenty years. They had been close in recent years, having already lost in 2007 and 2009, but in 2010 against Down, there was to be no mistake and Cork were All-Ireland champions.

Pat Gilroy and Dublin looked on and wondered, *What if?* They knew they had the beating of Cork, they knew how close they were, they were gaining confidence in each other and in the system, another year and they knew an All-Ireland final was there for them.

'In that Cork semi-final, the football they played was the first time that season they broke out from the unattractive blanket defence,' says Moran. 'You could see for the first time that they were building something that could win an All-Ireland. Gilroy knew he had to take a step back to take hopefully two steps forward and there was a lot of rumblings in the camp that year. He was hearing rumours that guys were going to walk and just had had enough of it. Things had to change.'

Wholesale change wasn't required. The building blocks had

been established, the team knew what was expected and required of them. If 2010 had ended with them knowing how close they were, 2011 was about going that extra mile. In January, the 6 a.m. sessions started again, and with a year's conditioning behind them, they were even fitter entering the 2011 season. Dublin reached the league final – their first since 1999 – but as on that occasion, Cork were once again their nemesis.

It was the kind of chastening experience that was to be the making, not the breaking, of Gilroy's Dubs and after the game, he came out fighting.

'This team has more character and more guts to put up with the sort of stuff that surrounds them every day and they still get back out there and train and work,' he said determinedly. 'They're the most honest guys you'll find. They'll get stick for this but we'll deal with that because it's our job.'

True to form, Dublin didn't let it set them back. Their mental resolve seemed to get stronger with each defeat. The Leinster title was regained after wins over Laois, Kildare and a three-point victory in the final against Wexford. They weren't blowing teams away but they were coming through when it counted and faced Tyrone in the All-Ireland quarter-final for the second year running. What was to follow, Gilroy described as the team's best seventy minutes of the entire year, when everything clicked into place, and Dublin ran out convincing seven-point winners. In the new decade, it was Dublin who were handing down seven-point drubbings to Tyrone. How times had changed. Now into a second successive All-Ireland semi-final, Dublin were being touted as serious title contenders.

From the high of the Tyrone victory, the semi-final against Donegal will go down in the annals of Gaelic football semi-finals for all the wrong reasons, and marked the low point of a decade of the blanket defence. Jim McGuinness, newly installed as Donegal's manager, was likewise a proponent of a defensive system of twelve men behind the ball when not in possession. Like Gilroy, a former All-Ireland winner with his county in the 1990s, McGuinness was an astute student of the game with a background in sports science, and was someone who was using his involvement with other sports to develop a style of play that would make Donegal just as watertight as Dublin had become.

'Jimmy would have looked at Dublin and seen what Gilroy did in the first two years to make them so defensive,' explains Val Andrews, who had coached McGuinness at Tralee IT. 'Jimmy McGuinness would basically look at how they did it, take it, copy it and then improve it.'

What occurred during that semi-final wasn't a meeting of two great expansive, attack-minded coaches. It was two detail-oriented managers who emphasised defence first and counter-attacking second. As Donegal parked the bus in front of their D, Dublin likewise retreated back and Croke Park was treated to the unseemly spectacle of two teams in possession and both going nowhere. By half–time, it was 0–4 to 0–2 to Donegal, and Dublin weren't to register their first score from play until the sixtieth minute.

Ironically, it was the sending off of Diarmuid Connolly that actually opened up some space for his team-mates on the Croke Park pitch, and as Donegal's intensity and work-rate inevitably faded going into the last quarter,. Dublin were able to turn a 0–6 to 0–3 deficit in the forty-fourth minute to come through 0–8 to 0–6. It was the lowest winning total for an All-Ireland semi-final since Galway had beaten Tyrone in 1956, and Dublin's total had only featured two scores from play in the entire game.

'I've seen the apocalypse and heaven help us if this is the way the game of Gaelic football is going to go,' said Pat Spillane, reeling in horror at the defence-first game he had just witnessed.

'Like watching paint dry' was the general tenor of fans leaving

Croke Park that day and while Dublin were into their first All-Ireland in sixteen years, many were also asking, 'Was this what it had to take?' Many in Gaelic football believe that the GAA's subsequent establishment of the Football Review Committee was a consequence of what happened between Donegal and Dublin. Was this to be the culmination and defining game of the tactical evolution that had been occurring for the last ten years? More pertinently, where were the attack-minded coaches who believed there was another way, rather than a one-dimensional philosophy of defence first, attack second?

The fallout and criticisms continued for the rest of the year and into the next championship season and, in many ways, some were wondering if we were at an existential moment that could see the game changed forever resulting in games of 0–8 to 0–6 becoming the norm, or was it merely a case of the game's evolution and other ways to counteract the defensive system just needed to be found?

But Dublin and Gilroy had found a way through Donegal's defensive blanket and they had performed what was necessary to get to the end result and were into an All-Ireland final. Jack O'Connor's Kerry faced them in September and while it was the first meeting in a final between these two counties since 1985 and reminiscences of the Heffernan–O'Dwyer years came up, there was no talk of glory years or the beginning of dynasties and a rivalry to compare with the 1970s. Football had moved on too much since then, there were now five or six counties competing at the top table regularly each year, and the game was a different sport to that of forty years previously.

The final was never going to be a defensive repeat of the Donegal semi-final, and while it wasn't a free-flowing, high-scoring game either, there was enough tension and drama to make it memorable for all the right reasons. Going into the last ten minutes, Kerry were four points ahead and for a team of Kerry's experience, in their seventh final in eight years, it should have been enough to see them through. However, substitute Kevin McManamon scored a vital goal on sixty-four minutes and suddenly Dublin had the Hill and the momentum behind them. Like Armagh, they didn't give up going into the closing stages of games and, having been knocking on the door for two years, their self-belief and mental toughness saw them hit Kerry with the winner in stoppage time with goalkeeper Stephen Cluxton coolly slotting over the winning free.

From a seventeen-point humiliation at the hands of the same team just two years previously, Pat Gilroy had set down a new plan, a new way of doing business, and turned the team around to become All-Ireland winners. It wasn't quite the Heffernan turnaround from 1973–1974, but it was remarkable all the same. What's more, the team had an average age of just twenty-three, with the biggest change in the team coming in defence.

Five new faces were in Dublin's backline compared to that which shipped 1–24 in 2009. There were only two changes in the forward line, with the main thrust of attack and supply focusing on the two Brogans, but key to the shape and tightness of the team was the fact that two of the half-forwards, Barry Cahill and Bryan Cullen, had previously featured in the half-back line. Defenders who became forwards so they could tackle and track back was key to Dublin's shape.

It was no coincidence either that it was a substitute, Kevin McManamon, who set Dublin on their way with his sixty-fourth-minute goal, as all through the season Gilroy was emphasising the thirty-man squad and not just the starting fifteen.

The biggest thing I've learned is the importance of the second fifteen. While I would have believed in it before, I

*really learned how important it is, because ten days before
the final, we were facing being down six of the fellas who
played the previous two games. The panel is so critical to
success, if you don't have that backup, I don't think you can
win it.*

The future for Dublin football was looking bright and Gilroy spoke
of a hunger and attitude from the squad of players that augured well.

*There are so many fellas here who are under twenty-three
and they are mad for football and training. I think there's
been a sea change in the whole attitude towards physical
fitness compared to seventeen years ago. These guys want
to be fit permanently, they are not looking for breaks, they
just want to train and if they are not training with us, they
will train on their own and I think that is a big difference.*

*We made a lot of mistakes against Kerry, like when they
outscored us 8–1, but there was a lot to be learned because
it was an intriguing match. Getting to the final after all
those years had been progress, so this was always going to
be the start – and it should be the start because it is such a
young team.*

However, as ever, the following year was to prove more difficult
and in Dublin where the hype and the media increase tenfold, there's
even more of a spotlight and demands on the players. Dublin have
only retained the All-Ireland once in ninety years, and that was at
the peak of Heffo's Dubs in 1976 and 1977; in fact, since the 1920s
– and excluding the 1970s – Dublin have never won an All-Ireland
more than once in a decade.

2012 was to be no different, and despite a Leinster final victory
over Meath and a third successive All-Ireland semi-final, a three-

point defeat to Mayo, was the culmination of a season that never got going for Dublin. Just weeks later, Pat Gilroy stepped down and his hugely successful four-year spell, resulting in three Leinster titles and one All-Ireland, came to an end.

After that five-goal hammering at the hands of Meath and the seventeen-point mauling by Kerry in his first year in charge, who could have foreseen the turnaround in Dublin's fortunes in the subsequent years? As Colin Moran suggests, the humiliation to Kerry was probably the best thing that could have happened, resulting as it did in a complete overhaul of the approach and system that Dublin needed to play. In the modern context, tweaking around the edges was no longer sufficient.

But can Dublin prove that they're not just one-hit wonders and establish a legacy to compete in finals on a regular basis over the next part of the decade, as Tyrone and Kerry did in the 2000s? One Sam Maguire a decade has been their lot so far and how radical and far-reaching the Gilroy template has been will be seen over the coming years.

'What Pat Gilroy did was get rid of the surface part of the Dublin bandwagon, bringing a bit of steel to them,' believes Tommy Carr. 'It was a no-nonsense approach on top of the flamboyancy that finally got them over the line. But you know you also need that bit of luck – at the end of the day should Kerry have lost that All-Ireland final? If they hadn't misplaced the hand-pass in the middle of the pitch, then would we be asking the same question as to why are Dublin still flat and why are they still the bridesmaids? I would have liked it if Dublin had followed up the following year with a really concrete performance – even getting into an All-Ireland final and being beaten by a point to be able to say, "Okay, they were a really, really good team."

'In the GAA, every player likes the big day and likes the headlines and the articles in the paper and Dublin gets so much

of that. They don't have to win All-Irelands to be as 'famous' as
Meath, Cork, Galway or Mayo teams. They get it handed to them
on a plate and they don't need to achieve to get recognition.'

For Val Andrews, it goes back ultimately to the development of
talent.

'Dublin don't dominate because we don't produce enough
technically and tactically good footballers,' he says. 'Therefore we
are only going to win one every ten years or so when we meet a
Kerry, they fall asleep for eight minutes and we get the score. The
bottom line is that technically Kerry are way ahead. Kerry's average
corner-back has more football skills than the average corner-back
in any county. The average corner-back in Kerry is going to score
with his left and right foot, he is going to score seven out of ten
in any given year, whereas the average corner-back say in Dublin
won't be two-footed and won't be comfortable if you put him near
the goals. And that's why Kerry win All-Irelands because skillwise, individually, they are always good.'

Gilroy made Dublin adapt to the top tier of Gaelic football, a game
where half-forwards were half-backs, where defence, tackling and
dispossession came first, and where two talented scoring forwards
were enough to win games. Coming up with the plan and then
putting it into place so successfully bore all the hallmarks of the
role of the MD and in the game of the twenty-first century, it was
such management skills that were now required for inter-county
teams to be successful. They were in a results-oriented business
and that's all that mattered.

'To say you want to go out and just play attacking football is
nice and well and good,' says Moran, 'but in reality when you get
to August and September and you are playing a top team at that
stage of the season, you are just going to do whatever it takes and
if that means playing ugly football, so be it.'

Chapter 19

Today's modern is tomorrow's traditional

Saviour or foe? Defensive stalwart or tactical genius? Whatever way you view his impact on the game, Jim McGuinness is the most talked-about manager in Gaelic football since Kevin Heffernan and his influence has been just as revolutionary. But, to some, while recognising his undoubted talents and skills, all that McGuinness has done is shown just how far behind Gaelic football coaching really is. McGuinness, leading coaches say, isn't twenty years ahead of everyone else, it's more that Gaelic football is twenty years behind the rest of sport. What he has achieved with Donegal, and through the wider recognition with his role at Celtic FC, is about the true modernisation of Gaelic football as it's brought firmly into the twenty-first century of modern sports coaching.

'In the evolution of sport you have flights of stairs and landings,' explains the renowned and innovative coach John Morrison. 'You are going up in tiers and, for me, Jim has gone from the top of one landing right onto the first rung of a new flight of stairs.'

'What Jim McGuinness has done is one of the best examples of teams and coaching,' believes Val Andrews, who saw McGuinness studying the game when he managed him at IT Tralee in the 1990s. 'He has got the complete system that is totally interchangeable where everybody knows exactly what they're doing in clearly defined roles and they all buy into it 100 per cent. It's incredible what he's done and it is only revolutionary by GAA standards.'

It was Clive Woodward, the English rugby World Cup-winning manager, who divided players into either sponges or rocks – those who were willing to soak up information and ideas against those who were closed off to learning. The modern player has to be a sponge, someone who digests and distils more information, stats and knowledge than ever before.

Sporting intelligence is the next frontier and an attribute that will see players make it to the top of their game, and while Jim McGuinness wasn't a star on the Donegal All-Ireland-winning team in 1992 (he was a sub on that panel), he was very much a sponge, looking, learning and listening, first to Brian McEniff, then Val Andrews and Pat Flanagan at IT Tralee and then John Morrison and Mickey Moran with Donegal in the early 2000s. Allied to his degree in sports science and psychology, he was seeing the practical application of man-management skills and forward-thinking techniques being developed by the likes of Andrews, Flanagan, Morrison and Moran, who were years ahead of their time.

'I definitely took to the studies with management in mind,' McGuinness said after his first season in charge. 'I went on to do a Master's in psychology because it was an area in which I felt I wasn't strong and it was something I wanted to know more about. When you're playing, you get a handle on training and get a handle on drills because you see other managers – and good coaches – doing them and you might feel you wouldn't be too bad in that area. Do your studies and that backs it up.'

'Game plans and structure to Gaelic football was only just being introduced by the likes of myself in the late 1990s,' explains

John Morrison. 'And what Jim has done was to make the structure watertight. He has also done what a lot of people don't do, he has moulded a system around the strengths of his players and taken their fitness level to a new high, plus the fact that all of the wee quirks that I used to be laughed at, he has taken, because he has recognised that football is played in the head. Mental fitness is the key – I keep psychology in the background – because if you clear the head, then you clear your feet. If your head is full of clutter, you're liable to stumble and Jim has taken it to those new levels.'

Jim McGuinness was a scraggly-haired lad they called 'Cher' when he first met Brian McEniff; with the long curls and dark looks there was the bit of the rock'n'roll about him. That was the thing about McGuinness, he stood out from the crowd, doing things in his own way and style. He was a minor on the county team, and despite his slight frame, McEniff saw enough to know there was something there and he invited him to a trial in Ballyshannon, where he got into the senior squad and witnessed from the bench Donegal's breakthrough success in 1992.

That was to be the peak of Donegal's success during McGuinness' playing career and, though he toiled for another eleven years with Donegal, they didn't win even an Ulster title, though they lost three finals along the way. As a mature student in his twenties, he re-energised himself, captaining Sigerson Cup teams at IT Tralee in 1998 and 1999 and following it up with a third in 2001 with Jordanstown University. It says something about his determination and focus that he went back to resit his Leaving Cert at the age of twenty-three, knowing he wanted to study and work in sport for his future career.

'He turned his life around and started to focus,' remembers McEniff. 'And my admiration for him grew from there. He was going to college in England for further studies and I recognised that he had a lot to give to the game and to Donegal.'

Like his mentor, Brian McEniff, and like others such as Pete McGrath and Mickey Moran, coaching and managing teams had always been part of his make-up, even as a young player. At just eighteen, he was coaching at underage level when Columba McDyer, a Glenties native who became the first Donegal man to win an All-Ireland medal when he played for Cavan in the 1947 Polo Grounds final, told him he was going to be a coach one day and presented him with a whistle, which he still uses to this day.

'I have never lost that whistle,' he said. 'Oil has been spilled on it. The pea is probably gone in it, and the boys slag me about it. But there would be panic in the dressing room if I mislaid it. It actually happened one day. All the boys could hear was, "Where's the whistle? Where's the whistle?" Now they know the full significance of it.'

His apprenticeship as a coach and manager was the Donegal club championship with Naomh Conaill. Having retired from the county setup and having spent months recuperating from a broken leg and cruciate injury, he was invited to train Naomh Conaill's seniors where his ideas for the defensive system began to be put in place.

Brendan Devenney, who was with Donegal for twelve years and is their record scorer, saw the McGuinness system of play as it was being introduced at club level in the Donegal championship. Devenney was captain of St Eunan's, the hot favourites, when they faced McGuinness' Glenties (Naomh Conaill) in the county final in 2005.

We came up against this team with all these players back and we were thinking, What the f is going on here? *The first game was 0–7 each and we should have won the match. We thought,* Right we've seen what they have, we'll go on and beat them now.

*But in the replay, a few things went right for them early
on and the next thing they get into the lead and we couldn't
break through – the more we tried, the more they sat back.
They hit us on the break, just like you see it nowadays with
Donegal. It was the most horrible final ever, it came out of
nowhere, was a pure freak event. I just walked out of there
that day wondering,* What the f just happened? *I felt sick,
it just wasn't football. That was the first time I'd ever seen
the blanket defence, nobody had seen it before. People were
just starting to do sweeper systems then, and this Glenties
team was playing a whole blanket system.*

But the system worked and Glenties won their first senior county
championship in Jim McGuinness' first season of management. It
was a remarkable introduction and showed, even then, just how far
ahead his ideas were. His years of playing, studying, thinking and
coming up with radical solutions to win games were coming to the
fore now.

For Devenney and those at Eunan's, however, the marker had
been laid down and they were determined to beat the Glenties
system with their own style of play.

'Every chance I got the was about smashing that system, finding
a way to do it, no matter what it took,' says Devenney. 'I thought,
*This is the most horrible thing I'd ever seen in football, these are
just a crowd who are scared of us and playing a way that nobody
wants to see.* So we perfected a way of holding the ball around
their forty-five and being so comfortable on the ball, at training we
did grids, grids, grids. Our main tactic was, when we got the ball
up to their forty-five, if we couldn't get the ball in quick, we held
on to it and waited and waited and waited and between a few of us
we would eventually smash the line.

'On top of that, if they broke us down, the biggest thing for us was our tackling and we tackled like mad to get it back. In those grids in training, we perfected the forwards tackling, we would hunt players down in twos and threes. After 2005, we played Glenties three times in the championship in my time and we beat them every time. In 2009, we faced them in the final and it was McGuinness' fifth year in charge of the club and I'll always remember we absolutely blew them off the park, it was a case of, "F you and that system, get away now."'

St Eunan's had found a way to beat Glenties and their system but, as Devenney points out, 'You'll get space at club level that you won't get at county.' Meanwhile, McGuinness had his sights set higher than club football and twice applied for the county senior position when it became available, but was turned down on both occasions.

'I wanted him to join me in 2005 to train the team,' remembers McEniff. 'Then he came to me when he was applying for the senior job and I remember he did a PowerPoint presentation in my kitchen, setting out the targets and goals and how it was going to be achieved, and it just blew me away. However, although I was on the county executive, I couldn't sit in on the interview panel because there were too many of my old players in for the job and, in the end, Brian McIver was appointed.'

However, the second time around, despite Jim McGuinness failing to get the plum job, the county board asked Brian McEniff to look after the hiring of the under-21 position.

'It was just before I left the county executive. Having done forty years with the county, the chairman asked if I would preside over the appointment of the under-21 team manager. There were three good applicants, but Jim stood out. I saw something in him. He wasn't like me, he would be a lot more academic then I was. The ability that I would have had would have been something that I brought in myself, that I wouldn't have learned. I wouldn't have had as much formal training, but that brought him to the level of intensity that he has.'

Intensity. It's an accurate description of McGuinness' philosophy on life and the game, reminiscent of the Roy Keane 110 per cent mentality. With the under-21s to look after, he had his chance to start testing himself at the next level.

Peter McGinley was a selector with McGuinness on that under-21 team and remembers the focus and the goals were there right from the start.

> *You could tell from listening to him. Jim would be saying, 'Right, we are going to win an Ulster with these lads for a start', and that was the attitude from day one. And the players themselves, they believed it too.*

Whereas the training wasn't necessarily revolutionary, what stood out in McGinley's eyes was the sheer intensity of it.

> *A lot of the training would have been old-school training, it would just be a lot of hard, hard running that a lots of clubs have always been doing but the intensity would have been taken to the next level. You would be training for longer periods and it would have been very intense, you would be training often and you would be told what to do from a strength and conditioning point of view. It's the time, the thought and research he puts into it. Jim has a really good knowledge of all sports and knows what makes people tick. He's a lot of experience from working with different teams.*
>
> *Ultimately, it's his drive and determination that he gets across to the players and just makes them believe that they are going to win; they are going to win Ulsters, they are going to win All-Irelands. When he is meeting the players*

*for the first time, it's not a casual approach, it's basically
'You are going to do this, and after you do this, this is what
is going to happen, you are going to work', so they all
bought into it from the start.*

Within two years, he had led them to their first Ulster title in fifteen
years and their first under-21 All-Ireland final in twenty-three
years. Their skipper and talisman (and future All Star), Michael
Murphy, had a penalty in stoppage time to win it for Donegal, but
his kick hit the crossbar and Dublin won by two points.

However, 2010 had shown that McGuinness' system could
succeed at inter-county level and with a talented group of players,
such as Murphy, coming through, further success could be had
if he was given the reins of the seniors. When John Joe Doherty
stepped down after another season in the wilderness for Donegal,
it was a matter of when rather than if McGuinness would step in,
and, within a month, his job as Donegal manager was confirmed.

Donegal were glad to see the back of the 2010 season; beaten
by Down in Ulster and then a nine-point thumping at the hands
of Armagh in the first round of the qualifiers was their lot for the
championship. The good old days back in 1992 were a distant
memory – Ulster titles, never mind All-Irelands, would have been
on their wish list, but since 1992 there had been five Ulster final
appearances with the county losing every single one.

That winter Jim McGuinness gathered the players together for
their first meeting.

*Look out the window. That's Donegal out there, that's the
homes and the people, the lakes and the mountains, they're
waiting for a team to cheer about and get behind. You need
to start thinking about where things went wrong before and
how it can be changed.*

The players split into groups and were asked for their feedback and reasons why Donegal hadn't succeeded.

'There's a lot made of management sometimes,' McGuinness said in an RTÉ documentary. 'But the bottom line is it has to come from the players. The seniors are a slightly different animal in that there was the psychological baggage of players carrying heavy defeats from previous games, so I knew early on that a different approach was needed. I believed deep inside I could do something. More importantly, the players were there to work with. Obviously, it was a low base to start from but that's not a bad thing either.'

For McGuinness, the key was self-belief and empowering the players. 'Come July, you'll have an Ulster medal in your back pocket,' he told them, looking around at a room of players, the older ones at least who must have thought he was half-mad or wondering what the hell he was on about. 'But you knew he had a plan and he had the belief that it was going to succeed,' said Colm McFadden, one of those who had been toiling for years on Donegal teams and seen managers come and go throughout that time. He, and the others in the room that day, knew this time was different.

Michael Murphy, who had witnessed McGuinness' techniques with the under-21s, knew the effect he was having: 'The penny dropped with a lot of people that day.'

'I have a very simple philosophy,' McGuinness says. 'You work extremely hard, do everything to prepare the team, try to educate them in relation to what you want to achieve, and trust them to go do it.'

He had four simple words to impart to his players: commit, focus, believe, achieve. Everything could be accomplished after that.

Just like Pat Gilroy with Dublin, so too Jim McGuinness introduced early-morning sessions – 7 a.m. starts, heavy training in the winter time, drill after drill after drill.

'I used to come home, go straight to bed, and couldn't even sleep I was that sore from training,' recalled Eamon McGee.

'It was the most grinding training you can imagine, it was brutal, repeating this drill over and over and over again,' said Joe Brolly, the former All-Ireland winner and RTÉ pundit. 'And the purpose was clear: Jim was breeding out of them the habits of a lifetime. In essence, they were being brainwashed.'

Training sessions would last for two and a half hours, the intensity being ratcheted up all the way through. Three on three situations, building to six on six, then twelve on twelve and fifteen on fifteen, for the whole night, which was a way to steel them for the battles ahead.

'You're here to work for the team, not yourself' was the McGuinness mantra. At every session, he spoke to them about winning Ulster, getting it inside their heads. He spoke about Tyrone and Armagh dominating and how he wanted his players to break that stranglehold. 'It's time to stop looking up to these guys and take them on,' he told them.

'Getting inside their heads' was what was most important for McGuinness. His background and studies in sports psychology told him that it was going to be won or lost in the mind. He would get them fitter than anyone else in the country, they would be playing a system that would win games, but ultimately it was about that timeless technique called 'buy-in' that had to come from the players themselves. Throughout the history of Gaelic football, it was the group that came together, that had that togetherness in the dressing room, that believed in themselves and each other, that came through – Armagh, Tyrone, Meath, Cork, Kerry, Dublin, Galway, Down … going right back through the decades it was there. McGuinness was putting a modern scientific slant to it, but it was still the same principle at heart.

Donegal won promotion back to Division One at the beginning of the year and then their opening game in the Ulster championship was against Antrim in Ballybofey and they won their first Ulster game in four years, coming through 1–10 to 0–7. Pat Spillane criticised the quality of play on offer on *The Sunday Game*, to which McGuinness reacted angrily:

> *Donegal seems to be this county that everyone can have a good laugh at because we're not that serious. I don't like my players or my county being disrespected. If people want to criticise how we play, I don't have an issue, but when it gets to your players ...*

For the players, it was obvious that McGuinness was going to back them to the hilt. They were all in it together, and if any slings and arrows were thrown their way, McGuinness was ready to protect his charges.

Cavan were seen off by nine points in the next round and then Tyrone were waiting in the semi-final – McGuinness had told his players that this was the team they were no longer going to look up to, but to stand alongside. Tyrone, led by Mickey Harte whose techniques and styles of play McGuinness had long watched and studied, picking up snippets where he could. Tyrone were going for their three-in-a-row in Ulster and were a significant marker on the road for his team's development.

They were only two points down at the break, due to Tyrone uncharacteristically misfiring with only six from eighteen scoring chances taken. Donegal took four of their five, and in the second half, with a draw looking likely, Donegal got late scores to see them through by three points.

'We needed to get back to what had got us this far, to forget about Tyrone, and the occasion and what was at stake, to just start playing the way we can,' said McGuinness afterwards, recognising that the victory was an important breakthrough for the team.

They faced Derry in the Ulster final – their first appearance in five years – and it was a game that they always controlled, their eleven-man shield outside the D giving Derry no inkling of space from which to score and Donegal ran out comfortable six-point winners.

From the wreckage of the Armagh defeat just thirteen months previously, it had been an incredible turnaround to become Ulster champions for the first time since 1992, but McGuinness had believed and, more importantly, he made the players believe too. During the winter, he had told them they were going to win an Ulster title, and now they had.

'It wasn't until they won it that I think they truly believed,' said McGuinness, and in that moment the hurt of 1993, 1998 and 2002 disappeared.

Their quarter-final clash against Kildare was one of the most emotional and exhilarating games that year. It went to extra time with nothing between the teams until Kevin Cassidy's miraculous long-range effort in stoppage time sealed the win by a point.

'From a coaching point of view, that game was one of the most memorable I have been involved in,' recalled McGuinness. 'There was a moment where there was no coaching, it was just in the hands of the players, the work they had done, it had come down to this and they had to work things out. It was a huge psychological challenge that night, they had been questioned about their desire and their commitment to play for Donegal. I feel a lot of our players went very deep then, they weren't going to come off that pitch beat and they laid everything on the line.'

Of course, the next round was the 0–8 to 0–6 semi-final loss to Dublin. Despite the criticisms all round, Donegal remained unrepentant about the tactics and style of play on the day.

'We wanted to just win games by any means possible,' said Michael Murphy.

Eamon McGee said, 'We weren't going to change just because the media and fans didn't like it.'

For McGuinness, all that mattered was they had lost, and why it had happened. It wasn't a question of aesthetics, it was a question of results.

> *For me as a coach, the bottom line was we didn't get over the line. Ultimately, we had fallen short. You see it in soccer but in Gaelic games it ruffles a few feathers. The reality is, every game in the world is moving and evolving. To be at the centre of that storm, well, it was something we just had to deal with.*

In Donegal even, from his old mentor Brian McEniff, it wasn't enough.

> *I didn't like the football that Donegal played. It wasn't what I grew up with, but he produced results and that was as much as we all expected. He gave Dublin a lot of respect in the match, and in hindsight maybe if we hadn't given them as much respect, we might have beaten them. But, as Jim said afterwards, it was a work in progress and from that I saw he had the ability to do what we needed to do and he had the players to do it.*

'You have to be pragmatic,' McGuinness told the *Sunday Independent*. 'After 2011, you had to say, "This is where we're at, but this is where we want to get to." We wanted to move the thing forward; you don't have to be perfect, you just have to be moving forward. A lot of that criticism was unrealistic. It would have been absolutely ridiculous on one level if we had been able to win an All-Ireland last year. It would not have made sense on a coaching level.'

Having established the foundation of a solid defence, Donegal were ready in the next season to play a quicker, more expansive

counter-attacking play, which was even to earn plaudits from
one of their staunchest critics, Pat Spillane, who remarked on
The Sunday Game after Donegal beat Derry by ten points in the
Ulster championship quarter-final that he 'saw something different
in Donegal – a more positive approach, moving the ball quicker,
playing with confidence, and if they're prepared to be more attack-
minded, they will be a very hard nut to crack'.

However, Joe Brolly begs to differ and refuses to buy into the
belief that Donegal were any different in their second year under
McGuinness.

> *They didn't play more expansively. The difference being*
> *that they were fitter; they did break out better and were*
> *psychologically ready for an All-Ireland. They scraped past*
> *a mediocre Kildare team first time around, whereas the next*
> *year they were beating an awesome team like Cork.*

The biggest challenge of McGuinness' managerial career came not
from outside the camp but from within when Kevin Cassidy, the
hero who pointed the winning free against Kildare in the previous
year, contributed to a book about the Ulster championship by
journalist Declan Bogue. *This Is Our Year* was an insider account
of a year in the championship as viewed by players from each of
the nine Ulster counties, and despite McGuinness demanding a
confidentiality clause from his players, Cassidy gave the Donegal
viewpoint for the book.

Cassidy wasn't revealing any insider secrets, but nonetheless
McGuinness' reaction was swift and uncompromising – his All
Star was kicked off the panel and all players were banned from
the book launch. He was laying down a clear line in the sand,
and anyone crossing it was going to suffer the consequences, no
matter what. 'I don't look back,' the Glenties man has said. 'It's

about moving forward.' And in relation to players, he had no exceptions.

The talk and media coverage might have continued long after the book had been launched and Cassidy had been banned but for McGuinness it was about focusing on the job at hand and preparing for the 2012 season.

'We had to be honest with ourselves,' said McGuinness. 'We had failed in 2011, we didn't get to an All-Ireland final. Two steps forward, one step back, it's that clinical, that's coaching.'

The ten-point victory over Derry in the Ulster championship woke people up to the fact that this Donegal team were a better version of the previous year's model and for the second year in a row, they beat Mickey Harte's Tyrone in what was a battle of tactical minds between two coaches similarly driven and sharing a similar playing philosophy. When they retained the Ulster crown – for the first time in their history – with an eleven-point drubbing of Down, their status as the new dominant force in Ulster was complete. Within two years, McGuinness had usurped Tyrone's place in Ulster football. Now all that was required was an All-Ireland to cement his place in Donegal footballing history.

To do it they would not only have to beat Tyrone in Ulster but also Kerry, the traditional superpower, and Cork, the most successful team over recent years with three league titles in a row and the 2010 All-Ireland.

'We felt pretty confident after being drawn against Donegal, having beaten them 2–16 to 1–08 in the league in Killarney,' said Jack O'Connor. 'But Donegal had our measure, the intensity of their tackling caught a few of our lads out. We had a lot of momentum coming back from five points down but then that was it, the deal was sealed. The game was being played on Donegal's terms, that was their strong point, they forced teams to play on their terms.'

For the Donegal players, Kerry were the benchmark of excellence, and when they found themselves ahead of the Kingdom in Croke Park, a degree of panic set in, McGuinness' game-plan was being forgotten about and they very nearly let Kerry back in the door. Once more an injury-time score sealed it for Donegal, this time it was Karl Lacey taking his chance and Donegal were through. For McGuinness, it was a real signal of how far the team had come.

Into their second successive semi-final, Donegal now faced Cork – a team that had destroyed them by fourteen points in 2009. But how the team had changed and the difference one man could make. Unlike the 2009 encounter, the two sides were nip and tuck for the first half but McGuinness wasn't happy – the players needed to get back to the script, back to what they had been doing in the previous rounds. In the second half, they responded and began to pull away, opening up a five-point lead at one stage before coming through by two points in the end.

Donegal were into an All-Ireland final, they were one stage better than 2011, now they just had to finish the job.

Mayo awaited, and while they were on their own mission to overcome five All-Ireland final defeats and were looking for a first Sam Maguire since 1951, McGuinness could picture nothing but a Donegal win.

'Every morning when I woke up, I saw the cup in the front of the team bus and it was a vision clear in my mind and I wanted it so much to come true,' he recalled. 'For me the best moment would be taking the cup home to the people of Donegal.'

Donegal exploded out of the traps that September Sunday, scoring 2–1 in the first ten minutes. Mayo were hit for six and were never again on level terms, though they did steady the ship to get within three, prompting McGuinness to read his team the riot act at half-time. 'It was very hard to take and it was probably the one time that I was very cross,' he remembered.

But Donegal never looked like letting it slip and they saw it through, winning out by four points. It was mission accomplished. Donegal were All-Ireland champions for only the second time, they were Kings of Ulster and now High Kings of Ireland, thanks to one man who single-handedly turned the players' minds and self-belief around based on a watertight system. Despite all the criticisms, it had never turned him or the players from the job at hand – winning an Ulster title and then an All-Ireland. Outside of their team circle, nothing else mattered.

'It was the best feeling in the world ever, to be honest,' McGuinness recalled in the documentary. 'It's something you dream about all your life and to be able to share it with the people of Donegal … Everything that happens in your life helps to make you what you are today.'

In the space of two years, Jim McGuinness had caused a storm in the GAA, dragging it into the modern. In fact his influence in sport beyond the GAA was confirmed when Celtic offered him a contract working with their youth players and when the Ryder Cup captain Paul McGinley name-checked his methods and approach to sport in general. McGuinness' success with Donegal has forced GAA people to reflect seriously on the state and future of Gaelic football, so much so that a Football Review Committee was charged to examine what changes, if any, were needed to ensure that the 'apocalyptic' vista as denounced from Kerry and elsewhere was not going to materialise.

But there are those who say that the critics in Kerry are only shouting loudest because they're not winning as much anymore.

'They just want to play the old game and win it their way. The number of teams in Ireland that are really afraid of Kerry is going down and down. Nobody is afraid of beating Kerry any more,' says John Morrison. 'People that are talking about the high catch, that's fine, but that was thirty years ago. Years ago, there were no mobile phones, it wasn't even in anybody's head, now look at the outcome. I was lucky enough to play in the 1980s and 1990s and our game has become unbelievably faster than some of the old greats who want to harp back to the catch-and-kick game. The game has moved on, but some teams don't want to accept that.'

What McGuinness did was bring the modern coaching ideas, in terms of systems, fitter athletes and an emphasis on sporting intelligence, to Gaelic football, which immediately put Donegal ahead of most other teams. Forward-thinking coaches, such as Morrison and Andrews, point to the likes of basketball, rugby and American sports, with their playbooks, hundreds of calls and ability of players to take all this information on board as proof of what inter-county footballers need to aspire to.

As for the criticism levelled at the emphasis on defensive play first and foremost, Andrews and others believe that this is a reflection of coaching standards overall. It is easier, they say, to coach how to stop an opponent playing than to coach someone to play creatively. 'There is no problem with the superior systems,' says Andrews. 'The systems that have evolved at the moment, they have a lot of fellas back, the only problem with that is the offensive coaching is abysmal.'

In 2010, Jim McGuinness summed up his simple football philosophy.

When you don't have the ball, you must do all you can to get it back. And when you have it, you have to make sure you do as much as you can with it. It's as simple as that.

Developing that into a team collective is the ultimate in man-management skills, to take thirty very different individuals, who are only as strong as their weakest link.

'I played on teams and have seen teams in which maybe "team" wasn't the key thing,' McGuinness told sports journalist Damian Lawlor. 'I've seen this in my own club, we had three or four very good county players in periods but we weren't able to win a county championship because we didn't have enough players around the edges to get us over the line. At times in the past, Donegal were like the old model – we had a couple of superstars in our ranks but the whole collective never seemed to give us traction. I felt it was important to address that. The collective always beats the opposition.'

'Jim is coming from such a different perspective with his game plan, other county managers are nowhere near to beating it,' believes Brendan Devenney. 'Maybe it's because we had five years of it and seen it that we were willing to really completely change our game around, from the physical, the tackling and ball retention. Glenties were the big challenge every year for us – it was about outworking them and outworking the system.'

The gauntlet has been thrown down by McGuinness and according to Brian McEniff there's more to come.

> There is a way around every system but it is up to each manager to find it and to devise their own schemes. We brought it up a bar in 2011, but we raised the bar again in 2012 and Jim feels he can raise the bar even more – and who is to doubt him? He maintains he can raise it, and I would say there is more in the players and he is going to probably find it.

Jim McGuinness has forced Gaelic football to re-evaluate itself and ask just where it really is in modern sporting terms, but ultimately the argument, now over 120 years old, has remained the same. Each generation finds the best way to succeed, and that way reflects a philosophy and attitude to the sport itself. For some,

Gaelic football is about the kicking game; for others, it's simple beauty is in the hand-passing and possession to gain scores. Debate has raged over the decades between counties who were winning about which way was better.

On the eve of the First World War, Kerry's Dick Fitzgerald wrote about the science of Gaelic football; a hundred years later, we still talk about the science of the game, it's just that society has developed a better knowledge and understanding in that time. But in a society that places an emphasis on systems, on the controllables, and what can be quantified, above everything else, what place is there then to be outside of that?

'We're trying to write the template for every game we play, and you can't do that,' believes Tommy Carr. 'Sport is not like that, sport has its geniuses because the geniuses thought outside the box and they were able to do things that other players weren't able to do.'

'There are young people all over the country and they can be whatever they want to be … as long as they believe,' said Jim McGuinness to a national audience on RTÉ television weeks after Donegal's All-Ireland success – the only problem now is, will the young footballers and coaches believe the only way is the McGuinness way?

Chapter 20

A question of faith

So which way is the right way? Is it the system above all else? Or is it a belief that Gaelic football is a catching-and-kicking game? If 'possession is the law' as espoused by Joe Lennon, should that be via short hand-passes, sideways and backwards, no matter what? Or can the modern game still be based on forward-thinking kicking principles?

The catch-and-kick evangelists like to paint themselves as the traditionalists, trying to save the game in the face of the onslaught of modernists who want to win at all costs, and yet the hand-passing philosophy is as old as the game itself. There were motions over 100 years ago trying to ban catching. But it's the winners who write the history and Kerry's ongoing success at football and their propensity for and love of writing about their achievements has invariably meant that their philosophy and approach to the game has been written and talked about in 'traditional lore'. Their tradition, we are told – and they tell themselves – is one to uphold.

And then you have the pragmatists, the counties that believed there was another way, through hand-passing and a short possession game. First there were the Leinster counties – Kildare and Dublin

– that developed and showed the way – and then there was the Ulster influence, from Antrim in the early days to Donegal and Tyrone in the modern. Theirs was a cerebral approach, influenced no doubt by the presence and popularity of soccer in the east and northeast before the culture of coaching in the GAA became hugely developed during the Troubles, becoming an outlet and an identity for many.

Just as the early teachers from Erin's Hope spread the gospel of the game far and wide in its early days, so too the Ulster influence is coming to bear on the game throughout the thirty-two counties. But as with any giant leap forward in development – think Kevin Heffernan in the 1970s or McGuinness in the 2010s – where one leads the way, the masses will eventually follow, seeking to imitate and have similar success. But as the herds fall into the trap of blindly following, one or two brave voices will seek another way.

Sadly for many of the catch-and-kick culture, the initiative is not being taken by Kerry (whom many feel have all too willingly sold their heritage down the river in the old 'if you can't beat them then join them' mentality) but by another Northern team, this time, not a county but a club: Crossmaglen of Armagh.

The rise of the Cross has already been documented in relation to Joe Kernan's emergence as a manager of talent and pedigree, but while Kernan brought success by inculcating a modern approach and winning mindset to their game which has resulted in unprecedented success at county, provincial and national level, their most recent evolution has seen them become standard-bearers for a kicking game that was once held aloft by Kerry.

Joe Brolly is one of Cross' biggest supporters, believing that their approach to and philosophy of the game is one that must be championed in the face of the modern obsession with possession and hand-passing. Ultimately, above all else, he says, it's about people enjoying their football, playing with a smile on their faces again and being given a creative freedom that brought them into the game as kids in the first place. And Brolly doesn't believe it's just romantic idealism that he's championing either. He points to Crossmaglen's success – two All-Ireland club titles in the past three years and four final appearances in the past six – as proof that their way is working, can succeed and should be the future blueprint for Gaelic football.

> For most teams, the preferred method of moving the ball is to hand pass or solo, the idea being not to give the ball away at all costs, but for Crossmaglen, there are two guiding principles to the way they play. The first is to play football the way it ought to be played and, secondly, to play the way boys enjoy playing it. Their ethos is man-to-man and the imperative is the traditional skills of the game, the skills we all enjoy: kicking the ball over the bar, kicking the long passes and catching the ball in the air.
>
> Crossmaglen have plotted a strategy which employs the laws of physics. It makes it virtually impossible, all other things being equal, for teams to beat them because what they do is really simple, and it is done brilliantly. It looks simple and there's no solo running or hand-passing in training at all.
>
> The template is that they set their team out exactly according to a programme. Their left corner-forward plays at the corner flag and their right corner-forward plays at the right corner flag and their full-forward plays full forward, and so on and so forth. The centre-forward plays between centre-forward and the two wing-forward positions and they are all interchangeable, at any one time anyone can be a centre-forward. The point is this: they play the width of the pitch.

The most important thing is their half-forward line stays in position. What that means is their keeper catches the ball, the corner-back gets the ball for Crossmaglen and nobody goes to him – the full-back doesn't go to him, the centre half-back doesn't drop in to support him, nor does the wing-back come towards him. They get out of his way. When the corner-back wins the ball, he's man-to-man and his job is to kick the ball sixty metres to the wing-forward area.

Whenever the wing-back gets the ball, his job is to kick the ball to the full-forward line. Never kick to the half-forward line. Don't give twenty- or thirty-yard passes. It is fifty- or sixty-yard passes. The important thing is the half-forwards, they stay in position, they don't go in on top of the full-forwards, they let the full-forwards play, the full-forwards all have forty metres of space. If you go to their training and you see their drills, they don't have any short drills. They have no short-sided pack in drills or any short drills at all and they don't do any hand-passing drills. Everything they do is the size of the pitch. They've got these drills that simulate their game plan. You just look at those and you realise, Sweet mother, this is just the way Gaelic football should be played.

For Brolly, who is one of the few to have seen up close the Crossmaglen training philosophy in action, it is and must be the future of the game. A constant criticism that comes up about the modern game is the practice of short, hand-passing drills that are so prevalent throughout the country and at all levels, but, says Brolly, the Cross way can be the way of the future, even one to counteract and defeat Jim McGuinness' system at Donegal.

For one to create an effective blanket defence strategy like Donegal's, you need to slow the ball coming out of the defence – teams are automatically doing that, they are getting the ball and coming out on a solo run. So now the Donegal boys have the two or three seconds they need. A solo run, a hand-pass and everybody is retreating back into position. You've moved maybe twenty yards altogether and could be going laterally because you're under pressure being tackled with the blanket defence now in position. Crossmaglen don't do that. The ball comes in, the keeper catches it, he kicks it sixty metres immediately into the wing-forward space, and he knows it is coming. What you've done immediately is you have cut out all the blanket defenders who have come forward in counter-attacking mode to try and support the opposition's team. They've all come forward but the ball's been kicked sixty metres over the top of them.

For Tony McEntee, who was co-manager of Crossmaglen during their most successful period when they reached three All-Ireland club finals in a row from 2010–2012, before stepping down after the 2013 club semi-final defeat to eventual winners St Brigid's of Roscommon, the style of play boiled down to one simple fact: how did they want to play the game?

We were trying to put together a system of play that we believed was the way that football should be played as individuals. We were trying then to get those players to buy into that system and develop and encourage them. As the years went on, we would try and tailor it to suit what we had available.

Uniquely perhaps, and running contrary to what most leading managers will tell you, for McEntee it wasn't about adapting to the players available to them but rather developing the philosophy first and making the players adapt in the long run.

> *We came up with the philosophy first. Then we got the players to buy into it and we got them to adjust to it. In our case, it's very much saying to them, 'This is the way we want it played.' This is the problem that we are seeing with the playing of Gaelic football, and we want to overcome it. We have moved from the win-at-all-costs mentality. Obviously, we want to win, but we've moved away from that mentality because we find we'd be restricted in our approach.*

It's a refreshing approach that is like a blast of fresh air on a stultifying coaching culture that has strangled the county scene in recent years. McEntee would be very critical of the path that Gaelic football has taken.

> *The disappointing aspect for me in relation to the game is it's taking a step backwards. There's a lack of invention or difference throughout the country with a large majority of coaches. None of them are willing to say, 'I'm going to try this and if it doesn't work we're going to try it differently', and see how it goes instead of just buying into the successful philosophy because a lot of the success of a team is on a year to year basis. The biggest disappointment in all of it is probably Kerry. Kerry have changed their system of play significantly over this past four or five years – it's affecting their game and it is affecting everybody else's game that Kerry play.*

As to the ailment affecting coaches nationwide, McEntee is quick to point to the low-risk possession philosophy.

Firstly there is laziness on coaches who aren't willing to put their heads down and try and develop a system of play. The second problem is you have damage limitation which gives you an increased chance of winning the match, so if you can keep it tight, keep it controlled, keep it focused in a smaller group, then the chance of you being there or thereabouts with ten or fifteen minutes to go is higher than if you try and play an expansive type of football where there's more risk or more chance of losing the possession. So I think a lot of coaches are looking at the players that they have. They see the job as a one, two or max three-year job and what they want to do is get quick results in a quick time span and it is very much moving towards that pressurised situation where if you don't perform and don't get the results, then you're out, as opposed to expanding and developing, coaching and moving on with the players.

The issue here is not with the systems and the players on those teams. Rather, it is the lack of variation throughout the country for style and for application, and part of the problem can be the coaching courses that the GAA itself provides. A lot of those coaching courses seem to promote high-intensity short drills in conditioned games and things like that. Then those coaches that they are breeding, they are doing the exact same thing when they go back – and all of a sudden you have a massive number of people out there doing the exact same thing.

Even in relation to training, the vogue for weights and strength and conditioning holds no truck with McEntee and Crossmaglen.

Weights programmes are not even on the agenda for their players; for McEntee, it's not about bulk or size, their playing philosophy is all about speed.

'We are unable to monitor such programmes appropriately, therefore the risk of injury is significant due to improper technique and too heavy weights,' explains McEntee as to why they don't advocate weight training. 'Some boys do some weights but these are specifically to reduce injury, i.e. they do not do weights for bulk, and, thirdly, we do not see a sufficiently significant benefit to weights compared to the negatives.'

And in relation to what Donegal and Jim McGuinness have achieved, McEntee would be, like Val Andrews, not one to see the achievements as being particularly far-reaching or revolutionary.

> *I wouldn't say that what McGuinness has done with those bunch of Donegal players was particularly advanced in relation to coaching. I think it's more advanced in relation to fitness and the whole buy-in from the team. That Donegal team, even in the All-Ireland final against Mayo, were particularly poor a lot of the time and struggled throughout. Looking at the side and being critical, although you don't want to be of any team, you would say that their skill level is no higher than many other teams and that their application was what was more impressive about them.*

'Like any serious watcher of football who goes to see Crossmaglen play and who knows it to be true, this is the way that Gaelic football ought to be played,' says Joe Brolly strongly. He is firmly in the aesthete's corner and backs Crossmaglen's philosophy to the hilt.

It is right and it is brilliant to watch. The boys love playing it and nobody is taking shortcuts; they are playing the game properly, the way it ought to be played. That means something. You are not doing these old negative copouts, filling your defence and covering over your weaknesses and stuff. Get out there, stick your chin out and go and play Gaelic football.

They go man-to-man and they put their heart and soul into it and enjoy the game so much. I was at the Glenswilly medal presentation when they won the Donegal Championship for the first time in 2011. Glenswilly play a very Donegal-style brand of football and they scored 1–09 with a lot of scores from frees.

I was talking to one of their forwards and I asked him, 'Well, what about Crossmaglen?' and this player replied, 'Jesus, I'd give my right arm to play on that forward line.'

It's about the sheer enjoyment players would get playing the Cross way. Gaelic football has become a serious chore for the players, because there's no fun in it. Players want to field a ball in the air, they want to stick a ball in the net, they want to show their skills and they can't do that playing a blanket defence.

The competitive instinct is so strong in the human being that the first question will be: can we win doing this? Can we win? We are relentlessly competitive and that is sort of marked I suppose by the ascent of man, we want to get better, we want to succeed at all costs. So Donegal have done what they've done and they've been up in the mornings doing weights at 6.30 a.m. and they've had three-hour training sessions because if boys are winning they will do anything. They will literally do anything if

*they are winning. Juan Márquez the boxer believed that
drinking his own pee would help him to win, so he drank
his own urine. Human beings will do whatever it requires
if they think it will help them to win.*

*The beauty of Crossmaglen is they are signalling to the
Gaelic footballing world that there is another way you can
win. You can win playing very attractively and most of all
your players will enjoy it. They will give their right arm to
be part of it. Jamie Clarke said to me that he loves playing
for Crossmaglen, he doesn't want to miss a league game. As
for Armagh, those boys have got lead in their boots when it
comes to Armagh, because it is all hand-passing and solo
running.*

*The game is becoming increasingly unattractive. And it
is becoming increasingly unwatchable. I go to watch Derry
play now and I don't miss Derry games. Myself and my
father call it our weekly punishment – this laborious hand-
pass, hand-pass, solo run, hand-pass, hand-pass, solo run,
everyone running around inside the blanket defence. When
you go to see Crossmaglen play you see people who go to
all their matches who are from other counties. There are
people from Louth, from Dublin, from Donegal, we meet
them and at half-time and full-time everybody's got a smile
on their face saying, 'This is great, this is crazy.' You can
just go and revel in what they're doing.*

Happily, and despite the dominance of Tyrone and Donegal in
recent years, Brolly doesn't see an apocalyptic future. He is an
optimist who believes that the kicking game as practised by
Crossmaglen will ultimately spread and in turn become the new
orthodoxy.

The Tyrone method and the Donegal method have had a very negative influence on Gaelic games. But this new method, this hub of invention in Crossmaglen, is starting to get serious focus and attention now. There are really good coaches like Ronan McGuckian who's down in Errigal Ciaran now and he's trying to convert them to be a kick-passing team. Ronan said to me he has wild cultural problems with converting Errigal Ciaran to a long-kick style. 'It's cultural,' he explained to me. 'The short game is deeply embedded in Tyrone's psyche now, it is just taking me time and it is going to take me more time to change things.' The reality is coaches are playing against Cross and they are getting their asses handed to them on a plate and they are saying, 'F–, look at how they're kicking that ball. Jesus Christ, how can we get back in the defence in time? Let's look at this, how are we going to deal with this?'

In the future, I believe Tony McEntee is going to take over Armagh, he'll take them and he'll transform them. They will play a brand of football that will be really, really attractive and, more importantly, the boys will genuinely, with all their heart and soul, put their shoulder to the wheel. Then everybody will have to sit up and pay attention. It has got to happen for the good of the game, because players are no longer enjoying the game. Players have a very strong competitive instinct and they enjoy the competition, but increasingly Gaelic football is becoming like a triathlon. It is becoming masochistic and the enjoyment is being taken out of it and players are being asked to be robots to do particular jobs in a particular way and generally speaking they're very mundane jobs. Crossmaglen are being asked to do particular jobs but it makes you feel young, makes you feel alive and in the end that's why we all play football.

It's what we're teaching the kids today that is so important, say the leading coaches. But, as Andrews and Morrison ask: who's coaching the coaches? Why is the emphasis on just verbal instruction, linear and mundane drills revolving around five-yard hand-passes? Where is the imagination?

'I could pick on one hand the number of coaches that could make a fella technically good,' says Val Andrews. 'Most of the coaches are good on defence, like locking and tackling and setting up systems, but there are very few coaches I know who could develop forwards. They don't know how to do it.'

'There is a time in a child's life where they learn to walk, to put a tie on, to close the buttons on their shirt, to use a knife and fork, to dress themselves, to wash their face, to walk to school, they are all muscle memory skills,' explains John Morrison. 'When you bring them into the sport that's the same thing, riding a bicycle, kicking a ball, they are all muscle memory and all the child needs is a buzz phrase and the picture to do it.

'There is a part of your brain called the limbic part, which has a top part, a middle part and a bottom part. The bottom part, which is for coping, is your muscle memory; the top part is for consciously thinking in a match when things go wrong, so if you are playing well, you won't need that part of your brain; the middle part is based on emotions and your memory bank, it's what I call the switchboard. You already see what is happening and it goes into the switchboard and your memory bank in there, so when you have a ball in your hand what do you do? In a flash, especially if your mind is in a positive state, your mind will actually flash up loads and loads of pictures of what you did successfully in the past in that situation and that's your decision made for you and away you go.'

Meanwhile, down in Kerry, having been confronted with successful football being played another way, they are having to look itself in the mirror and ask: is there such a thing as tradition any more? Mickey Ned O'Sullivan works with the Kerry minors, trying to develop the next crop of young talent to follow in the illustrious footsteps of their predecessors.

'There are no big things in life,' he impresses upon them. 'It is an accumulation of all the small things and you learn to focus logically on every small thing. Formula in itself is devoid of character. It's how you interpret it, how you project it and how the people buy into it that really counts.'

'You can't replicate what I am doing, you are not me,' says John Morrison, outlining the need for coaches to start to think for themselves once more. 'You need to take this, adapt it, worry about yourself and do it your way and when you do it your way it's not my work you're using, it's your own. And better than that, I will always get something back, because my father used to tell me, "The more you give, the more you get back."'

While all of the managers featured in this book have achieved the ultimate goal of All-Ireland success, it hasn't been without the pain of defeat along the way. Some were breakthrough successes, some only did it once, others multiple times, while some did it in different eras and with different players, but all made a mark that left an indelible legacy and pointed the way to the future.

The system versus the individual. Hand-passing versus catch-and-kick. One manager's philosophy versus another's values. Gaelic football's future is in its managers' hands.

Bibliography

Bogue, Declan, *This Is Our Year: A Season on the Inside of a Football Championship* (Ballpoint, 2011).

Bolt, Peter, *The Whole Manager: Achieving Success Without Selling Your Soul* (Oaktree, 1999).

Boylan, Seán & Quinn, John, *Seán Boylan: The Will to Win* (O'Brien Press, 2006).

Breheny, Martin, *Blessed and Obsessed: The Official Autobiography of Mick O'Dwyer* (Blackwater, 2007).
— *Joe Kernan: Without a Shadow of a Doubt* (Irish Sports Publishing, 2011).

de Búrca, Marcus, *The GAA: A History* (Gill & Macmillan, 1999).
— *Michael Cusack and the GAA* (Anvil Books, 1989).

Carbery, *Gaelic Football* (Gaelic Publicity Services, 1944).

Carr, Barney, *Summerhill, Warrenpoint: A Memoir* (Barney Carr, 2012).

Corry, Eoghan, *The History of Gaelic Football* (Gill & Macmillan, 2010).
— *Catch and Kick: Great Moments of Gaelic Football 1880–1990* (Poolbeg, 1989).

Cronin, Mike, *Sport and Nationalism in Ireland: Gaelic Games, Soccer and Irish Identity since 1884* (Four Courts Press, 1999).

Cronin, Mike, Murphy, William & Rouse, Paul, *The Gaelic Athletic Association 1884–2009* (Irish Academic Press, 2009).

Cronin, Mike, Duncan, Mark & Rouse, Paul, *The GAA: A People's History* (The Collins Press, 2009).
— *The GAA County by County* (The Collins Press, 2011).

Davin, Pat, *Recollections of a Veteran Irish Athlete: The Memoirs of Pat Davin, World's All-Round Athletic Champion* (Juverna Press, 1938).

Duggan, Keith, *House of Pain: Through the Rooms of Mayo Football* (Mainstream, 2007).

Fitzgerald, Dick, *How to Play Gaelic Football* (Guy & Co., 1915).

Flynn, T.J. & Ó Muircheartaigh, Joe, *Princes of Pigskin: A Century of Kerry Footballers* (The Collins Press, 2008).

Fogarty, Weeshie, *Dr Eamonn O'Sullivan: A Man Before His Time* (Wolfhound, 2007).

Foley, Michael, *Harte: Presence Is the Only Thing* (Poolbeg, 2010).
— *Kings of September: The Day Offaly Denied Kerry Five in a Row* (O'Brien Press, 2008).

Foley, P., *Kerry's Football Story* (The Kerryman, 1945).

Halberstam, David, *The Education of a Coach* (Hyperion, 2006).

Hayes, Liam, *Out of Our Skins* (Gill & Macmillan, 1992).

Healy, Tim, *Can You Manage? Everything You Need to Know About Managing Teams in Gaelic Football, Hurling and Other Sports* (Ballpoint, 2011).

Humphries, Tom, *Green Fields: Gaelic Sport in Ireland* (Weidenfeld & Nicolson, 1996).
  — *Dublin v. Kerry* (Penguin, 2007).
  — *Jack O'Connor: Keys to the Kingdom* (Penguin, 2007).

Lennon, Joe, *Coaching Gaelic Football for Champions* (J.F. & A. Lennon, 1964).
  — *Fitness for Gaelic Football* (Alba House,1969).
  — *Towards a Philosophy for Legislation in Gaelic Games* (Northern Recreation Consultants, 2000).

Lewis, Michael, *Moneyball: The Art of Winning an Unfair Game* (W.W. Norton, 2004).
  — *Coach: Lessons on Baseball and Life* (W.W. Norton, 2005).

Looney, Tom, *A King in the Kingdom of Kings: Dick Fitzgerald and Kerry Football* (Currach Press, 2008).

MacGabhann, Gearoid, *Big Jim Smith: Man of Breffni* (2012).

McAnallen, Donal, *The Cups that Cheered: A History of the Sigerson, Fitzgibbon and Higher Education Gaelic Games* (The Collins Press, 2011).

McCarthy, Finbarr, *Bainisteoir: The 10 Greatest GAA Managers* (Mentor Books, 2009).

O'Connor, Christy, *The Club* (Penguin, 2011).

Ó Riain, Séamus, *Maurice Davin, First President of the GAA* (Geography Publications, 1994).

O'Sullivan, Eamonn, *The Art and Science of Gaelic Football* (The Kerryman, 1958).

Ryan, Emmet, *Tactics Not Passion* (Original Writing, 2012).

Walsh, Denis, *Hurling: The Revolution Years* (Penguin, 2006).

Wilson, Jonathan, *Inverting the Pyramid: The History of Football Tactics* (Orion, 2009).

Winner, David, *Brilliant Orange: The Neurotic Genius of Dutch Football* (Bloomsbury, 2001).

GAAManagers.com

Who were Gaelic football's greatest managers? Suggest your own and vote in the fan poll on GAAManagers.com.

You'll also find more information on the managers featured in this book, hear a specially commissioned documentary and audio interviews with some of the subjects, as well as Daire's discussions of the book on radio and TV.

Join the discussion on GAAManagers.com.

Photograph Acknowledgements

Eamonn O'Sullivan: Weeshie Fogarty and the O'Sullivan family • **Maurice Hayes/Barney Carr**: Down GAA • **Barney Carr**: Down GAA • **Joe Lennon**: © Irish Photo Archive (www.irishphotoarchive.ie) • **Jim McKeever**: Jim McKeever • **John Dunne**: Cyril Dunne • **Kevin Heffernan**: © Connolly Collection/SPORTSFILE • **Mick O'Dwyer**: © INPHO/Billy Stickland • **Eugene McGee**: © INPHO/Billy Stickland • **Billy Morgan**: © INPHO • **Seán Boylan**: © INPHO/Billy Stickland • **Brian McEniff**: © INPHO/Billy Stickland • **Pete McGrath**: © INPHO/Billy Stickland • **John O'Mahony**: © INPHO/Billy Stickland • **Joe Kernan**: ©INPHO/Morgan Treacy • **Mickey Harte**: © INPHO/Andrew Paton • **Jack O'Connor**: © INPHO/Ryan Byrne • **Pat Gilroy**: © INPHO/Morgan Treacy • **Jim McGuinness**: © INPHO/Morgan Treacy • **John Morrison**: © INPHO/Andrew Paton • **Tony McEntee**: © INPHO/Presseye/Jonathan Porter

Acknowledgements

My thanks as always to those who gave of their time so willingly for interviews for this book. Meeting so many of Gaelic football's greatest managers, to hear their stories and delve into their methods and mindsets has been both a pleasure and a learning process. I realised quickly that, despite their different backgrounds, different locations and different eras, the one thing they all have in common is a 'glass half-full' approach to life in general. Every match, every day, every win and every loss is an opportunity. There is no such thing as sitting back and being a hostage to fortune, and it is this common thread that struck home to me as I travelled the country finding out about their philosophies of football and life. As John O'Mahony described it, 'Sport is a public examination of what you do behind closed doors for the rest of the year … every plan that's been hatched in those long winter nights is exposed, everything is there to be examined.' In such circumstances, only a positive mental attitude will succeed.

My gratitude and thanks also to the players and ex-players who gave valuable insights into just what it was like to play under these managers, and who gave a sense of the team spirit and ethos that is developed in the dressing room. Having team spirit is a vital part of any successful team and one that, as pointed out by players and managers throughout the book, must also come from the players themselves.

To Barney Carr, Maurice Hayes, Cyril Dunne, Liam Sammon, Brian Talty, Liam Gilmartin, Jim McKeever, Joe Lennon, Tony Hanahoe, Mick O'Dwyer, Weeshie Fogarty, Johnny Culloty, Mickey Ned O'Sullivan, Dave Weldrick, Billy Morgan, Eugene McGee, Seán Boylan, John Allen, Colm O'Rourke, Liam Hayes, Brian McEniff, Pete McGrath, Mickey Moran, John O'Mahony,

Ray Silke, Pat Comer, Kevin McStay, Joe Brolly, Art McRory, Joe Kernan, Enda McNulty, Philip Jordan, Jack O'Connor, John Morrison, Colin Moran, Val Andrews, Tommy Carr, Brendan Devenney, Peter McGinley, Tony McEntee, Paul Rouse and Donal McAnallen, my sincere gratitude and thanks.

Thanks also to the historians, journalists and writers, either through interviews or research from books already written – their work, dedication and passion for the sport is just as engaging. There is a canon of GAA writing that can be drawn on, which is being enriched each year with new works. It will be interesting to see if, over the next few years, there will be a genre of GAA writing focusing on the tactical, statistical and coaching revolution of recent years. My hope is that *The Managers* will find a place alongside these works.

To my agent, Peter O'Connell, and all those at Hachette Books Ireland who shared the vision for the book, especially Ciara Doorley, as well as my editor, Claire Rourke, who provided invaluable edit and draft suggestions, my sincere thanks.

Finally, writing a book is difficult enough – being away for stretches doing interviews and then locking yourself away in isolation to write, edit and draft – and if my head wasn't stuck at a laptop writing, then it was more than likely stuck in a book on management and tactics. Doing all of this while we had our first-born was a juggling act of patience and love that only a wife and family would endure, and my love and thanks as always to my parents in Dublin for their support, to Margaret – glad to have the conservatory back, I'm sure – and most especially Trina and Ryan. I couldn't have done it without you and, Ryan, you can have the best of both GAA worlds now I hope – Tipp for the hurling and Dublin for the football!

Index